LAWYERING AND ETHICS FOR THE BUSINESS ATTORNEY

Fourth Edition

■ ■ ■

Marc I. Steinberg

Rupert and Lillian Radford Professor of Law
Director, Corporate Counsel Externship Program
Dedman School of Law, Southern Methodist University

AMERICAN CASEBOOK SERIES®

WEST ACADEMIC PUBLISHING

American Casebook Series is a trademark registered in the U.S. Patent and Trademark Office.

© West, a Thomson business, 2002, 2007
© 2011 Thomson Reuters
© 2016 LEG, Inc. d/b/a West Academic
    444 Cedar Street, Suite 700
    St. Paul, MN 55101
    1-877-888-1330

West, West Academic Publishing, and West Academic are trademarks of West Publishing Corporation, used under license.

Printed in the United States of America

ISBN: 978-1-62810-120-1

ACKNOWLEDGMENTS

I owe many thanks to my research assistants, colleagues, and lawyer-friends for their assistance. My research assistants deserve kudos for their outstanding work—James Ames, Matt Brysacz, Rob Castle, Kelly Flanagan, Barrett Howell, Brooks Leavitt, Barrett Lidji, Dustin Mauck, Bobby Moore, Bipasha Mukherjee, Vanessa Murra-Kapon, Jason Myers, Emmanuel Obi, and Jonathan Rafpor. In particular, Mr. Howell and Mr. Myers, both now practicing attorneys, successfully undertook several challenging assignments with respect to this project.

I thank my friends and colleagues at SMU for their support on this project: Deans John Attanasio and Jennifer Collins, Professors Bill Bridge, Alan Bromberg, Linda Eads, Shubha Ghosh, Chris Hanna, George Martinez, and Fred Moss, as well as Ms. Jan Spann and Ms. Carolyn Yates. My thanks to the SMU Dedman School of Law for the award of summer research grants in connection with this project, including the Clark J. Mathews, II Faculty Research Endowment Fund. Also, I thank the SMU Maguire Center for Ethics and Public Responsibility for support of this project, and in particular, Mr. Cary Maguire, Professor Richard Mason, and Ms. Lorren Timberman. Moreover, my thanks to my lawyer-friends for their input on this project: Orrin Harrison, Ralph Janvey, Frank Razzano, Darrel Rice, and Bob Wise.

Law, The Law Governing Lawyers. Reprinted by permission of the American Law Institute; and (3) Aibel, Corporate Counsel and Business Ethics: A Personal Review reprinted by permission of the Missouri Law Review, Copyright 1994 by the Curators of the University of Missouri.

I dedicate this book with all my love to my wonderful children Alexandra (Alex), Avram (Avi) and Phillip (Bear) and to our terrific dog Teddy.

TABLE OF CONTENTS

TABLE OF CASES

The principal cases are in bold type.

LAWYERING AND ETHICS FOR THE BUSINESS ATTORNEY

Fourth Edition

SCENARIO I

WHO'S THE CLIENT?

∎ ∎ ∎

When an individual visits a lawyer's office and asks to be represented in a particular matter, the attorney normally has little difficulty identifying who is the client. Entity representation, however, renders the attorney's client-identification process more complex. The importance of ascertaining the identity of the client is underscored by the American Bar Association's (ABA) Model Rules of Professional Conduct. These Rules impose certain obligations that run from the attorney to the client.[1] For example, Model Rule 1.7 focuses on the loyalty owed by the attorney to each client.[2] Similarly, Model Rule 1.6, with certain exceptions, requires the attorney to maintain confidentiality with respect to information relating to the representation of a client.[3] This confidentiality is premised on two separate, but related, legal doctrines.[4]

The principle of confidentiality under the Model Rules is based *first* on the attorney-client privilege and the work product doctrine.[5] The *second* principle premised on lawyer-client confidentiality is found in the Model Rules themselves.[6] Lawyer-client confidentiality is more encompassing than the attorney-client privilege: Regardless whether the information is protected from disclosure under the attorney-client privilege, Rule 1.6 mandates (with certain exceptions) that all information relating to the representation of that client, irrespective of its source, be kept confidential.[7]

---

[1] *See, e.g.,* ABA Model Rules of Prof. Conduct, Rules 1.3–1.8.

[2] As comment 1 to Model Rule 1.7 states: "Loyalty and independent judgment are essential elements in the lawyer's relationship to a client."

[3] *See* Rule 1.6 of the Model Rules.

[4] *Id*. Rule 1.6 cmt. 3.

[5] *Id. See Upjohn Co. v. United States*, 449 U.S. 383 (1981).

[6] See Model Rule 1.6.

[7] *Id*. Rule 1.6 cmt. 3.

Both the privilege and the attorney's confidentiality obligation contain certain exceptions. For example, when the client gives informed consent to the disclosure of the otherwise protected information, such information is no longer within the scope of Rule 1.6.[8] As a second example, "lawyers within the same firm are generally deemed to have implied authorization to share client information with each other, to the extent necessary to carry out the representation."[9] As a last example, a lawyer under the Model Rules may reveal client information to the extent necessary "to prevent the client from committing a crime or fraud that is reasonably certain to result in substantial injury to the financial interests or property of another and in furtherance of which the client has used or is using the lawyer's services."[10]

Model Rule 1.6's obligations encompass communications between an attorney and a client.[11] An entity, such as a corporation, clearly cannot speak for itself; rather, it must rely on and speak through its representatives. Under the Model Rules, these corporate representatives are defined as constituents.[12] Constituents include directors, officers, employees, members, and shareholders.[13] The communications between the attorney and a constituent of the organization relating to the giving of legal advice to the organization are within the scope of Rule 1.6, so long as the communications relate to the constituent's role or position within the organization.[14]

In a situation where the organization's attorney becomes aware of a constituent's contemplated course of action that is a violation of law that reasonably may be imputed to the organization, the Model Rules provide a series of procedures

---

[8] *Id*. Rule 1.6(a).

[9] *Id*. Rule 1.6 cmt. 5.

[10] Rule 1.6(b)(2). A lawyer also may reveal client information to the extent necessary to establish a claim or defense on behalf of the lawyer in the event a controversy arises between the client and the lawyer. Rule 1.6(b)(5). For other exceptions to the principle of confidentiality, *see* Rule 1.6(b)(1), (3), (4), (6), Rule 1.13(c) & cmt. 6.

[11] *Id*. Rule 1.6(a).

[12] *Id*. Rule 1.13.

[13] *Id*. Rule 1.13(f).

[14] *Id*. Rule 1.13 cmt. 2.

that the attorney should follow, depending on the severity of the potential harm.[15] In the most extreme situation, the attorney may find it necessary to refer the matter to the organization's highest authority.[16] This issue is addressed in later Scenarios of this text. In the event that the organization's highest authority insists upon conduct that violates the law and that likely will result in substantial harm to the organization, the attorney may be obligated to withdraw from the representation and may reveal information concerning the representation to the extent the attorney reasonably views is necessary in order to prevent substantial harm to the organization.[17]

Closely held corporations (such as family corporations) may present complex scenarios. The attorney for such an enterprise often has significant contact with many, if not all, of the constituents.[18] As a result, some of the constituents may think that the attorney is representing them as individuals, in addition to the business enterprise.[19] Indeed, some sources argue that, due to the close nature of these corporations, the attorney's actions have a direct effect on each constituent and consequently, the attorney's obligations should run not only to the organization, but to each constituent as well.[20] In a family corporation, for example, the constituents are generally the employees, shareholders, officers and directors of the enterprise.[21] In addition, the business operations of a closely held corporation are oftentimes the sole source of livelihood for its shareholders. In such a situation, the corporation's success takes on paramount importance to each shareholder; if things go sour, such shareholders have no viable escape from their

---

[15] *Id.* Rule 1.13(b) & cmt. 4.

[16] *Id.* Rule 1.13(b)(3) & cmt. 5.

[17] *Id.* Rules 1.13(c), (d), 1.16(a), (b). *See* C. Wolfram, *Modern Legal Ethics* § 13.7 (1986).

[18] *See* Mitchell, *Professional Responsibility and the Close Corporation: Toward a Realistic Ethic*, 74 Cornell L. Rev. 466 (1989); Comment, *Once You Enter This Family There's No Getting Out: Ethical Considerations of Representing Family-Owned Businesses*, 75 UMKC L. Rev. 1085 (2007).

[19] *See* Haynsworth, *Competent Counseling of Small Business Clients*, 13 U.C. Davis L. Rev. 401 (1980); Mitchell, note 18 *supra.*

[20] Mitchell, *supra* note 18, at 506. *See In re Brownstein*, 602 P.2d 655 (Or. 1979). *But see Skarbrevik v. Cohen, England & Whitfield*, 282 Cal. Rptr. 627 (Ct. App. 1991).

[21] *See, e.g., Galler v. Galler*, 203 N.E. 2d 577 (Ill. 1964); *Triggs v. Triggs*, 385 N.E. 2d 1254 (N.Y. 1978).

investment.[22] These problems are exacerbated when individual shareholders have different personal interests, and each attempts to implement his/her individual goal within the company's policies and corporate framework.

It should be noted that in the partnership context, some courts have found that the attorney representing the organization also represents the individual partners.[23] As one court explained: "In the context of the representation of a partnership, the attorney for the partnership represents all the partners as to matters of partnership business."[24] Under this approach, an individual partner (even under privity principles) may bring a malpractice suit against the organization's attorney. For example, in one such case, the court allowed a limited partner to file a malpractice claim against the attorney that had been retained on behalf of the limited partnership.[25] Other courts, however, have adhered to the entity theory of

---

[22] *See* D. Branson, J. Heminway, M. Loewenstein, M. Steinberg & M. Warren, *Business Enterprises: Legal Structures, Governance and Policy* 405–494 (2d ed. 2012); Gross, *What Duties Does Corporate Counsel Owe to Minority Shareholders in a Closely Held Corporation*, 35 Ohio N.U. L. Rev. 987 (2009); Hendon, *Combatting Legal Theft: Arguments For Shareholder/Employees Terminated From Close Corporations*, 77 Or. L. Rev. 735, 737 (1998); Moll, *Shareholder Oppression v. Employment At Will in the Close Corporation: The Investment Model Solution*, 1999 U. Ill. L. Rev. 517 (1999); Siegel, *Corporate Inversions: The Interplay of Tax, Corporate, and Economic Implications*, 29 Del. J. Corp. L. 377 (2004).

[23] *See e.g. Metropolitan Life Insurance Company v. The Guardian Life Insurance Company of America*, 2009 WL 1439717 (N.D. Ill. 2009); *Adell v. Sommers, Schwartz, Silver and Schwartz*, 428 N.W.2d 26 (Mich. Ct. App. 1998).

[24] *Wortham & Van Liew v. Superior Court*, 233 Cal. Rptr. 725, 728 (Ct. App. 1987). *See also, Law v. Harvey*, 2007 WL 1280585, at *5 (N.D. Cal. 2007) (holding that attorney was representing the partnership and the partners in their individual capacity).

[25] *Adell v. Sommers, Schwartz, Silver and Schwartz*, 428 N.W.2d 26, 30 (Mich. Ct. App. 1998). Note that, depending on the circumstances, nonclients may bring negligence claims against the subject attorney. *See, e.g., McCamish, Martin, Brown & Loeffler v. F.E. Appling Interests*, 991 S.W. 2d 787 (Tex. 1999) (negligent misrepresentation claim based on issuance of defective opinion letter to nonclient); *Hines v. Data Line Systems Inc.*, 114 Wash. 2d 127, 787 P. 2d 8 (1990) (negligent preparation of private placement memorandum to investors in securities offering); Michels, *Third-Party Negligence Claims Against Counsel: A Proposed Unified Liability Standard*, 22 Geo. J. Leg. Eth. 143 (2009).

representation in the partnership setting.[26] Consequently, depending on the jurisdiction and the underlying circumstances, it may be uncertain whether an attorney for a partnership represents only the enterprise, or, absent an agreement otherwise, is deemed to represent the individuals as well.

An attorney for a newly forming or formed corporation should discuss potentially significant issues and conflicts before they arise. When representing a closely held corporation, the attorney should monitor the situations in which significant adverse interests may arise. The need for caution results from the fact that in close corporations the interests and rights of the organization and the constituents who control the organization often start off as consistent with one another.[27] Perhaps because of this alignment of interests, at least some courts take the position that, unless the parties agree otherwise, the attorney represents the constituents in their individual capacities as well as the organization.[28] This approach, however, is contrary to the generally accepted "entity" rule, according to which the entity (or the organization) is the client, and not the individual shareholders.[29]

Under the entity rule, "where a lawyer represents a corporation, the client is the corporation, not the corporation's shareholders."[30] As explained by one court:

> "[W]here an attorney represents a closely held corporation, the attorney [normally] ... owes no separate duty of diligence and care to an individual shareholder. ... [A]n attorney representing a

---

[26] *See, e.g., Hopper v. Frank*, 16 F.3d 92 (5th Cir. 1994) (applying Mississippi law); *Eurycleia Partners, LP v. Seward & Kissel, LLP*, 12 N.Y. 3d 553, 910 N.E. 2d 976, 883 N.Y.S. 2d 147 (Ct. App. 2009).

[27] *See, e.g., Wilkes v. Springfield Nursing Home, Inc.*, 353 N.E. 2d 657 (Mass. 1977).

[28] *See, e.g., In re Brownstein*, 602 P.2d 655 (Or. 1979), *citing, In re Banks*, 584 P.2d 284 (Or. 1978).

[29] *See, e.g., Skarbrevik v. Cohen, England & Whitfield*, 282 Cal. Rptr. 627 (Ct. App. 1991); *Egan v. McNamara*, 467 A.2d 733 (D.C. 1983); *Jesse v. Danforth*, 485 N.W.2d 63 (Wis. 1992); *Canegie Associates Ltd. v. Miller,* 2008 WL 4106907 (N.Y. Sup. Ct. 2008).

[30] *McKinney v. McMeans*, 147 F. Supp. 2d 898, 901 (M.D. Tenn. 2001). *See also,* Model Rule 1.13(a) ("A lawyer employed or retained by an organization represents the organization acting through its duly authorized constituents.").

corporation does not become the attorney for the individual stockholders merely because the attorney's actions on behalf of the corporation may also benefit the stockholders. The duty of an attorney for a corporation is first and foremost to the corporation, even though the legal advice rendered to the corporation may affect the shareholders."[31]

Contrary to the entity theory of representation,[32] some courts take the position that counsel represents individual shareholders in addition to the organization, based on that individual's reasonable expectation of being separately represented.[33] As one court explained: "Although, in the ordinary corporate situation, corporate counsel does not necessarily become counsel for the corporation's shareholders . . . where, as here, the corporation is a close corporation consisting of only two shareholders with equal interests in the corporation, it is indeed reasonable for each shareholder to believe that the corporate counsel is in effect his own individual attorney."[34] To hold otherwise, the court reasoned, would "exalt form over substance."[35]

Ascertaining whether such a reasonable expectation exists may hinge on the frequency and quality of encounters between the attorney and the individual. Elements that have been deemed relevant in this determination include: "[T]he extent and nature of the attorney's representation of the constituent in individual matters, the attorney's representation of entity clients with interests that diverge from those of the constituent, any oral or written representations made by the attorney

---

[31] *Brennan v. Ruffner*, 640 So. 2d 143, 145–146 (Fla. Dist. Ct. App. 1994). *See SEC v. Credit Bancorp, Ltd.*, 96 F. Supp. 2d 357 (S.D.N.Y. 2000).

[32] *See* cases cited *supra* notes 29–31.

[33] *See e.g.,* Comment, *An Expectations Approach to Client Identity*, 106 Harv. L. Rev. 687 (1993).

[34] *Rosman v. Shapiro*, 653 F.Supp. 1441, 1445 (S.D.N.Y. 1987), *citing, Westinghouse Electric Corp. v. Kerr-McGee Corp.*, 580 F.2d 1311 (7th Cir. 1978), *Glover v. Libman*, 578 F. Supp. 748 (N.D. Ga. 1983), *Bobbitt v. Victorian House, Inc.*, 545 F. Supp. 1124 (N.D. Ill. 1982).

[35] 653 F. Supp. at 1445. *See* Gross, *supra* note 22, 35 Ohio N.U. L. Rev. at 1005 (stating that in the small closely-held corporation setting, "if a lawyer leads an individual to [reasonably] believe she represents him, then the lawyer would owe him traditional obligations, including a duty of confidentiality").

regarding the representation, the person to whom the attorney's services were billed and who in return paid these bills, and the presence of independent counsel for the constituent."[36]

One of the corporate lawyer's tasks during the incorporation process is to draft the pertinent documents. These documents may include, for example, the articles of incorporation, bylaws, stock transfer restrictions, employment agreements, and the shareholder agreement. While documents such as the articles of incorporation and corporate bylaws may not give rise to an individual's reasonable expectation of being separately represented by the drafting attorney, the situation may become more problematic where the lawyer drafts documents that set forth the rights and interests of individual shareholders. Such documents may include buy-sell agreements, voting agreements, and employment contracts. Presumably, the attorney drafts such documents with the corporation's best interests in mind. One may ponder, however, whether the individuals, especially those who have had prior significant interactions with the attorney, have a reasonable expectation that the attorney is simultaneously protecting their personal best interests.[37]

If deemed to be concurrently representing the organization as well as an individual constituent, the attorney may be in a precarious position. As clients, each is owed the duties of loyalty and confidentiality.[38] If the attorney in fact is representing each of these common clients, then that attorney evidently is further bound by the obligations relating to intermediaries. For example, in a situation where an attorney is rendering legal advice to two clients who are organizing a business enterprise, the attorney is likely to be serving as an intermediary.[39]

---

[36] Comment, *supra* note 33, 106 Harv. L. Rev. at 691.

[37] *Id.* at 691–704. *See Minion v. Nagin*, 394 F.3d 1062, 1069 (8th Cir. 2005) (concluding that, as set forth in the complaint, attorney-client relationship existed between counsel for the corporation and individual shareholder-employee when counsel drafted key documents and rendered legal advice that focused on such shareholder-employee's personal interests, including his employment agreement with the corporation).

[38] *See* Model Rules 1.6, 1.7.

[39] Former Model Rule 2.2(a)–(c).

Former ABA Model Rule 2.2 set forth obligations assumed by an attorney serving as an intermediary.[40] These obligations today generally are set forth in Model Rule 1.7 and comments thereto. Accordingly, in this setting, the attorney must consult "with each client concerning the implications of the common representation" and procure "each client's consent to the common representation."[41] This consultation requires the attorney to present to each client the advantages, disadvantages, and risks involved, including the effect on the attorney-client privilege.[42] As an intermediary, the attorney must consult with each client regarding decisions to be made, so that each client is able to make adequately informed decisions.[43] In so doing, the attorney's obligation of confidentiality remains intact. Thus, confidences communicated to counsel by one common client ordinarily should not be revealed (absent that client's consent) to any of the other common clients. As a result, the attorney must strike a delicate balance between keeping each client adequately informed and maintaining the requisite confidentiality.[44] Nonetheless, in the event that litigation eventuates between the clients, communications between these common clients and the attorney intermediary generally will not be shielded from discovery by the attorney-client privilege.[45]

What steps an attorney representing a forming or just-formed closely held corporation should take to minimize potential conflicts of interest, liability exposure, and violation of the ethical rules at times are illusive.[46] One approach customarily used is for the attorney to have all the parties

---

[40] *Id.* Former Model Rule 2.2(a)–(c). Note that the 2002 amendments to the Model Rules, implementing the Ethics 2000 Commission's position, deleted Rule 2.2. Revised Rule 1.7 presumably encompasses the lawyer as intermediary dilemma. *See* Model Rule 1.7 cmt. 28. Scenario III herein addresses in greater depth the lawyer as intermediary.

[41] *Id.* Former Model Rule 2.2(a)(1).

[42] *Id.*

[43] *Id.* Former Model Rule 2.2(b).

[44] Model Rule 1.7 cmts. 28–33; former Model Rule 2.2 cmt. 6. *See AVR, Inc. v. Cemstone Products, Co.*, 1993 WL 104933, at *7 (D. Minn. 1993); *Hansen, Jones & Leta, P.C. v. Segal*, 220 B.R. 434 (D. Utah 1998); Rollock, *Professional Responsibility and Organization of the Family Business: The Lawyer as Intermediary*, 73 Ind. L.J. 567 (1998).

[45] *Id.* Former Model Rule 2.2 cmt. 6.

[46] *See* Mitchell, *supra* note 18, 74 Cornell L. Rev. 466 (1989).

involved agree that the attorney is representing only the organization, rather than the individuals. Such an agreement, of course, should be evidenced in writing. Although at times expensive, perhaps the safest way for the attorney to avoid potential liability resulting from multiple representation is to have each constituent seek independent counsel. At the arguable minimum, each shareholder should be informed to obtain the advice of his or her attorney. For example, language incorporated into a shareholder agreement for a closely held corporation may provide:

> "The Shareholders acknowledge that this Shareholder Agreement contains significant restrictions on their respective interests, and that they have been informed to seek their own legal counsel for themselves (and for the spouse, if any, of each individual Shareholder) and they represent and warrant that they are not represented by and are not relying on the Corporation's legal counsel for any legal advice concerning the meaning, interpretation, or legal effect of this Agreement."

However, retention of separate counsel for each shareholder is likely to make the process of organizing a business far more expensive. The constituent shareholders may well view these costs as prohibitive. Indeed, vigorous representation by separately retained counsel may "nix" the venture before it ever commences.

The following case provides an illustration where counsel for a closely-held corporation seeks to represent both the enterprise and minority shareholders in a dispute among the shareholders with respect to control of the corporation. As stated by the court: "Corporate counsel should . . . refrain from taking part in any controversies of factional differences among shareholders as to control of the corporation, so that he or she can advise the corporation without bias or prejudice."

WONG V. WONG
2013 WL 953865 (Ct. App. Cal. 2013)[47]

This litigation concerns the election of officers and directors of two related corporations, the Wong Family Investment Fund, Inc. (fund) and the Wong Family Benevolent Association, Inc., of Los Angeles (association). The association is a nonprofit mutual benefit association that owns the real properties that are managed by its wholly owned subsidiary, the fund. The association has several hundred members or shareholders who are the male descendants of the Wong family.

Each year, the association's governing council selects the members who will run for office. At the association's annual meeting in December, the members elect the association's officers and the fund's directors for the following year.

In 2010, the association's members were "factionalized" and embroiled in several lawsuits over control of the association. The disagreement arose in May 2010 when, according to one faction, the association's president Nam San Wong violated the bylaws by disbanding the association's governing council and installing a new council (the revised 2010 council) without the approval or vote of the shareholders. When the revised 2010 council selected the candidates for the annual election of officers and directors, a group of shareholders objected that the revised council was not authorized to perform that function and sought to conduct a separate election.

On November 20, 2010, the fund's 2010 board of directors retained Attorney Albert C. Lum as the fund's corporate counsel.

On December 27, 2010, Lum, while serving as the fund's corporate counsel, filed on behalf of five minority shareholders (plaintiffs) the present complaint for breach of fiduciary duty against association president Nam San Wong and four members of the revised 2010 council (defendants).

On January 15, 2011, the fund's newly elected board of directors terminated Lum as corporate counsel. However, Lum continued to represent the five individual plaintiffs in this action against the association's president Nam San Wong and the four members of the revised council.

---

[47] This decision is not officially published under the California Rules of Court.

On March 2, 2011, the fund and the individual defendants moved to disqualify Lum as plaintiffs' counsel. . . .

A Corporate Counsel's Duty of Loyalty to the Corporation Is Paramount to the Individual Interests of the Shareholders

To analyze the disqualification ruling in this case, we must first consider the duty of loyalty that Lum owed to his former client, the fund.

In *Metro-Goldwyn-Mayer, Inc. v. Tracinda Corp.* (1995) 36 Cal. App. 4th 1832, we stated that a corporate counsel's duty to the corporation takes precedence over the interests of the shareholders and that a corporate counsel must refrain from taking part in a dispute among shareholders over control of the corporation:

> "Case law provides the following guidelines: [A]s attorneys for [a] corporation, counsel's first duty is to [the corporation]. . . . Corporate counsel should, of course, refrain from taking part in any controversies or factional differences among shareholders as to control of the corporation, so that he or she can advise the corporation without bias or prejudice. . . . Even where counsel for a closely held corporation treats the interests of the majority shareholders and the corporation interchangeably, it is the attorney-client relationship with the corporation that is paramount for purposes of upholding the attorney-client privilege against a minority shareholder's challenge. . . . These cases make clear that corporate counsel's direct duty is to the client corporation, not to the shareholders individually, even though the legal advice rendered to the corporation may affect the shareholders. . . ."

It is undisputed that Lum advised two clients, the fund and the minority shareholder plaintiffs, with regard to the same matter, the election of officers and directors for 2011. While serving as the fund's corporate counsel, Lum applied for a TRO on behalf of the minority shareholders to halt the installation of the corporation's (the fund's) directors and the parent corporation's (the association's) officers. After the TRO was denied, the newly installed directors terminated Lum as corporate counsel and filed a cross-complaint for the fund against the minority shareholders. Based on these undisputed facts, we conclude, as a matter of law, that the interests of Lum's former and current clients with regard to the election were either adverse or potentially adverse. . . .

Because Lum advised two adverse or potentially adverse clients—the fund and the individual plaintiffs—with regard to the same matter without obtaining the fund's knowing and written consent as required under [the California ethical rules], he was properly disqualified from representing plaintiffs in this litigation.

Our determination that Lum was subject to disqualification for failing to obtain the fund's knowing and written consent to his representation of the minority shareholder plaintiffs is consistent with the general rule that "[c]orporate counsel should, of course, refrain from taking part in any controversies or factional differences among shareholders as to control of the corporation, so that he or she can advise the corporation without bias or prejudice. . . ." The undisputed facts of this case compel us to conclude that Lum violated his duty of loyalty to the fund when he agreed to represent the minority shareholder plaintiffs without obtaining the fund's informed written consent. . . .

As previously discussed, Lum should have refrained from representing the minority shareholders or, at the very least, should have obtained the fund's informed written consent before representing plaintiffs. Because the undisputed facts show, as a matter of law, that Lum did not obtain the fund's informed written consent . . . , we conclude, as a matter of law, the disqualification motion was properly granted regardless of the disclosure or nondisclosure of confidential information. . . .

The following Scenario highlights some of the significant ethical issues and dilemmas an attorney faces when attempting to represent a closely-held enterprise.

SCENARIO

Ashley and Alan Beasley are first cousins. A few years back, they started a small internet dating service. At first, the business was nothing more than an entertaining pastime. As the site's popularity grew, however, they became increasingly aware of its money-making potential. Although their dating service was offered free of charge, the site had enough daily visitors to warrant a call from a large restaurant chain inquiring about placing a banner advertisement on Ashley's and Alan's web page. They were thrilled at the proposition and the potential opportunities it presented. Before making any rash decisions, Ashley and Alan sought out professional legal advice.

The next day the two paid a visit to their old high-school friend, Buddy Buddanut, who had graduated from law school three years earlier. They explained to him their situation and asked what course of action he recommended. Since his admission to the Bar, Buddy had little experience with business planning or corporate formation; however, as a long-time friend of the Beasley family, and in need of the legal fees to be generated by corporate representation, he accepted the engagement. Having recently attended a CLE program on the advantages of incorporating business enterprises, Buddy suggested they incorporate the business immediately. He explained the tremendous advantages that he had heard a corporate structure provided and the liability shield it gave to Ashley and Alan. They agreed and Buddy pulled out an incorporation forms template that happened to be on his computer. "Double A Dating Services, Inc." thereupon became a validly formed corporation after filing the required documents with the State.

After being retained, Buddy suggested that members of the board of directors be named. Ashley and Alan decided to appoint themselves and one seemingly objective party. Ashley said that her younger brother David, who had just received his M.B.A., was not terribly busy these days, and would be happy to become a shareholder and board member. Wanting to keep the business in the family, Alan found this agreeable. Buddy next explained the necessity of corporate bylaws, allocation of control, and dispute resolution procedures.

Ashley and Alan decided that the corporation issue 100 shares of common stock, with Ashley and Alan each taking 48 shares, and thus each having 48% ownership of the corporation. The remaining four shares were issued to David, who was now a part-time employee of the business. Since their positions in Double A Dating Services, Inc. were going to be full time careers, Ashley and Alan decided that they would each fully participate in the daily management and operations of the corporation.

Business went swimmingly. Several large advertising site accounts were procured and the number of "hits" on Double A's site was increasing every day. With virtually no overhead cost, Ashley and Alan were brilliantly making out. Then Alan met his soul mate and suddenly lost much of his enthusiasm for the business. Ashley, although concerned, decided to say nothing in hopes that Alan would eventually come around. Instead, he announced that he was getting married, and wanted to work no more than thirty hours a week. Ashley was now extremely concerned. Rather than assisting Ashley in making significant business decisions, Alan was spending much of his time with his fiancée.

Even without Alan's input, things continued to go smoothly for the next six months. Ashley was becoming increasingly amenable to Alan's role, or lack thereof, as it allowed her the opportunity to run key aspects of the business largely on her own. One day, Ashley was approached by Sid Savvy, who owned an online service similar to that of Double A's Dating Services. Sid asked Ashley if Double A's Dating Services would be interested in acquiring another internet dating service. Sid explained that he was ready to retire and get out of the fast-paced life of a dotcom entrepreneur, and was willing to accept $375,000 for his company. After giving the idea careful consideration, Ashley concluded that this was the best thing that could happen to the business. An affordable source of financing was readily available, and Sid's internet site, Savvy Sid's Find-A-Date, Inc., was already a legend in its own time. It was the most popular dating service in the region. Ashley called Alan to tell him the exciting news. Alan, however, was furious with Ashley for even considering such a significant proposition without consulting him.

Perplexed, Ashley asked why it would even matter to him, considering that he had relatively little involvement in the business for nearly a year. Alan told Ashley that regardless of his diminished role in key operations, he was still a 48% owner and heavily dependent on his salary from their corporation, since Double A's Dating Service did not pay shareholder dividends. Alan felt the acquisition presented too much of a financial risk to their corporation, and that Ashley wanted to grow simply for the sake of growth. He reiterated that he, not Ashley, was the company's great visionary.

Ashley realized that Alan could use his 48% voting interest and position on the board of directors in attempts to thwart the planned acquisition. So she decided to make David her voting ally. The next stockholders' meeting was only one month away. Ashley phoned David and explained the situation. Not only did Ashley plan to defeat Alan in the vote, she also told David that it was time to remove Alan from the board and terminate his employment altogether. David agreed to go along with the plan, provided that he would receive a $5,000 monthly increase in his salary.

Ashley then called Buddy at his office. She explained to Buddy what was about to happen, and asked Buddy to do what was necessary as the Company's attorney to help effectuate Alan's removal from the board of directors and termination of his employment, due to the fact that he was no longer pulling his weight. Ashley also directed Buddy to draft a written offer by the Corporation to purchase Alan's 48% stock ownership at 50% of the stock's recently appraised value. Buddy, confused and a bit uneasy about being involved in a family squabble, began to carry out Ashley's requests. Two days before the stockholders' meeting, Buddy attended another CLE program. The topic of this one was shareholder oppression in a close corporation. Buddy walked out with a sick feeling in his stomach. He wondered, was he about to become one of Alan's oppressors and subject not only Ashley and David but also himself to serious liability exposure?

Did Buddy act properly in initially accepting the engagement and now following Ashley's directive? What steps should Buddy undertake at this time?

CONFIDENTIALITY OWED TO EXISTING AND FORMER CLIENTS

■ ■ ■

Attorneys sometimes face a tension between two fundamental principles of professional conduct. Lawyers owe a duty of confidentiality to their clients, a duty that, with certain exceptions, prohibits them from "reveal[ing] information relating to the representation of a client."[1] But attorneys cannot assist a client "in conduct that the lawyer knows is criminal or fraudulent."[2] The tension between these rules often arises when an attorney believes that she has a duty or wishes to remain silent regarding a client's representation, but also is concerned that such silence may facilitate a client's fraudulent or criminal act.

Under ABA Model Rule 1.6(b), a version of which has been adopted by the vast majority of states, an attorney has discretion to disclose information concerning the representation of a client to the extent that such attorney reasonably believes is necessary:

"(1) to prevent reasonably certain death or substantial bodily harm;

---

[1] Rule 1.6(a) of the ABA Model Rules provides: "(a) A lawyer shall not reveal information relating to representation of a client unless the client gives informed consent, the disclosure is impliedly authorized in order to carry out the representation or the disclosure is permitted by paragraph (b)."

[2] Model Rule 1.2(d). Rule 1.2(d) states: "A lawyer shall not counsel a client to engage, or assist a client, in conduct that the lawyer knows is criminal or fraudulent, but a lawyer may discuss the legal consequences of any proposed course of conduct with a client and may counsel or assist a client to make a good faith effort to determine the validity, scope, meaning or application of the law." *See also, United States v. Collins*, reported in, Wall St. J., Nov. 17–18, 2012, at B2 (former partner of law firm of Mayer Brown, who was held responsible for client's fraudulent statements, criminally convicted).

(2) to prevent the client from committing a crime or fraud that is reasonably certain to result in substantial injury to the financial interests or property of another and in furtherance of which the client has used or is using the lawyer's service; [or]

(3) to prevent, mitigate or rectify substantial injury to the financial interests or property of another that is reasonably certain to result or has resulted from the client's commission of a crime or fraud in furtherance of which the client has used the lawyer's services."[3]

The Securities and Exchange Commission (SEC) in its Standards of Professional Conduct for Attorneys likewise permits an attorney to reveal to the SEC, without the client's consent, such confidential information.[4]

The issue of disclosure becomes further complicated when the attorney's client is an organization, such as a corporation. Because a corporation is an artificial entity, it must act through its duly authorized constituents. Thus, if an attorney learns that an officer or employee of a corporate client is engaging or is about to engage in fraudulent activity, the attorney must ascertain whether such person is acting on behalf of or independently from the corporation. In this situation, Model Rule 1.13 directs the attorney to "proceed as is reasonably

---

[3] The overwhelming majority of states permit a lawyer to reveal a client's fraud or crime that threatens substantial financial loss. *See* American Law Institute, *Restatement (Third) of the Law Governing Lawyers* § 67, Reporter's Note at 514 (2000). *See also*, Model Rule 4.1(b) which provides that an attorney, when representing a client, shall not knowingly "fail to disclose a material fact to a third person when disclosure is necessary to avoid assisting a criminal or fraudulent act by a client, unless disclosure is prohibited by Rule 1.6."

[4] *See* 17 C.F.R. § 205.3(d)(2) of the SEC's Standards:

"(2) An attorney appearing and practicing before the Commission in the representation of an issuer may reveal to the Commission, without the issuer's consent, confidential information related to the representation to the extent the attorney reasonably believes necessary:

(i)To prevent the issuer from committing a material violation that is likely to cause substantial injury to the financial interest or property of the issuer or investors; . . . or

(iii)   To rectify the consequences of a material violation by the issuer that caused, or may cause, substantial injury to the financial interest or property of the issuer or investors in the furtherance of which the attorney's services were used."

necessary in the best interest of the organization" including, if warranted, referring the matter "to the highest authority that can act on behalf of the organization as determined by applicable law."[5]

A similar approach is taken by the Sarbanes-Oxley Act (SOX), enacted in 2002. Section 307 of SOX directs the SEC to adopt a rule:

> "(1) requiring a [subject] attorney to report evidence of a material violation of securities law or breach of fiduciary duty or similar violation by the company or any agent thereof, to the chief legal counsel or the chief executive officer of the company (or the equivalent thereof); and (2) if the counsel or officer does not appropriately respond to the evidence (adopting, as necessary, appropriate remedial measures or sanctions with respect to the violation), requiring [such] attorney to report the evidence to the audit committee of the board of directors of the issuer or to another committee of the board of directors comprised solely of directors not employed directly or indirectly by the issuer, or to the board of directors."[6]

Responding to this directive, the SEC's Standards of Conduct for Attorneys resemble existing ethical standards set forth in the ABA Model Rules. For example, the SEC's Standards

> "require an attorney to report evidence of a material violation, determined accordingly to an objective standard, 'up-the-ladder' within the issuer to the chief legal counsel or the chief executive officer of the company or the equivalent; [and] require an attorney, if the chief legal counsel or the chief executive officer of the company does not respond appropriately to the evidence, to report the evidence to the audit committee, another

---

[5] Model Rule 1.13(b). The highest authority within the organization ordinarily is the board of directors or similar governing body.

[6] SOX § 307, 15 U.S.C. § 7245. *See* Bainbridge & Johnson, *Managerialism, Legal Ethics, and Sarbanes-Oxley Section 307,* 2004 Mich. St. L. Rev. 299 (2004).

committee of independent directors, or the full board of directors."[7]

An important justification underlying the above pronouncements is that by bringing the potential fraud or illegality to light within the company, the attorney may be able to help prevent its occurrence.

Although the attorney may communicate with constituents of the corporation (such as directors, shareholders, and employees) in connection with learning about the potential fraud, she will be limited in terms of what information she may share with the constituents, particularly if their interests are adverse to the corporate client. As a comment to Rule 1.13 states, the "lawyer may not disclose to such constituents information relating to the representation except for disclosures explicitly or implicitly authorized by the organizational client in order to carry out the representation or as otherwise permitted by Rule 1.6."[8] Thus, when communicating with constituents associated with an organizational client, the business lawyer must be able to distinguish between those persons acting in their organizational capacity on behalf of the company and those acting in their personal constituent capacity, and must disclose confidential information relating to her representation of the client only to the former.

When a client, whether an individual or organization, during the course of a lawyer's active representation of that client uses or plans to use the attorney's work to perpetrate a fraud, the ABA Model Rules permit the lawyer to withdraw from the representation.[9] Indeed, when continued representation will result in a violation of applicable law or ethical rules, the

---

[7] SEC Press Release No. 2003–13 (2003). *See* 17 C.F.R § 205.3. The SEC Standards, as an alternative, permit a subject company to establish a "qualified legal compliance committee" (QLCC) for reporting and responding with respect to evidence of a material violation. *See* 17 C.F.R. § 205.3(c). Thus far, the QLCC alternative has not been widely adopted. *See* Rosen, *Resistances to Reforming Corporate Governance: The Diffusion of QLCCs*, 74 Fordham L. Rev. 1251, 1252 (2005) (pointing out that "97.5% of issuers have not yet adopted" the QLCC).

[8] Model Rule 1.13 cmt. 2. *See generally* Veasy & Di Guglielmo, *The Tensions, Stresses and Responsibilities of the Lawyer for the Corporation*, 62 Bus. Law. 1 (2006).

[9] *Id*. Rule 1.16(b)(2).

attorney must withdraw.[10] The attorney also may cease representation if the client has used the "lawyer's services to perpetrate a crime or fraud."[11] Given that an attorney may withdraw from representing a client when the lawyer's services are used to perpetrate an ongoing or completed fraud or crime, a key issue thus becomes how much "noise" ("noisy" withdrawal) the attorney can make in terminating the representation—that is, what can or should the attorney do or say to indicate that the client has acted or will act fraudulently or illegally? For example, may the lawyer disaffirm a legal opinion she rendered based on materially false information provided by her client? By disaffirming a previously issued legal opinion and making such a "noisy" withdrawal, a likely collateral consequence is the disclosure, inferentially, of information that relates to the representation. "Unlike a silent, unexplained withdrawal, a lawyer's explicit disaffirmance of work product [such as a legal opinion] prepared by the lawyer in the course of the representation, may well be understood as amounting to a representation by the lawyer that the client information on which the disaffirmed document relied is untrustworthy, thereby necessitating the withdrawal."[12]

Today, the ABA Model Rules, the SEC Standards, and the vast majority of states allow counsel to make a "noisy" withdrawal when the client uses such lawyer's services to commit an ongoing or completed fraud or crime.[13] Although the

---

[10] *Id.* Rule 1.16(a)(1).

[11] *Id.* Rule 1.16(b)(3).

[12] *See* ABA Comm. on Ethics and Professional Responsibility, *Withdrawal When a Lawyer's Services Will Otherwise Be Used to Perpetrate a Fraud*, Formal Op. 92–366 (1992) (setting forth the limited instances in which an attorney may "disaffirm documents prepared in the course of the representation that are being, or will be, used in furtherance of [a] fraud, even though such a 'noisy' withdrawal may have the collateral effect of inferentially revealing client confidences"). *See also*, Scannell, *The Stanford Affair: Top Lawyer's Withdrawal From Stanford Case Waves a Flag*, Wall St. J., March 6, 2009, at C2.

[13] *See, e.g.,* Model Rule 1.6(b)(2), (3), cmt. 10 to Model Rule 1.2, cmt. 3 to Model Rule 4.1; N.Y. Rules of Prof. Conduct, Rule 1.6(b)(3) (permitting an attorney "to withdraw a written or oral opinion or representation previously given by the lawyer and reasonably believed by the lawyer still to be relied upon by a third person, where the lawyer has discovered that the opinion or representation was based on materially inaccurate information or is being used to further a crime or fraud"); Texas Rules of Prof. Conduct, Rule 1.05(c)(7), (c)(8); SEC Standards, 17 C.F.R. § 205.3(d)(2).

SEC has declined to adopt a rule requiring that counsel make a noisy withdrawal,[14] a small number of states, such as Tennessee, mandate that counsel make a noisy withdrawal under specified circumstances.[15]

As noted at the outset of this Scenario, the rules governing an attorney's duty of confidentiality vary by jurisdiction and also may expand or restrict the grounds on which an attorney may or must disclose client confidences. California, for example, precludes attorney disclosure of client confidences to prevent or rectify financial harm.[16] Notably, the American Law Institute's (ALI) Restatement of the Law Governing Lawyers permits (but does not require) an attorney to disclose client confidences to prevent, rectify, or mitigate substantial financial loss, even if the fraud has already taken place.[17] Even more significant, as discussed earlier, many states pursuant to their ethical rules permit (and a small number of states mandate) disclosure of client fraud. Likewise, several states, including Michigan,[18]

---

[14] *See* Securities Exchange Act Release Nos. 42726, 47282 (2003).

[15] *See* Tenn. Rules of Prof. Conduct, Rule 4.1(b), (c). For further discussion, *see* M. Steinberg, *Attorney Liability After Sarbanes-Oxley* § 3.05 (2015); Cramton, Cohen & Koniak, *Legal and Ethical Duties of Lawyers After Sarbanes-Oxley*, 49 Vill. L. Rev. 725 (2004).

[16] *See* Cal. Bus. & Prof. Code § 6068(e).

[17] ALI, *Restatement of the Law Governing Lawyers* § 67 (2000), which provides in part:

"§ 67 Using or Disclosing Information to Prevent, Rectify, or Mitigate Substantial Financial Loss

(1) A lawyer may use or disclose confidential client information when the lawyer reasonably believes that its use or disclosure is necessary to prevent a crime or fraud, and:

(a) the crime or fraud threatens substantial financial loss;

(b) the loss has not yet occurred;

(c) the lawyer's client intends to commit the crime or fraud either personally or through a third person; and

(d) the client has employed or is employing the lawyer's services in the matter in which the crime or fraud is committed.

(2) If a crime or fraud described in Subsection (1) has already occurred, a lawyer may use or disclose confidential client information when the lawyer reasonably believes its use or disclosure is necessary to prevent, rectify, or mitigate the loss."

[18] Mich. Rules of Prof. Conduct, Rule 1.6(c)(3) ("A lawyer may reveal . . . confidences and secrets to the extent reasonably necessary to rectify the consequences of a client's illegal or fraudulent act in the furtherance of which the lawyer's services have been used").

Pennsylvania,[19] and Virginia,[20] permit an attorney under certain conditions to disclose client confidences to rectify financial harm. As stated in the ALI's Restatement of the Law Governing Lawyers:

> "A small minority of the states . . . strictly limit disclosure. . . . However, most jurisdictions—currently, 42—have . . . included substantial financial injury (or variant, but similar language) as a ground for permissible disclosure, in addition to substantial bodily harm."[21]

Thus, for example, in Texas, "[a] lawyer may reveal confidential information . . . [w]hen the lawyer has reason to believe it is necessary to do so in order to prevent the client from committing a criminal or fraudulent act . . . [or] to the extent revelation reasonably appears necessary to rectify the consequences of a client's criminal or fraudulent act in the commission of which the lawyer's services had been used."[22] Under these various state rules, for example, an attorney who represented a client when such client fraudulently obtained a loan would be allowed to disclose the fraud underlying the loan as a means of rectifying the consequences of the fraud.[23]

---

[19] Penn. Rules of Prof. Conduct, Rule 1.6(c)(3) ("A lawyer may reveal such information to the extent that the lawyer reasonably believes necessary . . . to prevent, mitigate or rectify the consequences of a client's criminal or fraudulent act in the commission of which the lawyer's services are being or had been used").

[20] Va. Rules of Prof. Conduct, Rule 1.6(b)(3) ("To the extent a lawyer reasonably believes necessary, the lawyer may reveal . . . such information which clearly establishes that the client has, in the course of the representation, perpetrated upon a third party a fraud related to the subject matter of the representation").

[21] ALI, Restatement of the Law Governing Lawyers, supra note 17, § 67, at 514.

[22] Texas Rules of Prof. Conduct, Rule 1.05(c)(7), (c)(8). Various Texas rules "indicate the underlying public policy of furnishing no protection to client information where the client seeks or uses the services of the lawyer to aid in the commission of a crime or fraud." Id. Rule 1.05 cmt. 10.

[23] Further note that under the Texas rule, an attorney does not have a duty to disclose the fraud. See id. Rule 1.05 cmt. 14 ("Although preventative action is permitted by paragraphs (c) and (d), failure to take preventative action does not violate those paragraphs."). See generally Symposium, The Evolving Legal and Ethical Role of the Corporate Attorney After the Sarbanes-Oxley Act of 2002, 52 Am. U. L. Rev. No. 3 (2003); Symposium, The Ethics 2000 Commission: The Adversary System and the Lawyer-Client

As another example, the New Jersey rule *requires* an attorney to reveal client confidences not only when the client's criminal, illegal, or fraudulent act would result in death or substantial bodily harm, but also when the client's actions are "likely to result in . . . substantial injury to the financial interest or property of another."[24] Also consider New York, which specifically addresses the issue of withdrawing previous opinions that may still be relied upon by a third party. In New York, a "lawyer may reveal . . . confidential information to the extent that the lawyer reasonably believes necessary . . . to withdraw a written or oral opinion or representation previously given by the lawyer and reasonably believed by the lawyer still to be relied upon by a third person, where the lawyer has discovered that the opinion or representation was based on materially inaccurate information or is being used to further a crime or fraud."[25]

Regardless of these various state rules permitting disclosure of client confidences, some states have not moved in this direction. The State Bar of California Standing Committee on Professional Responsibility and Conduct, for example, in directly addressing the issue of what an attorney can and should do in light of a client's fraud, has stated that the lawyer is prohibited from disclosing anything regarding the fraudulent activity without the client's consent. The attorney, however, must try to persuade the client from furthering the fraud. If the client persists in the misconduct, the lawyer must withdraw from the representation.[26]

Relationship, 70 Tenn. L. Rev. No. 1 (2002); Symposium, Ethics in Corporate Governance, 3 Wyo. L. Rev. No. 2 (2003); Langevoort, *Where Were the Lawyers? A Behavioral Inquiry Into Lawyers' Responsibility for Clients' Fraud*, 46 Vand. L. Rev. 75 (1993); Painter & Duggan, *Lawyer Disclosure of Corporate Fraud: Establishing a Firm Foundation*, 50 SMU L. Rev. 225 (1996).

[24] N.J. Rules of Prof. Conduct, Rule 1.6(b)(1).

[25] N.Y. Rules of Prof. Conduct, Rule 1.6(b)(3). *See* R. Simon, *Simon's New York Rules of Professional Conduct Annotated*.

[26] *See* State Bar of Cal. Standing Comm. on Prof. Responsibility and Conduct, Formal Op. 1996–146 (1996). *See also,* Cal. Bus. and Prof. Code § 6068(e)(1) ("It is the duty of an attorney . . . to maintain inviolate the confidence, and at every peril to himself or herself to preserve the secrets, of his or her client").

Much of the preceding discussion has focused on what may be considered as exceptions to the general rule of confidentiality owed to clients. Thus, if a lawyer resigned from representation of the client due to the client's fraudulent activity and wishes to disclose the former client's previous fraud, the lawyer would need to search for some basis within the SEC's Standards of Conduct or her jurisdiction's professional rules of ethics (or related commentary) to justify the disclosure of confidential information. This might lead some attorneys to believe that it may be best, and certainly ethically acceptable, if they were to keep knowledge of any previous or continuing fraud to themselves.

Nonetheless, an attorney may not be able to pursue an "ostrich" approach toward a client or former client's fraudulent activity in the name of preserving its confidences. Consider, for example, *In re OPM Leasing Services, Inc.*,[27] involving a law firm that, after learning of its role in closing one fraudulent transaction for a client, received assurances from the client's principals that they would not commit any further fraud. The law firm continued to close fraudulent transactions for the client despite "numerous additional facts . . . that should have raised suspicions about the bona fides of" the transactions.[28]

Although the law firm subsequently terminated its representation as outside general counsel, it agreed to mischaracterize the termination as a mutual decision between the firm and client.[29] After the law firm's resignation, the former client continued to close fraudulent transactions using either in-house counsel or another law firm that was oblivious regarding the actual reasons for the original law firm's resignation.[30]

---

[27] *In re OPM Leasing Services, Inc.* (1983) (Bankruptcy Trustee Report). *See also, In re O.P.M. Leasing Services, Inc.*, 40 B.R. 380 (S.D.N.Y. 1984); S. Taylor, "Ethics and the Law: A Case History," *N.Y. Times Magazine* at 31 (Jan. 9, 1983).

[28] O.P.M. Bankruptcy Trustee Report, *supra* note 27, at 359. *See id.* at 372 (considering these "red flags," the attorneys "should have proceeded with extreme caution" in closing the financings).

[29] *See id.* at 399 (stating that the law firm retained two law professors to counsel it on the ethical issues involved). *See also, id.* at 378–379 (The trustee also noted the close relationship between the law firm and the client, including that the law firm received up to 65% of its revenues from the client and that one of the attorneys served on the client's board of directors).

[30] *Id.* at 417–421.

The law firm's conduct in *OPM* "raise[d] issues beyond professional ethics. . . . No rule of professional ethics can or should exempt lawyers from the general legal proscriptions against willful blindness to the clients' crimes or reckless participation in them."[31] Or, to put the issue another way, "a lawyer is not privileged to unthinkingly permit himself to be co-opted into an ongoing fraud and cast as a dupe or a shield for a wrong-doing client."[32]

This leads to another question: What should an attorney do when the former client's prospective successor counsel calls to find out why she stopped representing the client. A useful measure is to reply, "I am unwilling to explain why I resigned unless the former client gives me permission to tell you." This statement, on its face, merely restates the general principle contained in the Model Rules and protects the former client's confidences. But it also should alert the prospective successor counsel to ask the client to grant permission for the predecessor counsel to discuss the representation. If the client refuses to give such permission, that should signal the prospective successor counsel that the client may be doing something unethical, and, accordingly, should prompt such counsel to decline the representation.[33]

Accordingly, the overwhelming majority of jurisdictions do not require an attorney to make a "noisy" withdrawal or otherwise "report-out" the client's ongoing illegal conduct. Is this the correct approach? Consider the following:

---

[31] *Id.* at 423.

[32] *Carter and Johnson,* [1981 Transfer Binder] CCH Fed. Sec. L. Rep. ¶ 82,847, at 84,172 (SEC 1981). *See In the Matter of Lapine,* [2010 Transfer Binder] CCH Fed. Sec. L. Rep. ¶ 89,039 (SEC 2010).

[33] *See* Brown, *Counsel With a Fraudulent Client,* 17 Rev. Sec. Reg. 913 (1984); Steinberg, *Attorney Liability for Client Fraud,* 1991 Colum. Bus. L. Rev. 1, 21–22 (1991).

SECURITIES AND EXCHANGE COMMISSION
V. SPIEGEL, INC.

Independent Examiner's Report
(U.S. Dist. Ct. N.D. Ill. 2003)

The Securities and Exchange Commission filed this civil action against Spiegel, Inc. on March 7, 2003. The SEC charged that Spiegel violated the federal securities laws by failing to file required periodic reports on Forms 10–K and 10–Q during 2002, and by failing to disclose advice from its auditor that Spiegel may not be able to continue as a "going concern." Upon commencement of this action, Spiegel consented to the entry of a partial final judgment of permanent injunction without admitting or denying the SEC's charges.

Spiegel likewise consented to this Court's appointment of the undersigned Independent Examiner to review Spiegel's financial records from January 1, 2000 to date, and to provide the Court and the parties with a written report (i) discussing Spiegel's financial condition and (ii) identifying any material accounting irregularities. The Court entered its order appointing the Independent Examiner on March 11, 2003. This report is respectfully submitted to the Court and served on the parties pursuant to that order as amended.

Summary of Findings

Facing the need to improve poor sales performance in its retail subsidiaries, Spiegel embarked by 1999 on a program that one of its audit committee members later called "easy credit to pump up sales." Through various techniques involving both its retail subsidiaries and its captive credit card bank subsidiary, Spiegel tilted its portfolio of credit card customers decidedly in the direction of high-risk subprime borrowers. These were customers who often could not get credit elsewhere and who could be counted on to respond to the opportunity to buy merchandise with the easy credit Spiegel offered them. [Subsequently, many of these customers did not pay their credit card bills.]

As Spiegel's financial condition worsened in late 2001, it breached all four loan covenants contained in its bank loan agreements. Spiegel tried desperately to renegotiate its financing with a consortium of 18 banks, but a myriad of problems frustrated this effort. As Spiegel was preparing to file its 2001 [SEC] Form 10–K annual report due in March 2002, its auditor KPMG advised that it would have to give Spiegel a "going concern" opinion, based on Spiegel's inability to conclude its bank refinancing arrangements and other problems.

Spiegel decided not to file its Form 10–K with a going concern opinion. Soon afterwards, Nasdaq indicated that it would delist Spiegel. At the delisting hearing, Spiegel assured Nasdaq that it was only days away from concluding its refinancing arrangements, and that it would then be able to file its Form 10–K without a going concern opinion. After several days, Nasdaq advised Spiegel that it had a last chance to file its Form 10–K and that otherwise it would be immediately delisted.

Spiegel's Chicago-based management—supported by Spiegel's outside counsel Kirkland & Ellis and its outside auditors KPMG—strongly recommended that Spiegel file its Form 10–K [with the SEC] in late May 2002. But the ultimate decision makers for Spiegel were in Germany. Spiegel was only 10% an American public company. About 90% of its equity and all of its voting stock were in the hands of Michael Otto and his family in Hamburg, Germany. Indeed, Spiegel operated in effect as the American division of Otto's huge multinational retail empire, including 89 companies with over 79,000 employees in 21 countries around the globe.

On May 31, 2002 in Hamburg, Spiegel's executive or "board" committee (consisting of Michael Otto and an executive of his private company Otto Versand GmbH) and Spiegel's audit committee (consisting of one present and one former Otto Versand executive) rejected the views of Spiegel's management, Kirkland & Ellis and KPMG, and directed Spiegel not to file its already-late first-quarter 2002 Form 10–Q. As time went by, they likewise directed Spiegel not to file its remaining 2002 Forms 10–Q.

Spiegel's German decision-makers had been fully briefed on the array of serious problems Spiegel faced, including at a seven-hour meeting with Spiegel's Chicago-based executives several weeks before. But they refused to allow Spiegel to file its reports with the SEC because they felt that a going concern opinion would cause Spiegel's suppliers to refuse to extend credit to Spiegel for the merchandise it purchased for resale. Such a result could lead Spiegel to bankruptcy. Likewise, Spiegel was concerned about the impact a going concern opinion would have on investors and employees.

It was only the prospect of an SEC Enforcement Division investigation that made Spiegel begin to belatedly file reports in February 2003—after not having filed a single periodic report since November 2001 (its third-quarter 2001 Form 10–Q). This 15–month hiatus in periodic reporting left investors without the disclosures and other protections mandated by the federal securities laws. All investors could do during this period was to attempt to piece together several incomplete pieces of information from a few press releases and news stories.

This matter involves not simply a failure to make required SEC filings. Rather, it involves a failure to make disclosure of material information about Spiegel's financial condition that investors needed to make their investment decisions about Spiegel. The SEC has already charged Spiegel with fraud for failing to disclose its auditors' going concern position. But . . . investors likewise failed to get a variety of other material information about Spiegel's financial condition. . . .

Ultimately, Spiegel was unable to dig itself out of this hole. Its financial condition just kept getting worse. On March 17, 2003, Spiegel filed a Chapter 11 bankruptcy case in the Southern District of New York.

Involvement of Spiegel's Professional Advisers

In the present case, the SEC charged Spiegel with fraud, and Spiegel consented (without admitting or denying liability) to a fraud injunction against the company. When a fraud charge hits a public company, the question naturally arises whether its professional advisers could have done anything to prevent this "train wreck" that hurt the company and its shareholders, creditors, and employees.

Spiegel's Legal Advisers. In evaluating the performance of Spiegel's lawyers, it is useful to consider rules adopted and other rules proposed by the SEC under Section 307 of the Sarbanes-Oxley Act, even though these SEC rules were not in effect at the time of conduct here. Under SEC rules effective August 5, 2003, lawyers representing a public company must report "up the ladder"—as high as the board of directors, if necessary—if the lawyers "become aware" of "evidence" of a "material violation" of federal or state securities law or a material breach of fiduciary duty by the company (or its officer, director, employee or agent).

In addition, the SEC has proposed (but not yet adopted [and, in all likelihood, will not adopt]) so-called "noisy withdrawal" rules that would require lawyers to assess whether the company has made an "appropriate response within a reasonable time" to the matter the lawyer has reported up the ladder, and if not, whether "substantial injury" to the financial interest or property of the issuer or investors has occurred or is likely. An outside attorney must then "withdraw forthwith from representing the issuer," and tell both the company and the SEC that the withdrawal was for "professional considerations." An inside attorney must cease participation in the matter. Both outside and inside attorneys must also disaffirm to the SEC any document the attorney assisted in preparing that "may be" materially false or misleading.

Robert Sorensen joined Spiegel as its general counsel at the end of June 2001. He brought in the firm of Kirkland & Ellis as principal outside counsel ... to provide additional depth in corporate and securities matters. ... As described above, by mid-May 2002, Kirkland & Ellis had plainly advised Spiegel that it was violating the law by not filing its Form 10–K, and that this illegal act could have serious consequences, including action by the SEC. Sorensen plainly concurred in this advice. The advice reached Spiegel's management, including its president Martin Zaepfel, who was also a member of Spiegel's board committee, which had the power to act for the full board. By the end of May, Zaepfel reported the advice to Michael Otto and Michael Cruesemann, the other two members of the board committee. Kirkland & Ellis also repeated this advice by phone to Spiegel's audit committee at the end of May. Plainly, Kirkland & Ellis and Sorensen reported "up the ladder" to Spiegel's audit committee and its board committee.

However, this was a case where reporting "up the ladder" was not enough. The advice from the lawyers here was rejected by Spiegel's audit and board committees, and the material information that should have reached investors was kept under wraps. White & Case became involved in Spiegel's affairs as counsel for Spiegel's "sole voting shareholder," Michael Otto and his corporate vehicles. Through its Hamburg partner Urs

Aschenbrenner, White & Case "interpreted" for the Otto interests the advice received from Spiegel's U.S. legal advisors, and it clearly played a substantial role in helping Otto and the Spiegel board committee evaluate that advice. Aschenbrenner consulted with White & Case's New York office on Spiegel issues, and lawyers from the firm's New York office were substantively involved on various Spiegel matters—again as representatives of Spiegel's sole voting shareholder—during much of 2002.

[White & Case lawyer] Aschenbrenner began accompanying Cruesemann to meetings with Spiegel's lender banks in Spring 2002, and also attended Spiegel's delisting hearing before Nasdaq on May 17, 2002. On May 31, 2002, the day Spiegel's audit and board committees made the final decision not to file the Form 10–K, Aschenbrenner was invited to be present at the audit committee meeting, and the audit committee had Aschenbrenner phone Kirkland & Ellis on a speakerphone for the committee to get advice. Aschenbrenner was heard to challenge Kirkland and Ellis' advice on the need to file Spiegel's form 10–K and the consequences of non-filing. In the days following the May 31, 2002 meeting, it appears that neither Aschenbrenner nor his New York partners did anything to express their agreement with Kirkland & Ellis' advice.

Whatever the conclusion as to the lawyers' performance around the time of the May 31, 2002 audit and board committee meetings, the question naturally arises as to what the lawyers did to press Spiegel to make its required SEC filings through the balance of 2002. . . . There does not appear to be a record of either Kirkland or Ellis or White & Case advising Spiegel of the dire consequences of its continuing failure to file its Form 10–K and make full disclosure to investors after May 31, 2002.

After May 2002, it appears that Spiegel's German directors considered Kirkland & Ellis and Sorensen, along with the rest of Spiegel's U.S. management, to be "black painters"—meaning pessimists who were exaggerating the seriousness of the situation. Over the summer, Cruesemann suggested that Kirkland & Ellis, and perhaps Sorensen, be replaced. The effort to replace Kirkland & Ellis failed only when U.S. management pointed out the cost of bringing in a new firm to draft documentation for the refinancing and other pending matters.

At the same time, while ostensibly still only counsel for Spiegel's sole voting shareholder, White & Case assumed a prominent role in negotiating on Spiegel's behalf with its banks on the refinancing effort . . . and with the insurer of the Spiegel securitizations. While still not technically retained as Spiegel's counsel, White & Case clearly enjoyed the confidence of Spiegel's sole voting shareholder, and an effort by White & Case to report "up the ladder" to Spiegel's audit and board committees that it shared the views of the "black painters" Kirkland & Ellis and Sorensen could have well caused Spiegel to comply with its obligations and avoid a fraud charge from the SEC.

As the months went by, Kirkland & Ellis continued to prepare and file Spiegel's Forms 12b–25 providing official notice of Spiegel's failure to file its remaining quarterly reports (Form 10–Q) for the balance of 2002. All of these recited that Spiegel was not filing its periodic reports because it was "not currently in compliance with its 2001 loan covenants and is currently working with its bank group to amend and replace its existing credit facilities," and thus "not in a position to issue financial statements . . . pending resolution of this issue." Of course, as Kirkland & Ellis knew, the real reason why Spiegel was not filing its periodic reports was that it did not want to disclose KPMG's going concern qualification and other material bad facts and circumstances threatening Spiegel's survival.

None of Spiegel's legal advisers withdrew—"noisily" or otherwise—from representing Spiegel. If the SEC's proposed withdrawal rule had then been in effect, the SEC would have been alerted to take action sooner, and investors would have received information they could have acted on to make informed investment decisions about Spiegel. In this case, the absence of a "noisy withdrawal" requirement allowed Spiegel to keep investors and the SEC in the dark.

HAYS v. PAGE PERRY, LLC
26 F. Supp. 3d 1311 (N.D. Ga. 2014)

This is a legal malpractice case arising out of services provided by the Defendants to Lighthouse Financial Partners, LLC [Lighthouse]. The Plaintiff, Lighthouse's Receiver, argues that the Defendants [who were legal counsel to Lighthouse] were aware that Lighthouse was not complying with applicable regulations; and that they were legally obligated to violate their duty of confidentiality and inform the regulatory authorities of the non-compliance. The Plaintiff argues that failure to do this allowed Benjamin DeHaan to continue stealing from Lighthouse's clients. . . .

Background

On February 1, 2013, Benjamin DeHaan—the former manager and majority owner of Lighthouse Financial Partners, LLC—pled guilty to one count of wire fraud. Lighthouse was in the business of providing investment advisory services to its clients, including investment of client funds. For years, DeHaan misappropriated funds from Lighthouse's clients. To accomplish this, he made several misrepresentations to federal and state regulatory authorities. To avoid stringent regulations, Lighthouse would report that it was not taking custody of its clients' funds. Lighthouse stated that the funds were immediately being transferred to qualified broker-dealers that served as custodians. . . . However, the funds placed in this Account were being misappropriated by DeHaan for his personal use.

From 2008 until 2012, the Defendant Page Perry, LLC represented Lighthouse. Pursuant to a retainer agreement, Page Perry agreed to "advise [Lighthouse] regarding all registration, licensing, and regulatory requirements, including, as applicable, the requirements of the Securities and Exchange Commission and all state securities and investment advisor regulators." . . .

The SEC filed a civil enforcement action against Lighthouse and DeHaan. Lighthouse's assets were frozen, and the Plaintiff S. Gregory Hays was appointed as Receiver for Lighthouse. The Plaintiff filed this lawsuit, arguing that the [attorney] Defendants knew, or should have known, that Lighthouse had custody of its clients' funds and that this posed a risk of theft. The Plaintiff further argues that the Defendants should have notified regulatory authorities of Lighthouse's non-compliance with applicable rules, and that such notification could have mitigated the ensuing damage. The Plaintiff asserts claims for professional malpractice, breach of fiduciary duty, and breach of contract. The Defendants move to dismiss.

Professional Malpractice

The Plaintiff claims that the Defendants' professional malpractice proximately caused the harm that Lighthouse suffered from DeHaan's theft of client funds. . . . To establish a legal malpractice claim, "the client has the burden of establishing three elements: (1) employment of the defendant attorney, (2) failure of the attorney to exercise ordinary care, skill and diligence, and (3) that such negligence was the proximate cause of damage to the plaintiff." . . . [T]he element of breach of duty in a legal malpractice case—the failure to exercise ordinary care, skill and diligence—must relate directly to the duty of the attorney, that is, the duty to perform *the task for which he was employed.* Additionally, "whether and to what extent the defendant owed the plaintiff a duty of care . . . are questions of law."

The Plaintiff asserts that the Defendants breached a duty to Lighthouse in at least three ways. First, the Plaintiff argues that the Defendants knew that Lighthouse likely had custody of client funds and that they failed to notify regulatory authorities. If the Defendants had done so, the argument goes, then DeHaan's scheme would have been stymied earlier on. In response, the Defendants argue that it is immaterial whether they knew that Lighthouse likely had custody of client funds. The Defendants argue that they were hired to perform an *advisory* role, and although they had a duty to perform *that role* with sufficient care and diligence, there was no independent duty to report regulatory non-compliance to a government agency. The Court agrees. The Plaintiff cites to no Georgia statute or state court case imposing such a duty on attorneys. Instead, the Plaintiff cites to Rule 1.13(b) of the Georgia Rules of Professional Conduct ("GRPC"), which states in relevant part:

> If a lawyer for an organization knows that an officer . . . associated with the organization is engaged in action . . . related to the representation that is . . . a violation of law that reasonably might be imputed to the organization, and that is likely to result in substantial injury to the organization, then the lawyer shall proceed as is reasonably necessary in the best interest of the organization. Unless the lawyer reasonably believes that it is not necessary in the best interest of the organization to do so, the lawyer shall refer the matter to *higher*

authority in the organization, including, if warranted by the circumstances, to *the highest authority that can act on behalf of the organization* as determined by applicable law.

To begin, the Georgia Supreme Court has made clear that the GRPC rules do not independently constitute legal duties which give rise to malpractice claims. Regardless, the exhibits attached to the Complaint show that the Defendants complied with this rule. The Defendants informed DeHaan—who, at the time, was the highest authority at Lighthouse—on at least three separate occasions that Lighthouse might not be in compliance with custody regulations. . . .

The Plaintiff tries to argue that the "highest authority" was the SEC or the Georgia Securities Commissioner. The Plaintiff cites no authority for this argument and it is entirely without merit. Rule 1.13 clearly states that "the lawyer shall refer the matter to higher authority *in the organization*, including . . . to the highest authority that can act on behalf of the organization." That the Receiver may now act on behalf of Lighthouse is immaterial. The Receiver did not have such authority when there was an attorney-client relationship between the Defendants and Lighthouse. GRPC Rule 1.13(c) makes clear that, in this circumstance, disclosure to an external agency is permissive but not mandatory: "if . . . the highest authority that can act on behalf of the organization . . . fails to address . . . an action . . . that is clearly a violation of law, and . . . the lawyer reasonably believes that the violation is reasonably certain to result in substantial injury to the organization, then the lawyer *may* reveal information relating to the representation. . . ." Thus, no legal duty was breached by the Defendants' failure to notify a regulatory authority of Lighthouse's non-compliance with custody rules.

The Bullard Affidavit relies upon a non-existent duty and can be entirely disregarded. The Plaintiff's central claim that Defendants were affirmatively required to reveal regulatory non-compliance to the government agencies regulating Lighthouse is unsupported by any legal authority. Significantly, in his response to the Motion to Dismiss, the Plaintiff fails to identify a single case or statute even intimating that Georgia lawyers have a duty to blow the whistle on their clients to regulators. In fact, Georgia law—preferring a policy that encourages the confidentiality of information obtained during the attorney-client relationship—never obligates a lawyer to report even the most serious client misconduct to regulators. A lawyer is not even permitted to report his client except in the most limited circumstances—circumstances Page Perry never faced during its representation of Lighthouse until the very end when the lawyers persuaded DeHaan to allow them to report his theft of client funds to the SEC.

The Plaintiff's theory—that Page Perry had to inform on Lighthouse of suspected or known regulatory violations—would put every corporate lawyer in a position of policing his client and turning it in to authorities despite the Bar Rules under which the attorney-client privilege is held sacrosanct. No rational client would seek compliance advice from a lawyer, knowing the lawyer would be obligated to report the client to regulators if the lawyer detected less than complete compliance with every relevant regulation. The Plaintiff's theory would convert private corporate lawyers representing financial advisers and other regulated industry participants into unwilling government auditors required to utilize information gained in the course of their representation to the potential detriment of their clients, all in the name of protecting the corporate client from itself. The concept is inherently objectionable and would actually require such corporate lawyers to routinely violate Bar Rules 1.6 and 1.13. The theory completely disregards the safeguards imposed in these Rules to render extraordinarily limited the circumstances in which a lawyer may be permitted, but not required, to bring a matter to the attention of regulatory authorities. . . . Under the Plaintiff's theory, the confidentiality of lawyer-client communications would no longer be held sacred because a lawyer's self-preservation interest would raise merely permissive reporting to mandatory reporting of a client to authorities outside of the organization itself. The Plaintiff provides no authority whatsoever for such a radical reversal of a lawyer's duty to a client. Outside corporate attorneys—with or without knowledge of suspicious activity—are not insurers of good behavior by the client.

Let us now consider how the above issues play out in the following Scenario.

SCENARIO

David Benedict has built up a successful finance company, Benedict Financing, Inc., in which he helps consumers and small businesses finance the acquisition of or the lease of household appliances, office equipment, and related furnishings. He is dedicated to improving his community and through his business has established a reputation as the most decent, caring, and honest businessperson in Plattensburg Oaks.

After Benedict Financing's longtime outside legal counsel retired and moved to Florida, David retained Oscar McMurray as outside counsel. Although he is more than 20 years Oscar's senior, David considers Oscar the brother he never had. Oscar used to be David's next-door neighbor and paperboy, and worked at Benedict Financing during high school and college. For Oscar's college graduation present, David paid Oscar's first year of law school tuition.

After many years in the business, David decided to retire so that he and his wife Clarissa could travel. David sold the business to his daughter Susan's husband, Pete Pistel, and gave up his seat as the Company's sole director to Pete. Unable to let go of the business he built up from scratch completely, however, David retained 5% stock ownership and an option to buy back from Pete an additional 20% of the Company's stock.

Unfortunately, Pete had neither David's business acumen nor his ethics. As the business began to falter, Pete tried to obtain a loan using the Company's finance leases as collateral, but was unable to secure the financing. Getting desperate, Pete took the form lease that Oscar had previously developed for Benedict Financing and used it to alter several existing leases and to forge false leases. Based on these fraudulent documents, Pete obtained a loan for Benedict Financing from an out-of-town lender seeking to establish itself in Plattensburg Oaks. Oscar provided an opinion letter for the transaction after reviewing the leases. Because they all conformed to the form lease he developed, Oscar believed that the leases were valid. In addition to the loan, Pete subtly nudged David into exercising his option to repurchase from Pete 20% of the stock in the Company. When David examined the fraudulent financial statements that Pete had prepared in connection with the loan closing, he decided to buy back the stock, not knowing that the financial statements were materially false.

With the loan proceeds in hand, Pete was able to keep the business barely surviving. He realized, however, that he would eventually need another loan. To make the Company appear profitable, over a period of several months, he forged additional leases. The pressure of keeping the business afloat started to get to Pete, and he began to drink heavily. One night about a year after the original loan, Pete had too much to drink at a gathering of David's family and friends to celebrate Clarissa's birthday. He inadvertently told Oscar about the fraudulently obtained loan.

Oscar confronted Pete the next day. Pete admitted his role in the previous fraudulent loan transaction but not to forging any leases since then. When Oscar said that he did not think he could represent Benedict Financing anymore, Pete told Oscar that he was working on another transaction with the lender, which had agreed to loan the Company more money and extend the debt, and asked Oscar to help him close the deal. Oscar said that he would not do any work in connection with closing the deal, but would stay on as outside general counsel for a short transition period. Pete also asked Oscar not to tell David anything about Pete's behavior because "it would break David's heart."

One day a few weeks later, after Oscar had concluded his representation of Benedict Financing, Oscar returned to his office after lunch. He checked his voice mail and found a message from the successor counsel that Pete retained to close the loan transaction. The attorney indicated that she was curious why Oscar was not closing the loan for Benedict Financing since he had been so well connected with the Company. The next voice mail message was from David, who found out that Oscar had terminated his representation of the Company and wanted to know why. David concluded his message: "Oscar, if there is something going on at my Company, I need to know and I trust you to tell me about it."

How should Oscar respond?

On the other hand, assume that Oscar has not resigned but is employed as Benedict Financing's inside general counsel. Assume also that Benedict Financing is a publicly-held company whose common stock is traded on the New York Stock Exchange and is subject to SEC regulation. The company has a nine-member board of directors, a majority of whom are independent directors. Upon discovering Pete's misconduct, how should Oscar proceed?

SCENARIO III

THE LAWYER AS INTERMEDIARY

∎ ∎ ∎

Elsewhere in this text, we consider the ethical issues facing an attorney who desires to simultaneously represent multiple clients in the business (or transactional) setting.[1] An attorney in this context will be challenged to aptly satisfy the obligations owed, including the duties of confidentiality and loyalty, to each client. In these situations, the Model Rules permit a lawyer to represent multiple clients in the business context where the parties' interests potentially may conflict. In undertaking such representation, the lawyer may be viewed as serving as an intermediary between two or more clients, playing more of a counseling role to facilitate the desired arrangement or transaction rather than ardently pursuing the interests of each client.

The Model Rules spell out the conditions in which an attorney may serve as an intermediary. Key elements are: consent from all clients after thorough consultation, the attorney's reasonable belief that all clients' best interests can be served, and the attorney's reasonable belief that she can be impartial. In addition, former Model Rule 2.2 requires that the attorney reasonably believe that the clients can make adequately informed decisions and obliges the lawyer to consult with each client regarding decisions to be made and their implications.

Pursuant to the recommendations made by the Ethics 2000 Commission, the 2002 amendments to the Model Rules deleted Rule 2.2. Nonetheless, Rule 2.2 serves as a useful benchmark to assess the propriety of the lawyer as intermediary. The provisions of Rule 2.2 and its commentary therefore continue to be helpful in our analysis of counsel's role in this setting.

---

[1] *See, e.g.*, Scenarios I, V, and VII herein.

Moreover, considerations relating to the lawyer as intermediary are now contained in the Comments to Model Rule 1.7.[2]

As noted in Rule 2.2's commentary, a "lawyer acts as intermediary in seeking to establish or adjust a relationship between clients on an amicable and mutually advantageous basis."[3] Two situations, for example, in which this may occur in the transactional setting are organizing a business between two or more entrepreneurs[4] and undertaking a financial reorganization of an entity in which two or more clients have an interest.[5] Factors that impact whether intermediation is appropriate in a given situation include: the likelihood of reducing the legal costs that otherwise would be incurred if the parties were each represented by separate counsel,[6] how amicable or contentious the parties' relationship is,[7] the degree of compatibility of the parties' interests,[8] whether the lawyer subsequently will represent the parties on a continuing basis, and "whether the situation involves creating a relationship between the parties or terminating one."[9] In other words, intermediation may be appropriate where the parties are best able to work together to achieve the mutual benefits associated with the contemplated arrangement or transaction. To the extent that the relationship has or may turn more confrontational, the clients ordinarily would be better served by procuring independent legal representation.

The lawyer serving as an intermediary entails significant consequences.[10] Certainly, client confidentiality is a paramount

---

[2] *See* Model Rule 1.7 cmts. 28–33.

[3] *Id.* Rule 2.2 cmt. 3.

[4] *See* Scenario I herein.

[5] Model Rule 2.2 cmt. 3

[6] *See id.* Rule 2.2 cmts. 1, 3.

[7] *See id.* Rule 2.2 cmt. 4 ("a lawyer cannot undertake common representation of clients between whom contentious litigation is imminent or who contemplate contentious negotiations").

[8] *See id.* Rule 2.2 cmt. 5.

[9] *Id.*

[10] *See id.* Rule 2.2 cmt. 8 ("In acting as intermediary between clients, the lawyer is required to consult with the clients on the implications of doing so, and proceed only upon consent based on such a consultation. The consultations should make clear that the lawyer's role is not that of partisanship normally expected in other circumstances."). *See generally Klemm v. Superior Court*, 142 Cal. Rptr. 509 (Cal. App. 1977); Dzienkowski,

concern. An attorney "acting as intermediary requires a delicate balance" between providing client A with sufficient information for A to make adequately informed decisions and protecting client B's confidences, and vice versa.[11] If A and B have an open and amicable relationship such that they freely exchange important information (including attorney-client communications) with respect to the subject matter at issue, counsel will more aptly balance each client's need-to-know. But the attorney's ability to balance these interests becomes precarious when B refuses to reveal confidential information to A and such information materially impacts key aspects of the contemplated arrangement or transaction. In such a situation, the lawyer may be compelled to terminate her role as intermediary.[12]

Moreover, if litigation subsequently arises between the clients, a related consequence is the probable loss of the attorney-client privilege. Under the prevailing view, the attorney-client privilege ordinarily does not protect communications between commonly represented clients and their attorney.[13] The commentary to Model Rule 2.2 cautions "it must be assumed that if litigation eventuates between the clients, the [attorney-client] privilege will not protect any such communications, and clients should be so advised."[14] Hence, unavailability of the attorney-client privilege further highlights the need for circumspection when determining whether counsel should serve as intermediary.

Another important consequence of using intermediation is its tenuous nature. The status of the attorney as intermediary

---

Lawyers as Intermediaries: The Representation of Multiple Clients in the Modern Legal Profession, 1992 U. Ill. L. Rev. 741 (1992); Rollock, *Professional Responsibility and Organization of the Family Business: The Lawyer As Intermediary*, 73 Ind. L.J. 567 (1998). *Cf.* Richmond, *Lawyers' Professional Responsibilities and Liabilities in Negotiations*, 22 Geo. J. Leg. Eth. 249 (2009).

[11] *See id.* Rule 2.2 cmt. 6 (citing to Model Rules 1.4 *Communication* and 1.6 *Confidentiality of Information*).

[12] *See id.*

[13] *See id.*

[14] *Id. See FDIC v. Ogden Corp.*, 202 F.3d 454, 461 (1st Cir. 2000) (applying Massachusetts law) ("[W]hen a lawyer represents multiple clients having a common interest, communications between the lawyer and any one (or more) of the clients are privileged as to outsiders but not *inter sese*.").

may be quite fragile and susceptible to termination.[15] For example, any client may terminate the relationship by demanding that the attorney withdraw from the representation.[16] Moreover, if any of the conditions precedent necessary for establishing the intermediary relationship cease to exist, that too will terminate the relationship. Thus, (1) if the parties' relationship becomes less amicable and significantly more contentious, (2) if the lawyer does not believe the matter can be resolved in the clients' best interests, or (3) if the attorney no longer can be impartial—any of those events, among others, will necessitate termination of the intermediation.[17] Finally, if the intermediation is terminated, the lawyer must walk completely away from the matter, as the Model Rules forbid her from representing any party in the matter thereafter.[18]

Let us consider the issues that a lawyer may face when acting as an intermediary under the following Scenario.

SCENARIO

Lana Lazaras received a phone call from her client, Sarah Safar, asking Lana to meet her at the country club. Lana has known Sarah since high school and has been her primary business attorney for approximately 15 years. During that time, Sarah has built up a property management company ("SPMCo") from scratch and has become one of the most prominent businesspersons in the community.

When Lana arrived, Sarah was sitting with Bennie Belonger, Sarah's brother-in-law. Bennie moved to town approximately five years ago and has been working primarily as a business consultant. Lana was recommended to Bennie by Sarah and has performed some legal work for him, successfully helping him with respect to some real estate investment partnerships. After Lana joined her clients at the table, Sarah announced that she was going to sell her property management

---

[15] *See* Model Rule 2.2(c).

[16] *Id.* Rule 2.2(c) & cmt. 10.

[17] *See id.* & cmts. 4, 7, 10.

[18] *Id.* Rule 2.2(c). *See generally* American Law Institute, *Restatement of the Law Governing Lawyers* §§ 122, 130 (2000).

company to Bennie. They had already reached an agreement on the fundamental terms of the transaction (including price and structure) and wanted Lana to draft the documents necessary to complete the transaction. The following is an excerpt of their conversation.

Sarah: We've already agreed on the price, the payment terms, and everything else. All we need from you, Lana, is to put the paperwork together.

Bennie: We're also going to split your bill 50–50. Sarah has spoken highly of you ever since I came to town, and you did a great job helping me on those real estate investments. We know that you'll be able to get the work done quickly and reasonably.

Lana: Sarah, why are you selling?

Sarah: Well, um, I just decided that I want to enjoy life more. With [my daughter] Sally going to college next year, [my husband] Sammy and I want to do more traveling.

Lana: What about you, Bennie? Do you know anything about running a property management company?

Bennie: Not specifically, but I do know how to market and grow a business, and I have a few ideas along those lines. Besides, Lana tells me that the guy in her office, Chris Castlebaum, has been managing the daily matters for her for the last few years. So, I'll make it worth his while to run the business for me.

Lana: What are you going to do—bring him in as an equity partner?

Bennie: I might down the road, but I'll start with a nice raise. I like the guy, and I think we can have a good working relationship.

Sarah: In fact, I originally talked to Chris about him buying the Company, but he's not in a financial position to do that now.

Lana: Well, it does not sound like it should be any problem for me to do this work. But I should talk with the two of you about some of the implications of me representing both of you at the same time. First of all, I am required by professional ethics to maintain each of your confidences and . . .

Sarah: Lana, you know that I think "legal ethics" is an
        oxymoron. You don't need to talk to us about
        confidences and the like. Bennie and I have been very
        open and frank in negotiating this deal, and I think
        we're both comfortable with the process.

Bennie: I've seen the Company's financials, tax returns,
        budgets, everything. She's seen my income tax returns
        and net worth. We're okay on all that.

Lana: Well, fine, as long as you don't think there will be a
        problem.

Following the meeting, Lana started drafting the necessary
documents for the transaction. She also assigned an associate of
her firm, Allan Nussbaum, to complete a due diligence review of
SPMCo's corporate documents and management contracts. Lana
previously had either drafted or reviewed all the relevant
documents, so she assumed that Allan would not have a difficult
time following a due diligence checklist that she prepared for
him. With checklist in hand, Allan trudged off to SPMCo's
offices. Sarah was out of the office, so Chris Castlebaum put
Allan in a conference room with all the necessary documents.

When Lana arrived at her office the next morning, Allan
was waiting to talk with her. "I wasn't sure if I should tell you
this, but I decided I should," Allan started. "I was at SPMCo's
offices pretty late last night, and Chris Castlebaum was the only
other person there. We decided to order some pizza, and when
we went into his office to get a phone book, he had a picture on
his desk of him and Sarah in—well, let's say a very friendly
position. When he saw that I saw the picture, he fell into his
chair and started crying. He told me how they had gotten really
close. He told her about a month ago that he loved her, but she
said that she couldn't go on anymore cheating on her husband.
That's why she's selling the business, out of guilt or something
like that. Anyway, he said that without her, there's nothing
keeping him in this town and that his brother could help him get
a great job in Chicago. So, he said he's probably going to move
there."

Lana was floored by this information. She thanked Allan for
his diligence and for telling her the information. She also asked

that he not tell anyone, even in the firm, about what he found out; Allan said he would keep quiet.

Later on that day, Lana arranged for Sarah to come over to her house that evening on the pretense of discussing some of the documents necessary for the sale. When Sarah arrived and sat down, Lana asked her about her affair with Chris. Sarah asked, "How do you know?" Lana told her about Allan's conversation with Chris. "Don't worry, I asked him not to tell anyone else," Lana finished. "But we do have to discuss what we're going to do about this."

Sarah: What do you mean, "what we're going to do about this?" It's over—*we* are not going to do anything.

Lana: Sarah, I understand that you do not want this to get out, but it puts me in a difficult situation. The fact that Chris is probably going to leave the Company is something that Bennie would want to know.

Sarah: Bennie can't know. If he did, he would tell Sammy and my marriage would be a real mess. You're my lawyer and my friend. You're not supposed to tell my secrets to anyone. You're the one always throwing your professional ethics in my face. Well, now I'm going to hold you to them: I forbid you to tell Bennie about this!

Focusing on Lana's decision whether to accept the intermediation arrangement and the facts as they developed, what were and are Lana's options?

SCENARIO IV

CORPORATE INTERNAL INVESTIGATIONS: WHAT ABOUT CONFIDENTIALITY?

■ ■ ■

An attorney's ability to render effective legal advice largely depends on the client's willingness to provide detailed and truthful information. Absent such candor, it frequently becomes impractical for the attorney to conduct a meaningful analysis of the client's possible legal rights and remedies. Toward that end, Model Rule 1.6 recognizes the essentiality of the client providing truthful information to his attorney.[1] Rule 1.6 generally protects from revelation confidences and secrets of the client (including communications coming within the attorney-client privilege). As the commentary to the Model Rules explains, the protection of a client's confidential information facilitates the development of facts that are necessary for effective representation.[2] The principle of lawyer-client confidentiality encourages the client "to communicate fully and frankly with the lawyer even as to embarrassing or legally damaging subject matter."[3]

In the context of organizational representation, the principle of lawyer-client confidentiality (and the specific communications it protects) becomes more complex. When retained to represent an entity, the attorney's professional duties generally run only to that entity, and not to the constituents through whom the entity communicates.[4] Generally, corporate clients receive the same level of protection of confidentiality as an individual client; however, difficulty arises due to the fact that the corporation

---

[1] Model Rules of Prof. Conduct, Rule 1.6. Rule 1.6 is addressed at length also in Scenario II.

[2] *Id.* Rule 1.6 cmt. 2.

[3] *Id. See Willy v. Administrative Review Board*, 423 F.3d 483, 495 (5th Cir. 2005).

[4] Model Rule 1.13. *See Orbit One Communications, Inc. v. Numerex Corp.*, 255 F.R.D. 98, 104 (S.D.N.Y. 2008). For further discussion on this topic, *see* Scenarios I, II, VII, XI herein. *See generally* S. Martyn & L. Fox, *The Ethics of Representing Organizations* (2009).

must speak through its constituents.[5] Since it is the constituents who must speak on behalf of the organization, communications between the organization's attorney and the organization (through the constituents) must receive some level of protection in order for the organization to benefit from the attorney-client privilege.

The U.S. Supreme Court examined the degree of protection these communications should receive in the landmark *Upjohn* case.[6] In its analysis, the Court focused more on the subject matter of the communications and less on the particular organizational constituent from whom the communications were made.[7] As the Court explained, "[t]he communications concerned matters within the scope of the employees' corporate duties, and the employees themselves were sufficiently aware that they were being questioned in order that the corporation could obtain legal advice."[8] As a result, the Court reasoned, "[c]onsistent with the underlying purposes of the attorney-client privilege, these communications must be protected against compelled disclosure."[9] Thus, the Supreme Court held that, while the constituents themselves were not in an attorney-client relationship with the corporation's attorney, their communications on behalf of the corporation were nevertheless protected by the privilege existing between the corporation and the corporation's attorney.[10]

---

[5] Mulroy & Thesing, *Confidentiality Concerns In Internal Corporate Investigations*, 25 Tort & Ins. L.J. 48, 49 (1989).

[6] *Upjohn Co. v. United States*, 449 U.S. 383 (1981).

[7] *Id.* at 394.

[8] *Id.*

[9] *Id. See In re Kellogg Brown & Root, Inc.*, 756 F.3d 754 (D.C. Cir. 2014); J. Gergacz, *Attorney-Corporate Client Privilege* (2d ed. 1990); Schipani, *The Future of the Attorney-Client Privilege in Corporate Criminal Investigations*, 34 Del. J. Corp. L. 921 (2009).

[10] The *Upjohn* Court also addressed the work product doctrine's application to documents prepared in connection with employee interviews conducted by an attorney during an internal investigation. To the extent that these documents reflect privileged communications, they are protected by the attorney-client privilege. To the extent that these documents reflect the mental impressions of the attorney conducting the interview, they are protected by the work product doctrine. *Id.* at 401. The Court did not, however, grant an absolute privilege to such documents; rather it held that the moving party is required to make a sufficient showing of necessity and unavailability in order to compel disclosure. *Id.* at 402.

Hence, the attorney-client privilege protects subject communications from compelled disclosure to an outside third party. Consequently, the *Upjohn* decision ultimately deals with the degree to which the attorney-client privilege protects communications made on behalf of an organizational client by the organization's constituents. The situation becomes more ambiguous, however, with respect to whether such communications also are protected from disclosure to other constituents within the organization. This issue may arise, for instance, in the context of an internal investigation within an organization.[11]

In *Hickman v. Taylor*, 329 U.S. 495 (1974), the Supreme Court recognized the work product doctrine, which was subsequently codified in Rule 26 of the Federal Rules of Civil Procedure. The work product doctrine ultimately protects from compelled discovery tangible items that are prepared "in anticipation of litigation or for trial" (FRCP 26(b)(3)). Essentially, the doctrine has been interpreted to protect a lawyer's mental impressions and legal analysis. In conducting an internal investigation, attorneys will inevitably keep written records of information gathered during employee interviews. To prevent these tangible items from being subject to future discovery, some commentators have suggested that the attorney should attempt to mix as many mental impressions and legal analyses as possible among the acquired and recorded information. *See* Kenny & Mitchelson, *Corporate Benefits of Properly Conducted Internal Investigations*, 11 Ga. St. L. Rev. 657, 667 (1995). *See also, Redvanly v. NYNEX Corp.*, 152 F.R.D. 460, 466 (S.D.N.Y. 1993) (holding that the corporation's attorney's notes were discoverable because they were "a running transcript of the meeting" and failed to reflect the attorney's mental impressions). Note, however, that if the corporation ultimately might elect to waive the attorney-client privilege and work product doctrine during the course of a government investigation, counsel should consider confining the interview notes to solely factual matters. *See also, Ryan v. Gifford*, 2008 WL 43699 (Del. Ch. 2008) (due to that defendant directors and their lawyers were present when the corporation's special committee and such committee's attorney met with the corporation's board of directors, work product protection held to be waived).

[11] *See generally* ABA Task Force on the Attorney-Client Privilege, *Report of the American Bar Association's Task Force on the Attorney-Client Privilege*, 60 Bus. Law. 1029 (2005); M. Steinberg & S. Yeager, *Inside Counsel— Practices, Strategies, and Insights* 279–305 (2015); D. Webb, P. Tarun, & S. Molo, *Corporate Internal Investigations* (2015); Cohn, *The Organizational Client: Attorney-Client Privilege and the No-Contact Rule*, 10 Geo. J. Leg. Eth. 739 (1997); Kenny & Mitchelson, *supra* note 10, 11 Ga. St. L. Rev. at 663–667; Mustakoff, *The Pitfalls of Waiver in Corporate Prosecutions: Sharing Work Product with the Government and the Uncertain Future of Non-Waiver Agreements,* 37 Sec. Reg. L.J. 3 (2009); Stucke, *In Search of Effective Ethics & Compliance Programs*, 39 J. Corp. L. 769 (2014);

Internal investigations can assist an organization's management in ascertaining the advantages and disadvantages of certain corporate policies.[12] In other instances, internal investigations may be aimed at uncovering suspected wrongful and/or criminal acts perpetrated by certain company employees during the course of employment.[13] In such a situation, the internal investigation can take on paramount importance in the corporation's attempt to fend off or minimize the imposition of criminal or serious civil sanctions as a result of the wrongful acts. Indeed, in the aftermath of the Sarbanes-Oxley Act of 2002 (SOX) and the Dodd-Frank Act of 2010, internal investigations have become more common due to: (1) SOX's directive to audit committees to establish procedures that relate to complaints received by the company regarding accounting or auditing matters; and (2) the Acts' protection given to whistleblowers who suffer termination or other retaliatory consequences as a result of engaging in protected conduct.[14] Hence, as a consequence of an increase in the number of employee whistleblower complaints and the recognition by audit committees of their enhanced responsibilities, internal investigations today are conducted with greater frequency.

Internal investigations generally are comprised of two courses of action: a document review and employee interviews.[15] It is in the area of employee interviews that the investigating attorney particularly must exercise caution with respect to representations (or the lack thereof) made to the individual employee. This is especially true where the individual

---

Thornburg, *Rethinking Work Product*, 77 Va. L. Rev. 1515 (1991); Zacharias, *Harmonizing Privilege and Confidentiality*, 41 S. Tex. L. Rev. 69 (1999).

[12] *See* Kenny & Mitchelson, *supra* note 10, 11 Ga. St. L. Rev. at 661.

[13] *See Ryan v. Gifford*, 2007 WL 4259557 (Del. Ch. 2007); Mulroy & Thesing, *supra* note 5, 25 Tort & Ins. L.J. at 48.

[14] *See* SOX §§ 301(m), 806; Dodd-Frank § 922, *adding*, § 21F of the Securities Exchange Act; J. Bostelman, R. Buckholz and M. Trevino, *Public Company Deskbook—Sarbanes-Oxley and Federal Governance Requirements* (2015); Steinberg & Kaufman, *Minimizing Corporate Liability Exposure When the Whistle Blows in the Post Sarbanes-Oxley Era*, 30 J. Corp. L. 445 (2005). For discussion on the role internal investigations play in helping an organization avoid criminal liability, *see Sentencing Commission Amends Guidelines, Calls for Improved Compliance Officer Access*, 42 Sec. Reg. & L. Rep. (BNA) 914 (2010); Valukas & Stauffer, *Internal Investigations Of Corporate Misconduct*, 6 Insights No. 2, at 17 (Feb. 1992).

[15] *See* Kenny & Mitchelson, *supra* note 10, 11 Ga. St. L. Rev. at 665–667.

employee's interests appear adverse to the interests of the organization.[16]

While Model Rule 1.13 provides that the attorney's loyalty is to the organizational client, the rule also obliges the attorney to "explain the identity of the client [namely, the organization] when the lawyer knows or reasonably should know that the organization's interests are adverse to those of the constituents with whom the lawyer is dealing."[17] An internal investigation designed to uncover possible employee wrongdoing may place the organization's interests and certain employees' interests at odds, thereby potentially invoking the attorney's Rule 1.13(f) obligation to explain the identity of the client to the interviewee-employee.[18]

As discussed above, one of the main objectives of the privilege is to encourage clients to speak freely and candidly with their attorney.[19] In conducting an internal investigation, the attorney should seek to obtain as much truthful and factual information from interviewees as practicable.[20] The corporation and the subject attorneys nonetheless must not impede an employee being interviewed from communicating as a whistleblower to the government. In one recent SEC proceeding, a company incurred a money penalty as well as other sanctions for using a confidentiality agreement signed by interviewees during its internal investigations that allegedly violated the Dodd-Frank whistleblower provision.[21] This proceeding is contained later in this Chapter.

Oftentimes employees may possess material information pertaining to the attorney's fact-finding investigation that they do not feel comfortable disclosing for fear of repercussions. If, for example, an employee had done something that could jeopardize her position within the organization, it is unlikely that the

---

[16] *See* Model Rule 1.13.

[17] *Id*. Rule 1.13(f).

[18] *Id*. *See* Rule 4.3 ("In dealing on behalf of a client with a person who is not represented by counsel, a lawyer shall not state or imply that the lawyer is disinterested.").

[19] *See* discussion *supra* notes 1–10 and accompanying text.

[20] *See e.g.* Kahn, *Preserving The Confidentiality of Internal Corporate Investigations*, 1 J. Corp. Disclosure & Confidentiality 155, 155–158 (1989).

[21] *See In the Matter of KBR, Inc.*, Securities Exchange Act Release No. 74619 (2015) (settlement).

employee will share the information with the attorney, unless the employee knows, or at least thinks, that her communications are confidential and will not be disclosed even to other constituents. Nonetheless, as counsel for the organization, the attorney is obligated to remain steadfastly loyal to the organization's best interests, and act in a manner intended to further those interests.[22] As one source explains:

> "Counsel for the corporation owes an allegiance to the corporation as an entity rather than to the employee being interviewed. In many circumstances, the interests of individual employees may be adverse to the interests of the corporation. . . . In the interest of candor, counsel should instruct employees that he represents the corporation, that he is not their attorney, that employees cannot assert the attorney-client privilege to bar disclosure of the interview, and that the corporation possesses the attorney-client privilege but may waive it and disclose the information."[23]

Under this approach, the attorney may well be obligated to give the employee-interviewee a Miranda-style warning. Indeed, the Association of Corporate Counsel recommends that, prior to their interviews, employees be required to sign an acknowledgment that they received this type of warning.[24] Moreover, in certain factual contexts, an attorney may incur liability based on negligent misrepresentation for failing to provide such a sufficient notice to a non-client third party.[25]

From the organizational-client's perspective, the problem is that such a warning could result in the employee being less than truthful, thus having a chilling effect on the employee's

---

[22] *See* Model Rule 1.7.

[23] Mulroy & Thesing, *supra* note 5, 25 Tort & Ins. L.J. at 49.

[24] *See* Hechler, *Upjohn Warning Is a Vital Tool*, Nat. L.J., Jan. 16, 2006, at 8; Martin, *When Corporate Counsel Get Caught in the Middle*, Cal. Law. at 75 (Dec. 1989); Steinberg, *Attorney Liability for Client Fraud*, 1991 Colum. Bus. L. Rev. 1, 19–20 (1991); Valukas & Stauffer, *supra* note 14, 6 Insights No. 2, at 19.

[25] *See Pendergast-Holt v. Sjoblom and Proskauer-Rose, LLP*, 2009 WL 890343 (N.D. Tex. 2009) (complaint); *Parker v. Carnahan*, 772 S.W.2d 151 (Tex. App. 1989); *Collin County v. Johnson*, 1999 WL 994039 (Tex. App. 1999). For further discussion, *see* C. Wolfram, *Ethical Considerations For Corporate Counsel: Advising And Disclosing In An Uncertain Legal World*, 796 PLI/Corp. 235 (1992).

willingness to candidly cooperate with the investigation.[26] Consequently, warning the non-client employee with respect to the consequences of making unprivileged self-incriminating statements could compromise the attorney's ability to fulfill her investigative responsibilities. In other words, the constituents may "not confide information the attorney feels is critical to competent representation."[27] It is for this very reason that some disagreement prevails as to whether employee-constituents should be given a warning regarding the limits of confidentiality. As the former Executive Vice President and Chief Legal Officer of the ITT Corporation explained:

> "There has been a good deal of discussion among corporate counsel as to whether an employee should be given a 'Miranda' type warning before being questioned in an internal investigation, or if not that, be given an opportunity to consult his or her own lawyer before submitting to interrogation. I have concluded that carrying out my professional responsibility to the corporate entity requires that neither of such courses be followed. It is my task to find out what the facts are as fully and as quickly as possible. It is the obligation of an employee to respond truthfully to questions put to him by the corporation as to activities in the course of his employment for which the corporation may be held responsible, whether civilly or criminally."[28]

Nonetheless, today this view no longer has widespread acceptance.

As internal investigations are frequently initiated to uncover facts related to suspected wrongdoing within the organization, it normally is in the corporation's best interest to retain counsel to conduct the investigation in an attempt to preserve the

---

[26] Pizzimenti, *The Lawyer's Duty To Warn Clients About Limits On Confidentiality*, 39 Cath. U. L. Rev. 441, 484 (1990).

[27] *Id. See generally* Fischel, *Lawyers and Confidentiality*, 65 U. Chi. L. Rev. 1 (1998).

[28] Aibel, *Corporate Counsel and Business Ethics: A Personal Review*, 59 Mo. L. Rev. 427, 438 (1994). *See United States v. Int'l Brotherhood of Teamsters*, 961 F. Supp. 665, 673 (S.D.N.Y. 1997) (allowing an employee not provided with warning to invoke the attorney-client privilege would preclude counsel "from disclosing the employee's communications . . . thus thwarting the investigation").

confidentiality of any detrimental communication that comes within the privilege.[29] In order to avoid potential ethical and malpractice issues, the investigating attorney in this setting ordinarily should avoid individual representation of an organizational constituent-employee. As counsel for an individual employee, the attorney would be bound by additional confidentiality obligations to that employee.[30] Therefore, prior to conducting employee interviews, prudent counsel should provide a "Miranda-type" warning. As one court held, "[i]n the absence of any advice by [corporate counsel] to the contrary, defendants were justified in believing that [corporate counsel] were there to protect their individual interests as well as those of the corporation."[31] Hence, a key objective of providing a "Miranda-type" warning is to avoid the impression that the attorney somehow misled the individual employee to believe that the attorney represented such employee's personal interests as opposed to those of the corporation.[32]

---

[29] As one source explains, "[t]he best method of ensuring that the results of the investigation remain within the company's control is to conduct the investigation in a manner specifically designed to maintain both the confidentiality of the investigative results and the attorney-client or work product privileges associated with them." Kenny & Mitchelson, *supra* note 10, 11 Ga. State Univ. L. Rev. at 663–664.

[30] *Id.* at 666.

[31] *United States v. Hart*, 1992 U.S. Dist. LEXIS 17796, at *5 (E.D. La. 1992). *Cf. In re Grand Jury Subpoena Under Seal*, 415 F.3d 333 (4th Cir. 2005) (concluding that employee interviewed in an internal investigation did not have attorney-client relationship with the attorney conducting the interview).

[32] *See, e.g., Westinghouse Electric Corp. v. Kerr-McGee Corp.*, 580 F.2d 1311 (7th Cir. 1978) (holding that the employees' communications to the corporation's attorney were privileged and confidential based on the reasonable belief that they were being individually represented by the corporation's attorney). In determining whether the individual corporate employee has an attorney-client relationship with the corporation's legal counsel, numerous courts adhere to a more rigorous standard, requiring that the individual establish that: (1) he approached the corporate attorney to procure legal advice; (2) the corporate attorney knew the employee was seeking legal advice in his individual capacity; (3) corporate counsel communicated to the employee in his individual capacity while recognizing the conflict dilemma; (4) the communications between corporate counsel and the employee were confidential; and (5) the substance of the communications with the corporate attorney did not concern matters within the corporation or the corporation's general affairs. *United States v. Graf*, 610 F.3d 1148, 1159 (9th Cir. 2010), *relying on, In re Bevill, Bresler & Schulman Asset Management Corp.*, 805 F.2d 120, 123–125 (3d Cir. 1986).

For example, in one relatively recent case, the subject employee claimed that he believed that corporate counsel also represented him when he gave incriminatory statements in an interview during an internal corporate investigation.[33] During that interview, the employee was not given notice that the law firm did not represent him. Subsequently, corporate counsel provided the employee's statements to the government. Prohibiting the government from using these statements, the district court asserted that the interviewee-employee "was never told, nor did he ever contemplate, that his statements to the lawyers [conducting the interview] would be disclosed to third parties, especially not the Government in connection with criminal charges against him."[34] The court also referred the lawyers to the State Bar Association for possible disciplinary action.[35] On appeal, the Ninth Circuit reversed.[36] Taking a very different view of the circumstances than the court below, the Ninth Circuit held that the employee's statements during the internal investigation interview were not protected under the attorney-client privilege. This was due to the appellate court's conclusion that the employee's statements to the attorneys conducting the internal investigation interview "were not 'made in confidence' but rather for the purpose of disclosure to [third parties, namely, the] outside auditors."[37]

In view that (as a matter of customary practice) a warning today is given to the employee being interviewed, the next question is what should the warning contain. Tension exists between providing sufficient information to the employee to render the warning effective, without deterring the employee from providing accurate and truthful information. For example, the attorney simply could inform the employee that she is the lawyer for the corporation. Alternatively, counsel could tell the employee that she represents the corporation, not the employee

---

[33] *United States v. Nicholas*, 606 F. Supp. 2d 1109 (C.D. Cal. 2009), rev'd, *United States v. Ruehle*, 583 F. 3d 600 (9th Cir. 2009).

[34] 606 F. Supp. 2d at 1112. See Scannell, For Corporate Lawyers, There's Just One Client, Wall St. J., April 13, 2009, at p. B1 (stating that the decision in Nicholas suggests that attorneys "need to issue more explicit warnings during internal investigations that they don't represent individual employees").

[35] 606 F. Supp. 2d at 1121.

[36] *United States v. Ruehle*, 583 F. 3d 600 (9th Cir. 2009).

[37] Id. at 609.

individually, and as such, nothing that the employee says to her need be kept confidential within the organization.[38]

The following two recent cases highlight important developments in this area. The first is an enforcement action instituted by the SEC against a company that allegedly violated the whistleblower provisions of federal law when conducting interviews of its employees during internal investigations. The second is a major decision by the U.S. Court of Appeals which reinforces and apparently expands the invocation of the attorney-client privilege during an internal investigation.

IN THE MATTER OF KBR INC.
2015 WL 1456619 (SEC 2015)

I.

The Securities and Exchange Commission ("Commission") deems it appropriate that cease-and-desist proceedings be, and hereby are, instituted pursuant to Section 21C of the Securities Exchange Act of 1934 ("Exchange Act") against KBR, Inc. ("KBR" or "Respondent").

II.

In anticipation of the institution of these proceedings, KBR has submitted an Offer of Settlement (the "Offer") which the Commission has determined to accept. . . .

III.

On the basis of this Order and Respondent's Offer, the Commission finds that:

Respondent

1. KBR, Inc. is a Delaware corporation headquartered in Houston, Texas. KBR's common stock is registered with the

---

[38] When conducting employee interviews in an internal investigation, the Association of Corporate Counsel recommends that the attorney use a written script. *See* Hechler, *Upjohn Warning Is a Vital Tool,* Nat. L.J., Jan. 16, 2006, at 8. *See generally* American College of Trial Lawyers, *Recommended Practices for Companies and Their Counsel in Conducting Internal Investigations,* 46 Am. Crim. L. Rev. 73 (2009).

Commission pursuant to Section 12(b) of the Exchange Act and trades on the New York Stock Exchange. . . .

Facts

A. *Statutory   and   Regulatory   Framework   Protecting
Whistleblowers*

2.   The Dodd-Frank Wall Street Reform and Consumer Protection Act, enacted on July 21, 2010, amended the Exchange Act by adding Section 21F, "Whistleblower Incentives and Protection." The congressional purpose underlying these provisions was "to encourage whistleblowers to report possible violations of the securities laws by providing financial incentives, prohibiting employment-related retaliation, and providing various confidentiality guarantees." . . .

3.   To fulfill this congressional purpose, the Commission adopted Rule 21F–17, which provides in relevant part:

> (a) No person may take any action to impede an individual from communicating directly with the Commission staff about a possible securities law violation, including enforcing, or threatening to enforce, a confidentiality agreement . . . with respect to such communications.

B.   *KBR's Confidentiality Statement*

4.   As part of its compliance program, KBR regularly receives complaints and allegations from its employees of potential illegal or unethical conduct by KBR or its employees, including allegations of potential violations of the federal securities laws. KBR's practice is to conduct internal investigations of these allegations. KBR investigators typically interview KBR employees (including the employees who originally lodged the complaint or allegation) as part of the internal investigations.

5.   Prior to the promulgation of Rule 21F–17 and continuing into the time that Rule 21F–17 has been in effect, KBR has used a form confidentiality statement as part of these internal investigations. Although use of the form confidentiality statement is not required by KBR policy, the statement is included as an enclosure to the KBR Code of Business Conduct Investigation Procedures manual, and KBR investigators have had witnesses sign the statement at the start of an interview.

6. The form confidentiality statement that KBR has used before and since the SEC adopted Rule 21F–17 requires witnesses to agree to the following provisions:

> I understand that in order to protect the integrity of this review, I am prohibited from discussing any particulars regarding this interview and the subject matter discussed during the interview, without the prior authorization of the Law Department. I understand that the unauthorized disclosure of information may be grounds for disciplinary action up to and including termination of employment.

7. Though the Commission is unaware of any instances in which (i) a KBR employee was in fact prevented from communicating directly with Commission Staff about potential securities law violations, or (ii) KBR took action to enforce the form confidentiality agreement or otherwise prevent such communications, the language found in the form confidentiality statement impedes such communications by prohibiting employees from discussing the substance of their interview without clearance from KBR's law department under penalty of disciplinary action including termination of employment. This language undermines the purpose of [the statute and SEC rule] which is to "encourage individuals to report to the Commission."

Remedial Steps Taken By KBR

8. KBR has amended its confidentiality statement to include the following statement:

> Nothing in this Confidentiality Statement prohibits me from reporting possible violations of federal law or regulation to any governmental agency or entity, including but not limited to the Department of Justice, the Securities and Exchange Commission, the Congress, and any agency Inspector General, or making other disclosures that are protected under the whistleblower provisions of federal law or regulation. I do not need the prior authorization of the Law Department to make any such reports or disclosures and I am not required to notify the company that I have made such reports or disclosures.

Violation

9.   Through its conduct described above, KBR violated Rule 21F–17 under the Exchange Act.

Undertaking

10. KBR has agreed to make reasonable efforts to contact KBR employees in the United States who signed the confidentiality statement from August 21, 2011 to the present, providing them with a copy of this Order and a statement that KBR does not require the employee to seek permission from the General Counsel of KBR before communicating with any governmental agency or entity, including but not limited to the Department of Justice, the Securities and Exchange Commission, the Congress, and any agency Inspector General, regarding possible violations of federal law or regulation. . . .

11. KBR has agreed to certify, in writing, compliance with the undertaking set forth above. . . .

IV.

In view of the foregoing, the Commission deems it appropriate to impose the sanctions agreed to in Respondent KBR's Offer.

Accordingly, it is hereby ORDERED that:

A. Pursuant to Section 21C of the Exchange Act, Respondent KBR cease-and-desist from committing or causing any violations and any future violations of Rule 21F–17 of the Exchange Act;

B. Respondent shall, within thirty (30) days of the entry of this Order, pay a civil money penalty in the amount of $130,000 to the Securities and Exchange Commission for transfer to the general fund of the United States Treasury. . . .

IN RE KELLOGG BROWN & ROOT, INC.
756 F.3d 754 (D.C. Cir. 2014)

KAVANAUGH, *Circuit Judge*: More than three decades ago, the Supreme Court held that the attorney-client privilege protects confidential employee communications made during a business's internal investigation led by company lawyers. *See*

Upjohn Co. v. United States, 449 U.S. 383 (1981). In this case, the District Court denied the protection of the privilege to a company that had conducted just such an internal investigation. The District Court's decision has generated substantial uncertainty about the scope of the attorney-client privilege in the business setting. We conclude that the District Court's decision is irreconcilable with *Upjohn*. We therefore grant KBR's petition for a writ of mandamus and vacate the District Court's document production order.

I

Harry Barko worked for KBR, a defense contractor. In 2005, he filed a False Claims Act complaint against KBR and KBR-related corporate entities, whom we will collectively refer to as KBR. In essence, Barko alleged that KBR and certain subcontractors defrauded the U.S. Government by inflating costs and accepting kickbacks while administering military contracts in wartime Iraq. During discovery, Barko sought documents related to KBR's prior internal investigation into the alleged fraud. KBR had conducted that internal investigation pursuant to its Code of Business Conduct, which is overseen by the company's Law Department.

KBR argued that the internal investigation had been conducted for the purpose of obtaining legal advice and that the internal investigation documents therefore were protected by the attorney-client privilege. Barko responded that the internal investigation documents were unprivileged business records that he was entitled to discover. . . .

After reviewing the disputed documents *in camera*, the District Court determined that the attorney-client privilege protection did not apply because, among other reasons, KBR had not shown that "the communication would not have been made 'but for' the fact that legal advice was sought." . . . KBR's internal investigation, the court concluded, was "undertaken pursuant to regulatory law and corporate policy rather than for the purpose of obtaining legal advice." . . .

KBR vehemently opposed the ruling. The company asked the District Court to certify the privilege question to this Court for interlocutory appeal and to stay its order pending a petition for mandamus in this Court. The District Court denied those requests and ordered KBR to produce the disputed documents to

Barko within a matter of days. . . . KBR promptly filed a petition
for a writ of mandamus in this Court. A number of business
organizations and trade associations also objected to the District
Court's decision and filed an amicus brief in support of KBR. We
stayed the District Court's document production order and held
oral argument on the mandamus petition.

II

We . . . consider whether the District Court's privilege ruling
was legally erroneous. We conclude that it was.

Federal Rule of Evidence 501 provides that claims of
privilege in federal courts are governed by the "common law—as
interpreted by United States courts in the light of reason and
experience." Fed. R. Evid. 501. The attorney-client privilege is
the "oldest of the privileges for confidential communications
known to the common law." *Upjohn Co. v. United States*, 449
U.S. 383, 389 (1981). As relevant here, the privilege applies to a
confidential communication between attorney and client if that
communication was made for the purpose of obtaining or
providing legal advice to the client. . . .

In *Upjohn*, the Supreme Court held that the attorney-client
privilege applies to corporations. The Court explained that the
attorney-client privilege for business organizations was essential
in light of "the vast and complicated array of regulatory
legislation confronting the modern corporation," which required
corporations to "constantly go to lawyers to find out how to obey
the law, . . . particularly since compliance with the law in this
area is hardly an instinctive matter." The Court stated,
moreover, that the attorney-client privilege "exists to protect not
only the giving of professional advice to those who can act on it
but also the giving of information to the lawyer to enable him to
give sound and informed advice." That is so, the Court said,
because the "first step in the resolution of any legal problem is
ascertaining the factual background and sifting through the
facts with an eye to the legally relevant." In *Upjohn*, the
communications were made by company employees to company
attorneys during an attorney-led internal investigation that was
undertaken to ensure the company's "compliance with the law."
The Court ruled that the privilege applied to the internal
investigation and covered the communications between company
employees and company attorneys.

KBR's assertion of the privilege in this case is materially indistinguishable from Upjohn's assertion of the privilege in that case. As in *Upjohn*, KBR initiated an internal investigation to gather facts and ensure compliance with the law after being informed of potential misconduct. And as in *Upjohn*, KBR's investigation was conducted under the auspices of KBR's in-house legal department, acting in its legal capacity. The same considerations that led the Court in *Upjohn* to uphold the corporation's privilege claims apply here.

The District Court in this case initially distinguished *Upjohn* on a variety of grounds. But none of those purported distinctions takes this case out from under *Upjohn*'s umbrella.

First, the District Court stated that in *Upjohn* the internal investigation began after in-house counsel conferred with outside counsel, whereas here the investigation was conducted in-house without consultation with outside lawyers. But *Upjohn* does not hold or imply that the involvement of outside counsel is a necessary predicate for the privilege to apply. On the contrary, the general rule, which this Court has adopted, is that a lawyer's status as in-house counsel "does not dilute the privilege." . . . As the [American Law Institute] Restatement's commentary points out, "Inside legal counsel to a corporation or similar organization . . . is fully empowered to engage in privileged communications." 1 Restatement [The Law Governing Lawyers] § 72, cmt. c, at 551.

Second, the District Court noted that in *Upjohn* the interviews were conducted by attorneys, whereas here many of the interviews in KBR's investigation were conducted by non-attorneys. But the investigation here was conducted at the direction of the attorneys in KBR's Law Department. And communications made by and to non-attorneys serving as agents of attorneys in internal investigations are routinely protected by the attorney-client privilege. . . .

Third, the District Court pointed out that in *Upjohn* the interviewed employees were expressly informed that the purpose of the interview was to assist the company in obtaining legal advice, whereas here they were not. The District Court further stated that the confidentiality agreements signed by KBR employees did not mention that the purpose of KBR's investigation was to obtain legal advice. Yet nothing in *Upjohn* requires a company to use magic words to its employees in order to gain the benefit of the privilege for an internal investigation. And in any event, here, as in *Upjohn*, employees knew that the company's legal department was conducting an investigation of a sensitive nature. . . .

In short, none of those three distinctions of *Upjohn* holds water as a basis for denying KBR's privilege claim.

More broadly and more importantly, the District Court also distinguished *Upjohn* on the ground that KBR's internal investigation was undertaken to comply with Department of Defense regulations that require defense contractors such as KBR to maintain compliance programs and conduct internal investigations into allegations of potential wrongdoing. The District Court therefore concluded that the purpose of KBR's internal investigation was to comply with those regulatory requirements rather than to obtain or provide legal advice. In our view, the District Court's analysis rested on a false dichotomy. So long as obtaining or providing legal advice was one of the significant purposes of the internal investigation, the attorney-client privilege applies, even if there were also other purposes for the investigation and even if the investigation was mandated by regulation rather than simply an exercise of company discretion.

In the context of an organization's internal investigation, if one of the significant purposes of the internal investigation was to obtain or provide legal advice, the privilege will apply. That is true regardless of whether an internal investigation was conducted pursuant to a company compliance program required by statute or regulation, or was otherwise conducted pursuant to company policy. . . .

In this case, there can be no serious dispute that one of the significant purposes of the KBR internal investigation was to obtain or provide legal advice. In denying KBR's privilege claim on the ground that the internal investigation was conducted in order to comply with regulatory requirements and corporate policy and not just to obtain or provide legal advice, the District Court applied the wrong legal test and clearly erred.

In reaching our decision here, we stress, as the Supreme Court did in *Upjohn*, that the attorney-client privilege "only protects disclosure of communications; it does not protect disclosure of the underlying facts by those who communicated with the attorney." . . .

Although the attorney-client privilege covers only communications and not facts, we acknowledge that the privilege carries costs. The privilege means that potentially critical evidence may be withheld from the factfinder. Indeed, as the District Court here noted, that may be the end result in this case. But our legal system tolerates those costs because the privilege "is intended to encourage 'full and frank communication between attorneys and their clients and thereby promote broader public interests in the observance of law and the administration of justice.'"

We grant the petition for a writ of mandamus and vacate the District Court's . . . document production order. . . .

The following Scenario highlights some of the ethical considerations facing an attorney conducting an internal investigation on behalf of an organizational client.

SCENARIO

As a child, Tim Eddy loved to travel with his father who worked as a technical support analyst for an amusement park. Eddy always knew that one day he would own his very own amusement park, and it would attract visitors from all over the globe. At the age of 30, he received his break. A heavy-hitter investor by the name of Josh Willy had heard of Eddy and decided to provide the needed capital to get the park (named Eddy-Willy Amusement Park, Inc.) off the ground. Eddy, it turned out, was a natural when it came to amusement park operations. Within five years, the park was generating $35 million in annual revenues. At that time, although not publicly traded, the Company had 87 shareholders, with Eddy and Willy each owning 26% of the stock.

The most popular ride was the "Hyper Wave." It was a huge wave that would catapult the riders several feet in the air, and then allow them to come crashing down with a giant splash. Eddy designed the ride himself and knew that it had to be operated with precision in order to avoid accidents. The only drawback to operating the ride was that in order to ensure safety, the operator's control booth had to be placed within the reach of the wave's incredible force. As a result, every time the wave came down, the operator was inundated with a water wall that left him/her drenched. For the first few months after the ride's inception, Eddy insisted that he operate the controls himself to make sure nothing went wrong. As business grew, however, Eddy had to spend more time attending to Company-related matters. Eddy realized the time had come to hire several people to be responsible for operating the "Hyper Wave." For the next two years, the park was extremely successful, and the Company's board of directors began inquiring into the possibility of opening another amusement park.

Then things took a turn for the worse. The operators of the "Hyper Wave" were becoming increasingly disgruntled with their job. The constant battering they took under the huge wave proved to be more than many of them could psychologically bear. As a result, their performance began to suffer, and accidents began to occur. While none of the accidents were catastrophic, rumors were rampant within the Company. Eddy and the board of directors realized that they needed to act, and fast.

Eddy suggested hiring an outside consulting firm to figure out what the source of the problem was. The board of directors (advised by legal counsel), however, realized that, if there was some rogue element within the organization, it could lead to serious liability in the event of a lawsuit. The board thereupon reasoned that whatever information was uncovered needed to be kept confidential. So they suggested hiring a law firm to conduct an internal investigation. Eddy, having heard that lawyers were rogue elements themselves, was not overly enthused with the idea, but acquiesced in order to maintain confidentiality over any information uncovered. [Note that "facts" are not entitled to protection under the attorney-client privilege. Nonetheless, disclosure of certain information may be a confidence or secret, thereby implicating Model Rule 1.6. *See* Scenario II herein.]

The Company's board of directors retained a law firm that specialized in amusement park litigation to conduct the internal investigation. Before commencing, the lawyers met with the board members to mutually agree on a course of action. The board directed that as many employees as possible should be interviewed by counsel and that, to avoid raising suspicion that might thwart the investigation, counsel should not focus solely on the "Hyper Wave" operators. Furthermore, the board wanted the employees to be as truthful as possible, and if that meant allowing them to think that their conversations with the lawyers were completely confidential, that was just fine.

The lawyers explained that since the investigation's purpose was to uncover potential wrongdoing by employees, there was a strong chance that certain employees' interests would become adverse to those of the corporation, in which case the lawyers would be ethically obligated to tell any such employee that he/she is not being represented individually by the interviewing lawyer. Upon hearing this, Eddy became agitated and responded, "Listen, we are paying you guys a ridiculous amount of money to do a really simple task, so you will tell our employees exactly what we want you to tell them, understood?" The lawyers assured Eddy that they would "do their best" to avoid saying or doing anything that would risk compromising their ability to successfully conduct the investigation.

Then the employee interviews began. First, the lawyers started with the roller-coaster operators, then moved onto the Ferris wheel, and then felt the time was right to interview the "Hyper Wave" operators. The first two interviews were disappointing, as the employees seemed no different than any of the other operators. The third interview, however, changed the tone of the entire investigation. This operator told the lawyers how he, and several of the other Wave operators, felt like second-class operators because of the location of their control booth. Being right under the path of the wave, they were bombarded all day by the very waves they were helping to create. This employee told the lawyers that some of the operators' "friends" would come to watch them on the job, just to get a laugh when the wave came crashing down, knocking the operator out of the chair and into the padded wall that had been erected immediately behind the control booth. When asked why there was a padded wall there, the lawyers were told that it was to keep the operators from being carried away by the tremendous force of the wave.

The fourth and fifth interviews went about the same as the third interview. The sixth, however, really got interesting. This operator, Jessica Hendry, initially attempted to deny the story told by the previous operators, but after the lawyers explained that they already knew the truth, she came clean. Hendry, however, not realizing that the lawyers had only heard the first part of the truth, continued into uncharted territory. She said, "Well, if you guys already know all this, and I guess if you're a bunch of lawyers you can't tell anyone what we tell you, yeah, we operators decided to try to cause a few wrecks." The lawyers could not believe their ears. They were so carried away with what they had just heard that all they could think about was getting more information.

Hendry then saw Ivan Inglas, a fellow Wave operator, walking by. She called him over and said, "These guys are some lawyers that want to hear about our little pact to cause wrecks on the Wave. They have to keep their mouths shut about what we tell them."

Feeling sort of relieved about finally being able to express his resentment towards his job, Inglas began to tell his story. Just then, however, the lawyers were hit with the implications of what Hendry had said about their vow of secrecy. They decided to end the interview immediately, and told the two employees that they would get back to them as soon as possible. The lawyers realized they were in a predicament and needed time to meet with the other attorneys to explain what had happened and figure out what to do. They knew they would have to tell the other lawyers exactly what had transpired and what had been communicated during the employee interviews. But they were also aware that their actions, or lack thereof, may have jeopardized the entire investigation.

In light of the above developments, did counsel act appropriately? What actions should now be taken by counsel in continuing the investigation?

Scenario V

Parent-Subsidiary Related Party Transactions

■ ■ ■

Attorneys who are hired by a business enterprise may have more than just one entity as their client. The parent corporation may have numerous subsidiaries that will direct their legal work to the attorney's law firm. In most dealings, this multiple representation will not pose a problem, as the interests of the wholly-owned subsidiaries normally will be aligned with those of the parent. With some frequency, the parent corporation and its subsidiaries may engage in transactions between themselves. Generally, except where the wholly-owned subsidiary is *insolvent*, these transactions are not problematic. As stated by the Delaware Court of Chancery: "When a controller [such as a parent corporation] owns 100% of a corporation's equity and the subsidiary is solvent, the interests ... are fully aligned.... Therefore, when the subsidiary is solvent—that in a parent and wholly-owned subsidiary context—the directors of the subsidiary are obligated only to manage the affairs of the subsidiary in the best interests of the parent and its shareholders."[1]

Nonetheless, when the subsidiary corporation is insolvent or has minority shareholders, transactions between the parent corporation and its subsidiary may raise concern. An attorney who simultaneously represents the parent company and its majority-owned subsidiary must seek to ensure that each client complies with its legal obligations.

In terms of the lawyer's professional obligations, the Model Rules of Professional Conduct demand loyalty to a client. To this end, the Model Rules generally prohibit a lawyer from representing a client whose interests are directly adverse to another client or if a significant risk exists that the lawyer's representation would be materially limited by the lawyer's

---

[1] *Quadrant Structured Products Company, Ltd. v. Vertin*, 102 A.3d 155, 184 (Del. Ch. 2014).

71

responsibilities owed to another present (or former) client, a
third party, or the lawyer's own interest.[2] Attorneys may
undertake an otherwise problematic dual representation if they
reasonably believe that their representation will not materially
harm either client *and* each client "gives informed consent,
confirmed in writing."[3]

Given the above, counsel should be cautious when requested
to represent both the parent and a majority-owned (but not
wholly-owned) subsidiary corporation in a self-dealing
transaction.[4] Two basic inquiries should be made by counsel.
First, are the interests of the parent and subsidiary directly
adverse to each other, which would give rise to the proscription
set forth in Model Rule 1.7(a)(1)? Second, do the responsibilities
that the attorney owes to one client, such as the parent
company, materially limit the lawyer's ability to represent the

---

[2] Model Rule 1.7 provides:

"(a) Except as provided in paragraph (b), a lawyer shall not represent
a client if the representation involves a concurrent conflict of interest.
A concurrent conflict of interest exists if:

> (1) the representation of one client will be directly adverse to
> another client; or

> (2) there is a significant risk that the representation of one or more
> clients will be materially limited by the lawyer's responsibilities to
> another client, a former client or a third person or by a personal
> interest of the lawyer.

(b) Notwithstanding the existence of a concurrent conflict of interest
under paragraph (a), a lawyer may represent a client if:

> (1) the lawyer reasonably believes that the lawyer will be able to
> provide competent and diligent representation to each affected
> client;

> (2) the representation is not prohibited by law;

> (3) the representation does not involve the assertion of a claim by
> one client against another client represented by the lawyer in the
> same litigation or other proceeding before a tribunal; and

> (4) each affected client gives informed consent, confirmed in
> writing."

[3] *Id.* Rule 1.7(b) & cmts. to Rule 1.7.

[4] A self-dealing transaction in this context generally is defined as the
parent corporation, due to its control and domination over the subsidiary,
receives a benefit to the detriment and exclusion of the subsidiary and its
minority shareholders. *See Sinclair Oil Corp. v. Levien*, 280 A.2d 717 (Del.
1971). A related party transaction in this context generally is a transaction
between the parent corporation and its subsidiary which may or may not be
viewed under the applicable corporate law as a self-dealing transaction.

subsidiary, thereby implicating Model Rule 1.7(a)(2)? For example, if the lawyer's primary relationship is with the parent, can she effectively also represent the subsidiary in a self-dealing transaction, such as a cash-out merger whereby the subsidiary's public shareholders would be eliminated?

Even if the attorney is concerned that she cannot ethically represent both entities in a corporate self-dealing transaction, she may face pressure to do so. For example, the executive officers in the parent corporation may be opposed to hiring a second law firm to represent the subsidiary due to apprehension that retention of more lawyers will further complicate and impede the "deal." The officers might even threaten to terminate entirely the relationship with the attorney and her law firm unless she represents both sides. Along the same lines, the attorney may be reluctant to bring in a second full-service law firm fearing that the other firm will take away some or all of the client's future business. Furthermore, the attorney may want the revenue that she would receive from both clients and thus be willing to minimize her ethical obligations.[5] In theory and hopefully in practice, professional responsibility dictates that the attorney must hold firm against these pressures.

When a lawyer is involved in a transaction between a parent corporation and its subsidiary, his ethical responsibilities become highly intertwined with the substantive corporate law rules governing such dealings. In addition to being concerned about his own behavior, the business lawyer also must provide advice with respect to his client's conduct to assist such client's officers and directors in fulfilling their fiduciary duties to the affected corporation and shareholders.[6] With this in mind, let us first review some of the substantive law governing related party or self-dealing transactions and then examine relevant implications for an attorney's ethical duties.

In the context of parent and majority-owned subsidiary self-dealing transactions, courts tend to examine the decisions made by a subject corporation's board of directors with more scrutiny than the normally deferential business judgment rule would

---

[5] *See* Rule 1.7 cmt. 10 ("The lawyer's own interest should not be permitted to have an adverse effect on representation of a client."). *See generally* Richmond, *Lawyers' Professional Responsibilities and Liabilities in Negotiations,* 22 Geo. J. Leg. Eth. 249 (2009).

[6] *See, e.g.,* R. Clark, *Corporate Law* §§ 3.4–4.2 (1986).

allow.[7] Most notably, in Delaware (the most popular state where "large" publicly-held companies opt to incorporate), such transactions must meet the standard of *entire fairness*, with the burden of persuasion falling on the defendants.[8] The standard of entire fairness has two components—fair dealing and fair price—that must be assessed given the pertinent facts and circumstances involved; even though the two components may be analyzed separately, they should not be bifurcated when concluding whether the entire fairness standard has been met.[9]

The concept of fair price seems straightforward. It "relates to the economic and financial considerations of the proposed [transaction, such as a] merger, including all relevant factors: assets, market value, earnings, future prospects, and any other elements that affect the intrinsic or inherent value of a company's stock."[10] Depending on the circumstances, a court may find that the duty of fair price was violated if the price itself involved in the transaction was deemed egregiously low.[11]

---

[7] *See A Handbook of Basic Law Terms* 27 (B. Garner ed. 1999) (defining the business judgment rule as "[t]he presumption that in making business decisions not involving direct self-interest or self-dealing, corporate directors act on an informed basis, in good faith, and in the honest belief that their actions are in the corporation's best interest").

[8] *See Kahn v. Tremont Corp.*, 694 A.2d 422, 428 (Del. 1997) ("Ordinarily, in a challenged transaction involving self-dealing by a controlling shareholder the substantive legal standard is that of entire fairness, with the burden of persuasion resting upon the defendants."); *Weinberger v. UOP, Inc.*, 457 A.2d 701, 710 (Del. 1983) ("The requirement of fairness is unflinching in its demand that where one stands on both sides of a transaction, he has the burden of establishing its entire fairness, sufficient to pass the test of careful scrutiny by the courts.").

[9] *See Weinberger*, 457 A.2d at 711; *Valeant Pharmaceuticals International v. Jerney*, 921 A. 2d 732, 746 (Del. Ch. 2007). *But see Glassman v. Unocal Exploration Corp.*, 777 A.2d 242 (Del. 2001) (holding that, absent fraud or illegality, appraisal is a minority shareholder's exclusive remedy in a short-form merger—namely, a merger with respect to which the majority shareholder owns 90% or more of the subsidiary corporation's stock). In a subsequent decision, the Delaware Supreme Court held that the quasi-appraisal remedy is available in a short-form merger when the controlling shareholder breaches its duty of disclosure. *See Berger v. Pubco Corp.*, 976 A. 2d 132 (Del. 2009). *See generally* Steinberg, *Short-Form Mergers in Delaware*, 27 Del. J. Corp. L. 489 (2002).

[10] *Weinberger*, 457 A.2d at 711.

[11] *See id.* at 709 (One report "show[ed] that a return on the investment at $21 [the actual purchase price] would be 15.7% versus 15.5% at $24 per share. This was a difference of only two-tenths of one percent, while it meant

The concept of fair dealing focuses on the process of the transaction. It "embraces questions of when the transaction was timed, how it was initiated, structured, negotiated, disclosed to the directors, and how the approvals of the directors and the stockholders were obtained."[12] The Delaware Supreme Court has noted that strong evidence of a fair process would be if both the parent and subsidiary "exerted its bargaining power against each other at *arm's length*."[13] Arguably, the best way for a parent corporation and its subsidiary to arrive at an arm's length transaction is to set up a special committee of the independent members of the subsidiary's board—that is, those board members who are independent from the parent—to negotiate and approve the proposed transaction with the parent.[14]

The mere establishment of such a committee of independent directors by the subsidiary is not sufficient in and of itself.[15] The committee must in fact be independent and function in that manner. Thus, there are a number of factors considered in deciding whether the subsidiary's board and/or special

---

over $17,000,000 to the minority."); *Kahn*, 694 A.2d at 432 ("When assigned the burden of persuasion, this test [of entire fairness] obligates the directors or their surrogates to present evidence which demonstrates that the cumulative manner by which it discharged all of its fiduciary duties produced a fair transaction.").

[12] *Weinberger*, 457 A.2d at 711.

[13] *Id.* at 709 n.7 (emphasis added).

[14] *Id. See* M. Steinberg, *Securities Regulation: Liabilities and Remedies* § 15.04[1] (2015); Gerstein & Faris, *Special Negotiating Committees*, 38 Rev. Sec. & Comm. Reg. 157 (2005); Weiss, *Balancing Interests in Cash-Out Mergers: The Promise of Weinberger v. UOP, Inc.*, 8 Del. J. Corp. L. 1 (1983).

[15] *Kahn v. M & F Worldwide Corp.*, 88 A.3d 635, 645 (Del. 2014) (emphasis in original) (holding that in "controller buyouts, the business judgment standard of review will be applied *if and only if*: (i) the controller conditions the procession of the transaction on the approval of both a Special Committee and a majority of the minority stockholders; (ii) the Special Committee is independent; (iii) the Special Committee is empowered to freely select its own advisors and to say no definitively; (iv) the Special Committee meets its duty of care in negotiating a fair price; (v) the vote of the minority is informed; and (vi) there is no coercion of the minority"); *Kahn*, 694 A.2d at 428 ("Entire fairness remains applicable even when an independent committee is utilized because the underlying factors which raise the specter of impropriety can never by completely eradicated and still require careful judicial scrutiny.").

committee failed to satisfy their duties of loyalty and care owed to the corporation and the shareholders:

- If some directors fail to share material information among all members of the subsidiary's directors, particularly among the independent committee, in accordance with the directors' duty of candor;[16]

- If interested directors affiliated with the parent corporation exert an overbearing influence on the transaction;[17]

- If the entire transaction occurred within an unduly narrow time frame and under conditions unduly beneficial to the parent;[18]

- If the "independent" committee members had previous significant dealings with the parent corporation so as to bring their "independence" into question;[19]

---

[16] See Weinberger, 457 A.2d at 709–711 (failure of subsidiary board members to disclose to other subsidiary board members stock valuation information that was generated from internal subsidiary data for the benefit of the parent and to which they were privy constituted breach of fiduciary duty); Kahn, 694 A.2d at 431 (stating that "the Court of Chancery correctly stated that a controlling shareholder . . . must disclose fully all material facts and circumstances surrounding the transaction"). See generally Hammermesh, Calling Off the Lynch Mob: A Corporate Director's Fiduciary Disclosure Duty, 49 Vand. L. Rev. 1087 (1998); Klock, Litigating Securities Fraud As a Breach of Fiduciary Duty in Delaware, 28 Sec. Reg. L.J. 296 (2000).

[17] See Weinberger, 457 A.2d at 710 ("Given the absence of any attempt to structure this transaction on an arm's length basis, [the parent] cannot escape the effects of the conflicts it faced, particularly when its designees on [the subsidiary's] board did not totally abstain from participation in the matter.").

[18] Id. at 711 ("For whatever reasons, and they were only [the parent's], the entire transaction was presented to and approved by [the subsidiary's board] within four business days."); Kahn, 694 A.2d at 431 ("Initiation by the seller, standing alone, is not incompatible with the concept of fair dealing so long as the controlling shareholder does not gain financial advantage at the expense of the controlled company.").

[19] See Kahn, 694 A.2d at 426 ("Although the three [individuals] were deemed 'independent' for purposes of this transaction, all had significant prior business relationships with [the controlling shareholder] or [his] controlled companies.").

- If the independent committee is not advised in an adequate manner by competent, independent professionals, such as lawyers and financial advisers; moreover, these professionals should not be selected by officers of the parent or because of a previous relationship with the parent;[20] and

- If certain members of the committee fail to participate actively in the negotiation and decision-making process and/or if they overly rely on the efforts of another committee member who may not be independent.[21]

Individually, any one of these may or may not constitute unfair dealing depending on the facts of the situation. But as more of these shortcomings begin to mount, a parent corporation will have greater difficulty establishing the fairness of the transaction.

How does this substantive law interact with counsel's ethical duties? As discussed above, the primary rule of professional responsibility invoked with respect to parent-subsidiary self-dealing transactions is Model Rule 1.7. The general thrust of the rule applied in this setting is that, if an attorney cannot adequately represent each of the parties, such dual representation constitutes an impermissible conflict of interest.

---

[20] *See Weinberger*, 457 A.2d at 712 (""We can only conclude from the record that the rush imposed on [the investment banker] by [the parent's] timetable contributed to the difficulties under which this investment banking firm attempted to perform its responsibilities. Yet, none of this was disclosed to [the subsidiary's] minority."); *Kahn*, 694 A.2d at 429 ("[T]he selection of professional advisors for the Special Committee doesn't give comfort; it raises questions."). *See generally* Baker, Butler & McDermott, *Corporate Governance of Troubled Companies and the Role of Restructuring Counsel*, 63 Bus. Law. 855 (2008); Davidoff, *Fairness Opinions*, 55 Am. U. L. Rev. 1557 (2006); Sharfman, *Kahn v. M & F Worldwide Corporation: A Small But Significant Step in the War Against Frivolous Shareholder Lawsuits*, 40 J. Corp. L. 197 (2014).

[21] *See Kahn*, 694 A.2d at 430 (Delaware Supreme Court finding fault with one member not attending negotiations or meetings with professional advisors; a second member only partially participating; and the third member, who conducted the negotiations, being "arguably the least detached member of the Special Committee"). *See also, Kahn v. Lynch Communication Systems, Inc.*, 638 A.2d 1110 (Del. 1994), *on remand*, 669 A.2d 79 (Del. 1995); *Rabkin v. Olin Corp.*, 586 A.2d 1202 (Del. 1990); *Rosenblatt v. Getty Oil Corp.*, 493 A.2d 929 (Del. 1985).

As discussed above, the initial question to consider under Rule 1.7 is whether the parent's and subsidiary's interests are directly adverse to each other. Even though both entities might benefit from a transaction between them, frequently any transaction between the two will be of a zero-sum nature: the benefit to one comes at the expense of the other. As a general proposition, the substantive law, for its part in self-dealing transactions in parent and majority-owned subsidiary transactions, calls for entire fairness, including procuring competent and independent advice from professionals.[22] As a result, Rule 1.7(a) arguably prevents the same counsel from representing both parties in the negotiations.[23] But even if the parent's and subsidiary's interests are not directly adverse, the substantive law requirement that the subsidiary receive competent and independent legal advice likely means that an attorney could not fulfill that role without materially limiting his representation to the parent, or vice versa. As a result, the prohibition of dual representation in this context normally should be implicated.[24]

Even if an attorney normally should refrain from representing both the parent and subsidiary corporations due to an apparent conflict of interest, Rule 1.7 does allow the attorney to continue the dual representation in this setting if two elements are satisfied. First, the lawyer reasonably believes that she can render diligent and competent representation to each client, here the parent and the subsidiary.[25] In many cases, an attorney may *subjectively* believe she can properly represent both the parent and subsidiary, particularly if she has an ongoing professional relationship with both entities. But the

---

[22] *See supra* notes 9–21 and accompanying text. *But see Glassman v. Unocal Exploration Corp.*, 777 A.2d 242 (Del. 2001) (discussed in note 9 *supra*).

[23] *See* Model Rule 1.7 cmt. 28 (stating that "a lawyer may not represent multiple parties to a negotiation whose interests are fundamentally antagonistic to each other, but common representation is permissible where the clients are generally aligned in interest even though there is some difference in interest among them").

[24] *See generally* Symposium, *The Role of Counsel in Corporate Acquisitions and Takeovers: Conflicts and Complications*, 39 Hastings L.J. No. 3 (1988); Rotunda, *Conflicts Problems When Representing Members of Corporate Families*, 72 Notre Dame L. Rev. 655 (1997).

[25] Model Rule 1.7(b)(1).

ethical mandates call for an *objective* standard—whether the lawyer "reasonably believes" that such lawyer under the circumstances would be able to provide "competent and diligent representation" to each affected client.[26] The second element requires each client to give informed consent to the representation, confirmed in writing.[27] Once again, the substantive law governing corporations interacts with counsel's ethical obligations. The subsidiary would need to provide its consent independently of the parent's determination. Thus, for the lawyer to comply with her ethical duties in rendering dual representation, she should seek to ensure that the subsidiary's "independent" directors are not under the parent's domination and control.[28]

Because directors in parent-subsidiary self-dealing transactions should be particularly mindful of their fiduciary duties, counsel representing either the parent or subsidiary corporation should seek to ensure that such directors fulfill their obligations. To the extent that the attorney fails in this task— for example, if he is too driven to promote the parent company's interests and renders improper legal advice—he subjects his client, his client's directors and executive officers, and himself to liability exposure. Certainly, if counsel has acted incompetently or assisted in a fraudulent transaction, he has violated the Model Rules as well as being subject to liability exposure for malpractice and aiding and abetting breach of fiduciary duty.[29]

---

[26] *Id.* & cmt. 15.

[27] *See id.* Rule 1.7(b)(4). "Informed consent requires that each affected client be aware of the relevant circumstances and of the material and reasonably foreseeable ways that the conflict could have adverse effects on the interests of that client. . . ." *Id.* Rule 1.7 cmt. 18. *See id.* Rule 1.0(e) & cmts. 6–7 (defining the term "informed consent" and setting forth comments thereto).

[28] *See supra* notes 16–21 and accompanying text.

[29] *See* Model Rules of Prof. Conduct, Rule 1.1 ("A lawyer shall provide competent representation to a client. Competent representation requires the legal knowledge, skill, thoroughness and preparation reasonably necessary for the representation."); Rule 1.2(d) ("A lawyer shall not counsel a client to engage, or assist a client, in conduct that the lawyer knows is criminal or fraudulent. . . ."). *Cf.* Rule 1.2 cmts. 9–10.

A recent decision illustrates the liability exposure that a corporate director, officer, or legal counsel can incur in this context. Indeed, in the following case, damages exceeding $148 million were awarded.

IN RE DOLE FOOD CO., INC. STOCKHOLDER LITIGATION
2015 WL 5052214 (Del. Ct. 2015)[30]

[In February 2013], the [Dole] Board agreed that [David H.] Murdock would start functioning as CEO, and [C. Michael] Carter would start functioning as President and COO. . . . Carter [also] retained his position as Dole's *General Counsel* and Corporate Secretary. [emphasis supplied] He also joined the Board. . . .

As a practical matter, responsibility for day-to-day management of Dole passed . . . to Carter in December 2012. Carter was Murdock's only direct report, which meant that the executive team reported to him. His job was to carry out Murdock's plans, and he did so effectively, even ruthlessly. When Carter set a goal for a division, they fell into line. Dole's executives could not envision anyone failing to carry out Carter's instructions. . . .

In November 2013, defendant Murdock paid $13.50 per share to acquire all of the common stock of Dole . . . that he did not already own. Before the transaction, Murdock owned approximately 40% of Dole's common stock, served as its Chairman and CEO, and was its *de facto* controller. . . . The Merger closed on November 1, 2013.

In his initial letter to Dole's board of directors (the "Board"), Murdock offered to pay $12.00 per share. . . . Murdock conditioned his proposal on (i) approval from a committee of the Board made up of disinterested and independent directors (the "Committee") and (ii) the affirmative vote of holders of a majority of the unaffiliated shares. [Nonetheless,] Murdock did not adhere to its substance. He and his right-hand man, C. Michael Carter, sought to undermine the Committee from the start, and they continued their efforts throughout the process.

---

[30] This decision is an "unpublished opinion." *See* Hoffman, *Dole CEO Must Pay Shareholders*, Wall St. J., Aug. 28, 2015, at B4.

Before trial, the allegations and evidence regarding Murdock and Carter's activities, together with the relationships between certain Committee members and Murdock, were sufficient to create triable questions of fact regarding the Committee's independence. The record at trial, however, demonstrated that the Committee carried out its task with integrity. The Committee was assisted in this effort by expert legal counsel and an investment bank—Lazard Frères & Co. LLC ("Lazard")—that likewise acted with integrity. . . .

Because of the diligence of its members and their advisors, the Committee overcame most of Murdock and Carter's machinations. The Committee negotiated an increase in the price from $12.00 to $13.50 per share, which Lazard opined fell within a range of fairness. Several market indicators supported Lazard's opinion. Stockholders approved the Merger, with the unaffiliated stockholders narrowly voting in favor in a 50.9% majority.

But what the Committee could not overcome, what the stockholder vote could not cleanse, and what even an arguably fair price does not immunize, is fraud. Before Murdock made his proposal, Carter made false disclosures about the savings Dole could realize after selling approximately half of its business in 2012. He also cancelled a recently adopted stock repurchase program for pretextual reasons. These actions primed the market for the freeze-out by driving down Dole's stock price and undermining its validity as a measure of value. Then, after Murdock made his proposal, Carter provided the Committee with lowball management projections. The next day, in a secret meeting that violated the procedures established by the Committee, Carter gave Murdock's advisors and financing banks more positive and accurate data. To their credit, the Committee and Lazard recognized that Carter's projections were unreliable and engaged in Herculean efforts to overcome the informational deficit, but they could not do so fully. Critically for purposes of the outcome of this litigation, the Committee never obtained accurate information about Dole's ability to improve its income by cutting costs and acquiring farms.

By taking these actions, Murdock and Carter deprived the Committee of the ability to negotiate on a fully informed basis and potentially say no to the Merger. Murdock and Carter likewise deprived the stockholders of their ability to consider the

Merger on a fully informed basis and potentially vote it down. Murdock and Carter's conduct throughout the Committee process, as well as their credibility problems at trial, demonstrated that their actions were not innocent or inadvertent, but rather intentional and in bad faith.

Under these circumstances, assuming for the sake of argument that the $13.50 price still fell within a range of fairness, the stockholders are not limited to a fair price. They are entitled to a fairer price designed to eliminate the ability of the defendants to profit from their breaches of the duty of loyalty. This decision holds Murdock and Carter jointly and severally liable for damages of $148,190,590.18, representing an incremental value of $2.74 per share. Although facially large, the award is conservative relative to what the evidence could support.

Let us consider how these issues play out in the following Scenario.

SCENARIO

Oneworld Corp. is a privately held holding company with interests in a variety of manufacturing and industrial businesses. Jonathan Evans founded the company and is now its Chief Executive Office (CEO) and Chairman of the Board. Evans is a very hands-on leader and demands a say in virtually every aspect of all his businesses, including Oneworld's subsidiaries. One of his most trusted advisers is his long-term outside general counsel, Chris Mathias, who has worked with Evans for over 20 years.

Evans decides that he wants Oneworld to buy out the minority interests in one of its subsidiaries, Mac & McGaw, Inc., a farm equipment manufacturer. Oneworld already owns 51% of Mac & McGaw, with the remaining stock in the Company publicly traded on the New York Stock Exchange. The value of Mac & McGaw's stock has declined over the past few years. Evans attributes this stock price decline to poor weather conditions, the relatively weak economy, and the current credit market crunch. These conditions have kept farmers from being able to afford new equipment. Believing that sales will pick up in the foreseeable future, he perceives that the stock is now significantly undervalued, thus giving rise to his desire to cash-out the minority shareholders. At the time, Mac & McGaw has a nine-member Board of Directors: Evans and three other officers from Oneworld; Harold Stanley, the president of one of Mac & McGaw's key suppliers; Melissa Brown, an investment banker who has an existing and ongoing professional relationship with Evans and Oneworld; Francine Baker and Leonard Collins, two highly respected business people from outside companies; and Albert Anson, the Dean of the business school from a major university who also has a $95,000 a year consulting contract with Oneworld. Evans calls Mathias over to his office and expresses his desire for Oneworld to acquire the minority interests in Mac & McGaw. Mathias suggests that Oneworld create a new subsidiary, Newco, in which Oneworld would be the sole owner and then execute a freeze-out merger in which Mac & McGaw would merge into Newco, with the public shareholders of Mac & McGaw receiving cash for their stock. He advises Evans that this structure would be the easiest way to accomplish Evans' goals.

Unfortunately for Evans, he learned earlier that day that one of Oneworld's European subsidiaries requires his immediate attention and he must leave for France the next day. Prior to leaving, he tells Mathias that he is relying on him to make sure that the Mac & McGaw transaction takes place and that he will make it worth Mathias' efforts. Mathias, who is under criticism by his law partners for not being a strong rainmaker, knows that the financial reward he will receive from getting the deal done for Evans will silence some of his critics in the firm (at least for a while).

That evening, Evans and Mathias finalize their plan. They arrange for the Mac & McGaw board of directors to set up a special committee to negotiate with Oneworld. The committee is to be comprised of Stanley, Collins, and Anson. Upon making this decision, Evans expresses his approval: "Collins is too busy with his own business to get too involved in this and Anson knows where his bread is buttered. Stanley is a bit of a wild card, but should not be too much of a problem." Evans and Mathias also decide that Mac & McGaw will retain the investment banking firm of Hornsby/Wagner. Although Hornsby/Wagner has never worked for Oneworld or any of its subsidiaries, Evans knows the firm through Melissa Brown, who has a strategic alliance with that firm. Evans also tells Mathias that since he also serves as Mac & McGaw's general outside counsel, Mathias must represent both companies in the transaction and that Evans will make sure that Mac & McGaw's board of directors signs off on that.

After hammering out those details, Evans calls in Oneworld's Chief Operating Officer (COO), Denton Young. Young also serves as Mac & McGaw's executive vice president and as one of its directors. The three review Oneworld's and Mac & McGaw's financials. Provided that the price of Mac & McGaw stock remains stable, they decide that Oneworld's initial offer in its negotiations with the members of the Mac & McGaw independent committee will be a 10% premium over that day's closing stock price and that Oneworld will go as high as an 18% premium if need be. They also realize that they could go as high as 25% without seriously hampering Oneworld's economic gain, but Evans rejects going that high: "We should get this done at most for an 18% premium. That's enough of a gravy train for those 'pain in the butt' shareholders."

Evans leaves for Europe the next day and expects to be gone for three weeks. He tells Mathias, "I want this done by the time I get back." Mathias immediately starts to work on the transaction: having Newco created and preparing its organizational documents; drafting the initial documents necessary for the merger transaction as Evans and he envisioned; having several phone calls with members of the Oneworld's and Mac & McGaw's boards of directors; and, of course, staying in continual contact with Evans. Ten days after Evans left, Mathias formally conveys the buy-out offer to Mac & McGaw's board of directors, which proceeds to select the pre-arranged special committee and approve Mathias as the subsidiary's counsel for the transaction. Two days later, after negotiations lasting seven hours between the Mac & McGaw special committee and Oneworld, the companies issue a press release announcing the contemplated merger between Mac & McGaw and Newco whereby the Mac & McGaw minority shareholders will receive a 20% premium above market price for the cash-out of their stock in Mac & McGaw.

When Evans returns from Europe, he is irate at the premium involved in the buy-out. He screams at Mathias, "I thought I told you 18% was the top." Mathias responds, "It was

Stanley. He was too much of a wild card. He kept pouring over the financials and asking for more and more, and saying that perhaps the committee should get another lawyer to get more input. It finally got to the point where I cut off how much information he was getting and forced the issue. Fortunately, we got Hornsby/Wagner to say that the 20% premium was a fair price, and I strong-armed Anson to get Collins to outvote Stanley. Otherwise, it could have been worse."

Subsequently, the merger is completed. Six months thereafter Evans' predictions regarding Mac & McGaw's increasing sales come true as farmers have bumper crops throughout most of the nation, with added benefits of a booming economy and improved credit markets. As a result, Newco (i.e., Mac & McGaw) performs more favorably. Ten months after the freeze-out merger is completed, Evans takes advantage of an eager buyer to spin off the subsidiary at a price that equates to a 45% premium above the stock price on the day that Oneworld and Mac & McGaw announced the merger with Newco. Shortly thereafter, a well-known plaintiffs' law firm locates a "representative" former minority shareholder who was frozen out in the merger. The class action lawsuit names Oneworld, Mac & McGaw (Newco), Mac & McGaw's board of directors, the investment banking firm of Hornsby/Wagner, and Mathias and his law firm as defendants. In particular, Mathias is sued allegedly for aiding and abetting Mac & McGaw's breach of fiduciary duty and for fraud.

What should have Mathias done to avoid this lawsuit? What arguments can he now make on behalf of his clients and himself to escape liability?

SCENARIO VI

THE CORPORATE OPPORTUNITY DOCTRINE AND THE LAWYER'S ROLE

■ ■ ■

A corporate attorney advising his client on a proposed transaction should seek to ensure that the transaction does not conflict with the client's existing fiduciary obligations. A client who serves as a director or executive officer in a corporation cannot engage in transactions that impermissibly conflict with his duty of loyalty to the corporation. One such way a fiduciary can breach his duty of loyalty to the corporation is by improperly taking a corporate opportunity. If a lawyer facilitates such a transaction, the lawyer subjects himself to malpractice exposure and also risks becoming an accessory to the client's breach of duty to the corporation.

Corporate directors and officers owe a fiduciary duty of loyalty to the corporation they serve.[1] A breach of the corporate opportunity doctrine constitutes a violation of this duty.[2] The corporate opportunity doctrine prohibits a director or officer from improperly taking advantage of a business opportunity that belongs to the corporation.[3] A corporate fiduciary breaches her duty of loyalty to the corporation if the fiduciary misappropriates a corporation's business opportunity for such fiduciary's own benefit.[4] The remedy that may be invoked for such a breach is the ordering of a constructive trust whereby the defendant fiduciary is deemed to hold in trust the subject

---

[1] *Guft v. Loft, Inc.,* 5 A.2d 503, 510 (Del. 1939).

[2] *Id. See* Brown, *When Opportunity Knocks: An Analysis of the Brudney & Clark and ALI Principles of Corporate Governance Proposals for Deciding Corporate Opportunity Claims,* 11 J. Corp. L. 255 (1986).

[3] *Guft,* 5 A. 2d at 510. *See Broz v. Cellular Information Systems, Inc.,* 673 A. 2d 148 (Del. 1996).

[4] *Guft,* 5 A.2d at 510. *See Unified Western Grocers, Inc. v. Twin City Fire Ins. Co.,* 457 F.3d 1106, 1113 (9th Cir. 2006); *Thorpe v. Cerbo, Inc.,* 676 A. 2d 436, 443 (Del. 1996).

property (or profit) for the benefit of the corporation.[5] Based on the rationale of unjust enrichment, a constructive trust may be ordered even where the corporation has not incurred any damages or injury.[6]

The doctrine thus prohibits officers and directors from using their privileged positions for personal benefit to usurp opportunities that properly belong to the corporation.[7] An expansive definition of what constitutes a "corporate opportunity" could prevent corporate fiduciaries from pursuing a wide array of business prospects for their personal advantage, thereby impairing economic competition.[8] Such an approach would further reduce an individual's incentive to become a director. Alternatively, an unduly narrow definition of corporate opportunity could induce these fiduciaries to focus less energy on the corporation and to use their corporate positions for personal gain.[9] The corporate opportunity doctrine should carefully balance the need to ensure director/officer loyalty to the corporation while not making these positions overly burdensome.[10]

Upon applying the prevailing test, if a circumstance is determined to present a corporate opportunity, then the subject fiduciary should offer it to the corporation before taking the

---

[5] *Guft*, 5 A.2d at 511. *See Cantor v. Perelman*, 414 F. 3d 430, 436 (3d Cir. 2005); *Genesis Technical & Financial, Inc. v. Cast Navigation, LLC,* 905 N.E. 2d 569, 576 (Mass. App. 2009); 3 W. Fletcher, *Fletcher Cyclepedia of the Law of Corporations* § 861.50 (2015).

[6] *See Thorpe v. Cerbco, Inc.*, 676 A. 2d 436, 455 (Del. 1996).

[7] *See Guft*, 5 A. 2d at 510.

[8] *See* A. Pinto & D. Branson, *Understanding Corporate Law* 272 (4th ed. 2013); Chew, *Competing Interests in the Corporate Opportunity Doctrine*, 67 N.C. L. Rev. 435, 452 (1989). *See also, Comedy Cottage, Inc. v. Berk*, 495 N.E. 2d 1006, 1011 (Ill. App. 1986) ("Defendant's duty is not inconsistent with his right to enter into competition with a former employer upon leaving such employment.").

[9] *See* Pinto & Branson, *supra* note 8, at 272; Chew, *supra* note 8, 67 N.C. L. Rev. at 442. *See also, Guft*, 5 A. 2d at 510 ("Corporate officers and directors are not permitted to use their position of trust and confidence to further their private interest." This duty includes both the obligation to "protect the interests of the corporation committed to his charge, but also to refrain from doing anything that would work injury to the corporation.")

[10] *See* Pinto & Branson, *supra* note 8, at 272; Chew, *supra* note 8, 67 N.C.L. Rev. at 451–452.

opportunity for such fiduciary's own interest.[11] Although a formal presentation to the board may not be required, such a presentation normally acts as a safe harbor and reduces the risk associated with an after-the-fact judicial determination.[12] The benefits of a formal presentation, however, depend on adequate disclosure of the relevant facts concerning the opportunity. When presenting on the subject corporate fiduciary's behalf a potential corporate opportunity to the board of directors, counsel should be mindful that only attractive opportunities are likely to be challenged, and the greater the potential success, the greater the scrutiny the presentation is likely to receive. As a general proposition, if the disinterested members of the board of directors exercising their independent business judgment reject the opportunity after full disclosure, the fiduciary may then pursue the corporate opportunity.[13]

The common law has developed and adopted several tests that define a corporate opportunity in order to balance the interests of the corporation and the subject officer or director.[14] The main tests, which are discussed below, are the interest test, the line of business test, the fairness test, the economic capacity test, and the American Law Institute (ALI) test.[15]

A number of states use different combinations of the tests for determining whether a corporate opportunity exists. For example, Minnesota combines the line of business and the fairness test in an attempt to increase the predictive nature of each test.[16] Delaware applies the economic capability test, the

---

[11] *See Broz v. Cellular Info. Sys.*, 673 A.2d 148, 157 (Del. 1996).

[12] *Id. See Today Homes, Inc. v. Williams*, 634 S.E. 2d 737, 743 (2006); *Telxon Corp. v. Meyerson*, 802 A. 2d 257, 263 (Del. 2002).

[13] *Broz*, 673 A.2d at 157. *See In re Cumberland Farms, Inc.*, 284 F.3d 216, 228 (1st Cir. 2002); *Northeast Harbor Golf Club, Inc. v. Harris*, 661 A. 2d 1146, 1150 (Maine 1995); American Law Institute, *Restatement of the Law of Corporate Governance* § 5.05 (1994).

[14] *See Broz*, 673 A. 2d at 155.

[15] *See Brandt v. Somerville*, 692 N.W. 2d 144, 155 (N.D. 2005) (stating that "a single test has not yet emerged [and that] four tests have been established as standards for identifying a corporate opportunity: the 'line of business' test, the 'interest or expectancy' test, the 'fairness' test, and the 'ALI' test"); *infra* notes 16–78 and accompanying text.

[16] *Miller v. Miller*, 222 N.W. 2d 71, 81 (Minn. 1974).

line of business test, and the interest test.[17] Hence, Delaware considers such factors as whether the opportunity is presented to the director in his individual or corporate capacity, whether the opportunity is essential to the corporation, whether the opportunity is within the so-called line of business of the corporation, whether the corporation has an interest in the opportunity, and whether the director employed the resources of the corporation to exploit the opportunity.[18]

Line of Business Test. Pursuant to the line of business test, a corporate opportunity exists if a fiduciary pursues a business endeavor that is within the same or perhaps closely related prospective line of business as the corporation.[19] The line of business test generally signifies that the company has the practical and financial ability to pursue the opportunity, and that such opportunity is consistent with its reasonable growth expectations.[20]

But determining whether an activity is within the company's line of business may be uncertain, which can lead to reasonable differences of opinion as to whether an activity is within a company's line of business.[21] The corporation's line of business will encompass the company's existing operations; many courts also include opportunities that are closely related to the current or *future* operations.[22] Because business enterprises often evolve in response to market forces, the line of business test may be extended to encompass related areas of business.[23]

---

[17] *See Broz v. Cellular Info. Sys.*, 673 A.2d 148, 154–155 (Del. 1996); *General Video Corporation v. Kertesz*, 2008 WL 5247120, at *18 (Del. Ch. 2008); *McGowen v. Ferro*, 859 A.2d 1012, 1038 (Del. Ch. 2004).

[18] *Broz.*, 673 A.2d at 154–155.

[19] *See Design Strategies, Inc. v. Davis*, 384 F. Supp. 2d 649, 672 (S.D.N.Y. 2005); *Broz*, 673 A.2d 148, 154 (Del. 1996).

[20] *Guft*, 5 A. 2d at 514. *See Miller v. Miller*, 222 N.W. 2d 71, 81 (Minn. 1974).

[21] *See Northeast Harbor Golf Club, Inc. v. Harris*, 661 A. 2d 1146, 1149 (Maine 1995); Gelb, *The Corporate Opportunity Doctrine—Recent Cases and the Elusive Goal of Clarity*, 31 U. Rich. L. Rev. 371, 377 (1997).

[22] *See PJ Acquisition Corp. v. Skoglund*, 453 N.W. 2d 1, 8 (Minn. 1990); Brown, *supra* note 2, 11 J. Corp. L. at 257–258.

[23] *See Miller*, 222 N.W. 2d at 81 (stating that a relevant criterion is whether "the opportunity embraces areas adaptable to its business and into which the corporation might easily, naturally, or logically expand"); Brown, *supra* note 2, 11 J. Corp. L. at 258.

An application of the line of business test is seen in *Burg v. Horn.*[24] In that case, the U.S. Court of Appeals for the Second Circuit, applying New York law, allowed the defendant to take a real estate opportunity without first offering it to a corporation for which he served as a director. Prior to the existence of the corporation, the defendant was a successful and active real estate investor who was on the board of several other real estate corporations. The defendant then urged the plaintiff to invest in a corporation with the intended purpose of purchasing a building.[25] After completion of the transaction, the defendant entered into other similar real estate deals without offering the opportunities to the new corporation.[26]

The issue in *Burg* was whether the defendant director had a duty to offer to the new corporation all real estate opportunities in the same line of business to which he became privy.[27] The court reasoned that the line of business test is not to be rigidly applied; rather, the scope of the conduct prohibited must be determined by the particular circumstances of the case.[28] The court held the opportunity was not a corporate opportunity because the defendant had served on several boards of companies involved in real estate investments prior to the formation of the company and there was no agreement that future opportunities belonged to the subject corporation.[29] *Burg* thus concerned an opportunity that, although within the company's line of business, was deemed not to constitute a corporate opportunity due to the special circumstances of that case.

The Interest Test. Under the interest test, a corporate opportunity exists if the corporation has an active interest in the business opportunity. Historically, the interest test relied on the concept of corporate property; that is, whether the company has a property interest in the opportunity in question.[30] Hence, early case law defined the interest test narrowly, "requir[ing] an accrued legal right, such as a binding contract with a third

---

[24] 380 F. 2d 897 (2d Cir. 1967).

[25] *Id.* at 898.

[26] *Id.* at 899.

[27] *Id.* at 897.

[28] *Id.* at 900.

[29] *Id.* at 900–901.

[30] *See* Brown, *supra* note 2, 11 J. Corp. L. at 262.

party."[31] The parameters of the interest test have since expanded.[32] Applying the modern standard, a corporate opportunity exists under the interest test when the opportunity is advantageous, fits into "a present, significant corporate purpose, as well as an ongoing corporate policy," and when "the corporation has an active interest in" the opportunity.[33]

In *Farber*, for instance, a corporate opportunity existed when two directors purchased land adjacent to the corporation's intended golf course.[34] The *Farber* case involved the prospective purchase of land by the Servan Corporation (Servan), whose corporate purpose was to build a golf course on property already owned by the corporation.[35] At a later meeting, the stockholders refrained from voting on whether to purchase a tract of land adjacent to the contemplated golf course until the corporate officers could investigate the opportunity.[36] Nonetheless, the principal officers and majority shareholders of Servan thereupon purchased the adjacent land for themselves.[37] Litigation thereafter ensued alleging that the corporate fiduciaries usurped a corporate opportunity that properly belonged to Servan.[38]

The court, applying Florida law, held that the fiduciaries usurped a corporate opportunity; the Servan Corporation had an active interest in the adjacent land because it had previously discussed purchasing the property at a board meeting.[39] The property also fit into a present significant corporate purpose because it was adjacent to the golf course that the corporation was building.[40] The fiduciaries were held liable to the corporation for their profits that resulted from the transaction.[41]

---

[31] *Id. See Colorado & Utah Coal Co. v. Harris*, 49 P.2d 429, 431 (Colo. 1935).

[32] Brown, *supra* note 2, 11 J. Corp. L. at 262. *See Litman v. Allen*, 25 N.Y.S. 2d 667, 686 (Sup. Ct. 1940).

[33] *Farber v. Servan Land Co.*, 662 F.2d 371, 378 (5th Cir. 1981).

[34] *Id.* at 372–373.

[35] *Id.* at 373.

[36] *Id.*

[37] *Id.*

[38] *Id.* at 374.

[39] *Id.* at 378.

[40] *Id.*

[41] *Id.* at 381.

The interest test and the line of business test are not coextensive. Corporations can have an interest in opportunities that are not within the same line of business. Where the opportunity is of interest to the corporation but unrelated to the corporation's line of business, the line of business test may be viewed as overly restrictive.[42] In *Farber*, for example, the acquisition of property adjacent to a golf course was not within the same industry as golf course construction but the corporation nonetheless had an active interest in the opportunity.[43]

Fairness Test. The fairness test examines the factual circumstances to determine both the fairness of the situation and whether the corporation's interests call for protection.[44] The fairness test "provides little or no practical guidance to the corporate officer or director seeking to measure her obligations."[45] In an attempt to make the fairness test more predictable, the Minnesota Supreme Court in *Miller* first applied the line of business test and then applied the fairness test. If the court found the opportunity to be a corporate opportunity under the line of business test, then the director under the fairness test would have the burden to show that she did not violate her duties of good faith, loyalty, and fair dealing by taking the opportunity.[46]

Applying this test, a court may analyze several factors in determining the fairness of the transaction, such as the executive's relationship to the corporation, whether the opportunity was presented to her in her individual or corporate capacity, whether corporate facilities were used to acquire the opportunity, the harm or benefit to the corporation that resulted from the acquisition, and the good faith and care exercised by the corporate fiduciary.[47] The *Miller* court thus listed several factors to determine the fairness of the fiduciary's conduct:

---

[42] *See* Pinto & Branson, *supra* note 8, at 275.

[43] *See* 662 F.2d at 378–379.

[44] *Durfee v. Furfee & Canning, Inc.,* 80 N.E. 2d 522 (Mass. 1948).

[45] *Northeast Harbor Golf Club, Inc. v. Harris,* 661 A. 2d 1146, 1150 (Maine 1995).

[46] *Miller* 222 N.W. 2d at 81. *See Today Homes, Inc. v. Williams*, 634 S.E. 2d 737, 744 (Va. 2006); Brown, *supra* note 2, 11 J. Corp. L. at 260.

[47] *Miller,* 222 N.W. 2d at 81–82

"[T]he nature of the officer's relationship to the management and control of the corporation; whether the opportunity was presented to him in his official or individual capacity; his prior disclosure of the opportunity to the board of directors or shareholders and their response; whether or not he used or exploited corporate facilities, assets, or personnel in acquiring the opportunity; whether his acquisition harmed or benefitted the corporation; and all other facts and circumstances bearing on the officer's good faith and whether he exercised the diligence, devotion, care and fairness toward the corporation which ordinarily prudent men would exercise under similar circumstances in like position."[48]

The *Miller* approach sought to enhance the predictive outcome of the test, but critics claim that, in practice, it causes further confusion. According to these critics, the solution is not to replace one vague test for corporate opportunity with two vague tests.[49]

Economic Capacity Test or Defense. The economic capacity test supplements, but does not necessarily replace, other tests for determining the existence of a corporate opportunity. Under this test, an opportunity is not improperly taken by the director or officer if the corporation is financially incapable of exploiting the opportunity, regardless of whether it is in the corporation's line of business or whether the corporation has an interest in the opportunity.[50]

Some courts have viewed the economic capacity test as a means to determine whether a corporate opportunity exists in the first instance.[51] Pursuant to this approach, the corporation, in claiming that a director improperly usurped a corporate opportunity, has the burden of establishing that the enterprise

---

[48] *Id. See* Chew, *supra* note 8, 67 N.C. L. Rev. at 462–464.

[49] *See* Brown, *supra* note 2, 11 J. Corp. L. at 260; Brudney & Clark, *A New Look at Corporate Opportunities*, 94 Harv. L. Rev. 997, 999 (1981).

[50] *See* Pinto & Branson, *supra* note 8, at 277, *citing, Klinicki v. Lungren,* 695 P.2d 906 (Or. 1985).

[51] *See PJ Acquisition Corp. v. Skoglund*, 453 N.W. 2d 1, 8 (Minn. 1990), *quoting, Miller*, 222 N.W. 2d at 81; *Brandt v. Somerville*, 692 N.W.2d 144, 156 (N.D. 2005); Brown, *supra* note 2, 11 J. Corp. L. at 263.

had the financial resources to take the opportunity.[52] Under this rationale, where a corporation does not have the financial ability to undertake the opportunity, it is effectively not available to the corporation, and hence, a corporate opportunity does not exist.[53] Under such circumstances, a director may personally pursue that opportunity.[54] Critics observe that unduly broad application of this principle allows corporate fiduciaries of a financially troubled, yet solvent, company to "cherry-pick" attractive opportunities in situations where the corporation may have been able to procure the necessary funds.[55]

Other courts have applied the financial inability test as a defense available to the officer or director.[56] Under this line of cases, a director can defend herself against a claim of corporate opportunity by showing that the corporation was financially insolvent. Hence, this defense "applies only [when] the corporation is actually insolvent to such a degree that it cannot carry on business or the corporation is legally disqualified from embracing the opportunity."[57]

American Law Institute Test. The American Law Institute (ALI) provides a recommended version of the corporate opportunity doctrine. [58] To date, a number of state courts have applied or quoted this ALI test.[59]

From a general perspective, the ALI test prohibits a director or senior executive officer from taking a corporate opportunity without first offering it to the corporation.[60] Under the ALI test,

---

[52] *See Miller* 222 N.W. 2d at 81.

[53] *Id. See PJ Acquisition Corp. v. Skoglund*, 453 N.W. 2d 1, 8 (Minn. 1990).

[54] *See Schildberg Rock Products v. Brooks*, 140 N.W. 2d 132, 138 (Iowa 1966) (stating that "where a corporation is unable to avail itself of an opportunity . . . an officer or director may embrace it as his own without accounting to the corporation").

[55] *See* Brown, *supra* note 2, 11 J. Corp. L. at 265.

[56] *See Irving Trust Co. v. Deutsch*, 73 F.2d 121, 124 (2d Cir. 1934); *Trieweiler v. Sears*, 689 N.W. 2d 807, 845 (Neb. 2004).

[57] *Trieweiler v. Sears*, 689 N.W. 2d 807, 845 (Neb. 2004) (also opining that "[c]orporate financial difficulty short of actual insolvency . . . is inadequate by itself to exonerate a fiduciary who appropriates the opportunity").

[58] *See* American Law Institute, *Principles of Corporate Governance* § 5.05 (1994).

[59] *See id.* § 5.05(b) cmt. & 2015 cumulative annual pocket part.

[60] *Id.* § 5.05(a).

a corporate opportunity is present: when a director or senior executive becomes aware of an opportunity through the performance of her role as a corporate fiduciary; when the circumstances "should reasonably lead the director or senior executive to believe that the person offering the opportunity expects it to be offered to the corporation;" *or* if, through the use of corporate information or property, the director or senior executive "should reasonably be expected to believe [that such opportunity] would be of interest to the corporation."[61] And, as a last example under the ALI test, a corporate opportunity exists when a senior executive knows that the opportunity is closely related to a business the corporation is currently engaged in or expects to enter into in the future.[62] The ALI test thus expands the scope beyond the traditional "line of business" test insofar as it includes endeavors the corporation expects to enter.[63]

Generally, a director or senior executive officer under the ALI test may not take a corporate opportunity. However, a director/senior executive may take advantage of a corporate opportunity, if the corporation first rejects the opportunity. Thus, the ALI test prohibits a director or senior executive from taking a corporate opportunity without first offering it to the corporation accompanied by disclosure of all material facts with respect to the conflict of interest and the corporate opportunity.[64] Even then, however, the offer to the corporation is not sufficient to entitle the officer or director to pursue the opportunity unless: (i) "[t]he rejection of the opportunity is fair to the corporation;" (ii) after adequate disclosure, the rejection occurs in advance of its taking by disinterested directors or, if the senior executive is not a director, by a "disinterested superior," in a manner that satisfies the business judgment rule; or (iii) after full disclosure, the project is rejected in advance or

---

[61] *Id.* § 5.05(b)(1).

[62] *Id.* § 5.05(b)(2).

[63] *Id.* § 5.05(b)(2) cmt. to § 5.05(b)(2) (stating that "Section 5.05(b)(2) expands the scope of corporate opportunity beyond the concept of an existing 'line of business,' which is utilized as a test in some decisions, to cover an existing or contemplated activity of the corporation").

[64] *See id.* § 5.05(a) & cmt. to § 5.05(a). The Comment to Section 5.05(a) provides that "under § 5.05(a)(1) disclosure of all material facts known to the director or senior executive concerning the conflict of interest and the corporate opportunity should be made to the corporate decisionmaker reviewing the matter."

subsequently ratified by disinterested shareholders and the rejection does not constitute a waste of corporate assets.[65]

The ALI test has some caveats regarding the offer and rejection of a corporate opportunity. Most significantly, unless required by the standards set forth above, directors who are not senior executives (namely, outside directors) do not have a duty to offer to the corporation opportunities that are closely related to the existing or contemplated lines of business of such corporation.[66] This conclusion, of course, assumes that the opportunity was not offered to the outside director with the expectation that the opportunity be offered to the corporation and that the outside director has not exploited corporate resources to access the opportunity. The ALI standard thus confines the line of business test to senior officers (who also may be directors) in order to help induce qualified individuals to serve as outside directors.[67]

SCENARIO

At his retirement press conference, the famous NFL Quarterback Luke Klut announced he was considering real estate as a future career. Luke said, "Bart Farr (another NFL Quarterback) was a role model both on the football field and in the business world so I would like to try my luck in real estate."

Sacked Property Company (SPC) is a publicly-traded commercial real estate corporation, headquartered in Pittsburgh, Pennsylvania, that develops commercial office and retail space. Due to Sarbanes-Oxley and the rules of the stock exchange, SPC is required to have independent directors on the board. After seeing the press conference, the CEO of SPC, realizing that Luke could increase community awareness of the Company, approaches Luke about becoming an independent director. The CEO wants Luke to serve as a SPC director because he is well known and highly regarded in the Pittsburgh community. Although Luke has never been a director and has no investments in real estate, Luke accepts the nomination and becomes a director for SPC.

---

[65] *See id.* § 5.05(a)(3).

[66] *See id.* § 5.05(b)(2).

[67] *See id.* § 5.05 cmt. at p 287.

After his election as a director, Luke finds that he enjoys the real estate business and is pleased that others at SPC value his opinion on company decisions. After six months as a director, Luke attended an SPC board of directors meeting where the CEO recommended that the SPC board of directors consider a strategic change for the Company. SPC should change its exclusive focus from commercial real estate to also encompass prime residential real estate. The CEO felt that prime residential real estate was profitable and would provide another avenue for growth. Although not directly applicable, the CEO was confident that SPC's skills, competencies, and experience would help the Company meet the demands of the residential real estate market. The CEO proposed that the Company should actively look for potential residential projects. The SPC board of directors approved the CEO's proposal that SPC expand into the prime residential real estate markets.

At a fundraising golf tournament the following week in Palm Springs, California, Luke ran into a childhood friend Benny Banker who is the CEO of Composite Bank. Mr. Banker had not seen Luke in years; however, Banker had followed Luke's football career and believed that Luke was a wealthy individual who was interested in real estate. Banker mentioned to Luke that the bank had recently foreclosed on a luxury residential apartment complex in Sarasota Florida and that the bank intended to unload the property within thirty days. Banker told Luke that he would sell the complex at an attractive price if Luke would commit to purchasing the property. Luke expressed his interest in the opportunity to Banker and said he would contact Banker in a few days with his decision whether to purchase the property.

As Luke's attorney, how would you counsel him in handling this opportunity? Is this a corporate opportunity? Should he present the proposal to SPC? Should he purchase the apartment complex on his own behalf?

SCENARIO VII

THE MULTIPLE REPRESENTATION DILEMMA FOR THE BUSINESS ATTORNEY

■ ■ ■

In many instances, it may be desirable for counsel to represent multiple clients during the course of an investigation, arbitration, mediation, trial, or administrative hearing. Indeed, from counsel's perspective, there are many benefits to representing multiple clients, such as enhancing the attorney's control over the subject proceeding (including the dissemination and collection of information), allowing for consistency in strategy, and avoiding duplication in the various efforts expended.[1] Likewise, for clients, multiple representation is cost effective, facilitates the effectuation of a "united" defense strategy, and reduces the unnecessary duplication of legal services. Despite the potential benefits, however, disadvantages also exist in multiple representation situations, including conflict of interest and ethical concerns. For example, representing multiple clients may dilute the lawyer's duty of loyalty to her clients. In other situations, the affected clients' interests may become sufficiently divergent so as to require the lawyer to withdraw from the representation.[2]

The ethical concerns of multiple representation are addressed in both The Model Code of Professional Responsibility ("Model Code") and The Model Rules of Professional Conduct ("Model Rules"). For example, Disciplinary Rule 5–105(b)–(c) of the Model Code states:

---

[1] *See* Brodsky & Zeena, *Multiple Representation of a Corporation and its Employees: Establishing and Protecting the Attorney-Client Privilege and Protecting Against Conflicts of Interest*, PLI No. B4–6970, 741 PLI/Corp 175, 185 (1991); Brodsky & Zeena, *Representing a Corporation and Its Employees*, 25 Rev. Sec. & Comm. Reg. 13 (1992); Veasey, *Separate and Continuing Counsel for Independent Directors: An Idea Whose Time Has Not Come as a General Practice*, 59 Bus. Law. 1413 (2004).

[2] *See* sources note 1 *supra*.

"A lawyer shall not continue multiple employment if the exercise of independent professional judgment in behalf of a client will be or is likely to be adversely affected by the lawyer's representation of another client, or if it would be likely to involve the lawyer in representing differing interests, except . . . if a disinterested lawyer would believe that the lawyer can competently represent the interest of each and if each consents to the representation after full disclosure of the implications of the simultaneous representation and the advantages and risks involved."[3]

Similarly, Rule 1.7 of the Model Rules addresses simultaneous representation. Model Rule 1.7(a) provides:

"Except as provided in paragraph (b), a lawyer shall not represent a client if the representation involves a concurrent conflict of interest. A concurrent conflict of interest exists if:

(1) the representation of one client will be directly adverse to another client; or

(2) there is a significant risk that the representation of one or more clients will be materially limited by the lawyer's responsibilities to another client, a former client or a third person or by a personal interest of the lawyer."[4]

Under Model Rule 1.7(b), multiple representation generally is allowed if the attorney "reasonably believes that [he/she] will be able to provide competent and diligent representation to each affected client . . . and each affected client gives informed consent, confirmed in writing."[5] Informed consent:

"requires that each affected client be aware of the relevant circumstances and of the material and reasonably foreseeable ways that the conflict could have adverse effects on the interests of that client. The

---

[3] Model Code of Prof. Responsibility DR 5–105(b)–(c).

[4] Model Rules of Prof. Conduct, Rule 1.7(a).

[5] *Id.* Model Rule 1.7(b)(1), (b)(4). *See generally* DiLernia, *Advance Waivers of Conflicts of Interest in Large Law Firm Practice,* 22 Geo. J. Leg. Eth. 97 (2009); Painter, *Advance Waiver of Conflicts,* 13 Geo. J. Leg. Eth. 289 (2000); Zacharias, *Waiving Conflicts of Interest,* 108 Yale L.J. 407 (1998); Task Force Report, *Conflicts of Interest Issues,* 50 Bus. Law. 1381 (1995).

information required depends on the nature of the conflict and the nature of the risks involved. When representation of multiple clients in a single matter is undertaken, the information must include the implications of the common representation, including possible effects on loyalty, confidentiality and the attorney-client privilege and the advantages and risks involved."[6]

Provisions pertaining to multiple representation in the American Law Institute's Restatement of the Law Governing Lawyers essentially mirror Model Rule 1.7. One provision, for instance, provides that "a conflict of interest is involved if there is a substantial risk that the lawyer's representation of the client would be materially and adversely affected by the lawyer's own interests or by the lawyer's duties to another current client, a former client, or a third person."[7]

Although addressed in other Scenarios of this text and not the principal focus of this Scenario, there are many situations in the corporate counseling context where multiple representation concerns exist. For example, conflicts may arise: (1) during the formation stage of an entity; (2) in situations involving closely-held enterprises; (3) in related party (such as interested director) transactions; and (4) in instances where conflicts between management and shareholders may exist, such as management self-dealing, proxy contests, leveraged buy-outs, and other alleged misconduct by management.[8] Multiple representation concerns also may arise in the litigation context. For example, potential conflicts—as illustrated by this

---

[6] Model Rule 1.7 cmt. 18. *See also,* Model Rule 1.0(e) cmts. 18–19 (defining the term "informed consent" and setting forth comments in regard thereto).

[7] American Law Institute, *Restatement of the Law Governing Lawyers* § 121 (1999). *See generally* Boyd, *Current Trends in Conflict of Interest Law,* 53 Baylor L. Rev. 1 (2001); Moore, *Restating the Law of Lawyer Conflicts,* 10 Geo. J. Leg. Eth. 541 (1997).

[8] *See Bernocci v. Forcucci,* 614 S.E. 2d 775 (Ga. 2005); *Bottoms v. Stapleton,* 706 N.W. 2d 411 (Iowa 2005); *Campellone v. Cragan,* 910 So. 2d 363 (Dist. Ct. Fla. App. 2005). *See generally* M. Steinberg, *Attorney Liability After Sarbanes-Oxley* §§ 9.01–9.07 (2015); Bassett, *Three's a Crowd: A Proposal to Abolish Joint Representation,* 32 Rutgers L.J. 387, 418 (2001); Scenarios I, IV, V, IX herein.

Scenario—may arise in shareholder derivative actions and government investigations and prosecutions.

Generally, the interaction between the corporation and its divergent constituencies, including shareholders, directors and officers, may give rise to conflict dilemmas.[9] For instance, although applicable ethical provisions provide that counsel owes allegiance to the entity,[10] determining an appropriate course of conduct that serves the corporation's best interests may be problematic.[11] The directors, shareholders, and other constituencies affected may disagree as to the appropriate action that is in the corporation's best interests. Moreover, counsel's own assessment of the situation may be blurred by the affinity felt toward the directors and executive officers, and by the desire to defend corporate transactions which likely resulted in part from her "lawyering."[12]

Derivative suits[13] thus implicate multiple representation problems. For example, conflicts may arise when a lawyer is faced with the dilemma of representing both the corporation and its officers and directors in a derivative action. The comment to Model Rule 1.13 provides only general guidance in this context:

> "The question can arise whether counsel for the organization may defend such an action. The proposition that the organization is the lawyer's client does not alone resolve the issue. Most derivative actions are a normal incident of an organization's affairs, to be defended by the organization's lawyer like any other suit. However, if the claim involves serious charges of wrongdoing by those in control of the organization, a

---

[9] *See* Elias, *Multiple Representation in Shareholder Derivative Suits: A Case-by-Case Approach*, 16 Loy. U. Chi. L.J. 613, 617 (1985). *See also*, G. Hazard, W. Hodes, & P. Jarvis, *The Law of Lawyering* §§ 12:14–12:18 (4th ed. 2015).

[10] *See* Model Rule 1.13.

[11] Elias, *supra* note 9, 16 Loy. U. Chi. L.J. at 617.

[12] *Id. See* C. Wolfram, *Modern Legal Ethics* 421 (1986); Landry, *Joint Representation of a Corporation and Director/Officer Defendants in Stockholder Derivative Suit: Is It Permissible?*, 18 J. Leg. Prof. 365 (1993).

[13] A derivative suit is "an action brought by one or more stockholders of a corporation to enforce a corporate right or remedy a wrong to the corporation in cases where the corporation, because it is controlled by the wrongdoers or for other reasons, fails and refuses to take appropriate action for its own protection." 19 Am. Jur. 2d, *Corporations* § 2250.

conflict may arise between the lawyer's duty to the organization and the lawyer's relationship with the board. In those circumstances, Rule 1.7 governs who should represent the directors and the organization."[14]

Under traditional ethical guidelines, multiple representation in derivative suits generally is permitted so long as the client provides informed and objective consent to the representation. In this setting, however—derivative litigation—consent in many cases would be given by directors or executive officers aligned as individual defendants in the suit. Consequently, "it would be a mere charade for the same directors to vote for the corporation's consent to representation of themselves and the entity."[15] Hence, it has been suggested that, although a corporation and individual defendants theoretically may consent to dual representation, "caution [should] be exercised when applying consent provisions to the corporate setting."[16] Additionally, Model Rule 1.13(g) provides guidance: "If the organization's consent to the dual representation is required by [Model] Rule 1.7, the consent shall be given by an appropriate official of the organization other than the individual who is represented, or [such consent shall be given] by the shareholders."[17]

Although multiple representation increases the potential for conflicts in derivative suits, many courts have held that the filing of a derivative action does not necessitate separate representation.[18] Indeed, in instances where a suit is without

---

[14] Model Rule 1.13 cmt. 14. Note that attorney conflict of interest dilemmas with respect to derivative litigation may arise in the close corporation setting. *See generally* Riccio, *Conflicts of Interest in Derivative Litigation Involving Closely-Held Corporations: An All or Nothing Approach to the Requirement of "Independent" Corporate Counsel*, 63 Bus. Law. 383 (2008).

[15] C. Wolfram, *supra* note 12, at 426.

[16] Elias, *supra* note 9, 16 Loy. U. Chi. L.J. at 617. *See Cannon v. U.S. Acoustics Corp.*, 532 F.2d 1118 (7th Cir. 1976); Dunshee, *Multiple Representation in Shareholder Derivative Suits: Do the Current Rules Do Enough to Promote Informed Consent?*, 9 Del. L. Rev. 213, 214 (2007); Ass'n of the Bar of the City of New York, Comm. On Prof. Ethics, Op. No. 842, 15 The Record 80 (1960).

[17] Model Rule 1.13(g).

[18] *See, e.g., Schmidt v. Magnetic Head Corp.*, 468 N.Y.S. 2d 649 (App. Div. 1983); *Schwartz v. Guterman*, 441 N.Y.S. 2d 597 (Sup. Ct. 1981); *Seifert v. Dumatic Indus. Inc.*, 197 A.2d 454 (Pa. 1964); C. Wolfram, *supra* note 12, at 426.

merit, seeks minor relief, or does not allege charges of serious wrongdoing against directors or officers, counsel generally may represent both the entity and the individual defendants with their respective informed consents.[19]

In instances where derivative actions allege serious wrongdoing by management and are found to be non-frivolous, courts have differed regarding the permissibility of multiple representation of the corporation and its representatives.[20] Early cases evidenced a certain deference to a corporation's decision to have counsel represent all parties. In *Otis & Co. v. Pennsylvania R. Co.*,[21] for example, the court concluded:

> "[T]here is no reason to require removal of counsel as petitioned. The corporation, as an interested party having a right to appear and defend, may select such counsel as it chooses. Moreover, there is no allegation of any breach of confidence or trust of which either the corporation or the individual defendants complain."[22]

More recent decisions, however, generally favor the retention of separate counsel.[23] Indeed, some courts have expressed the view that such multiple representation is impermissible. For instance, one court stated:

> "If the same counsel represents both the corporation and the director and officer defendants, the interests of the corporation are likely to receive insufficient protection. An increased recovery for the corporation is wholly

---

[19] *See* sources cited note 18 *supra*.

[20] *See, e.g., Messing v. FDI, Inc.*, 439 F. Supp. 776, 783 (D.N.J. 1977); *Cannon v. U.S. Acoustics Corp.*, 398 F. Supp. 209, 220 (N.D. Ill. 1975), *aff'd in part and rev'd in part*, 532 F.2d 1118 (7th Cir. 1976); *Lewis v. Shaffer Stores Co.*, 218 F. Supp. 238, 240 (S.D.N.Y. 1963); *Rowen v. LeMars Mut. Ins. Co.*, 230 N.W. 2d 905, 917 (Iowa 1975); *Schwartz v. Guterman*, 441 N.Y.S. 2d 597 (Sup. Ct. 1981).

[21] 57 F. Supp. 680 (E.D. Pa. 1944).

[22] *Id.* at 684.

[23] *See, e.g., Murphy v. Washington American Base Ball Club, Inc.* 324 F.2d 394 (D.C. Cir. 1963); *Campellone v. Cragan*, 910 So. 2d 363 (Fla. Dist. Ct. App. 2005); *Lower v. Lanark Mut. Fire Ins. Co.*, 448 N.E.2d 940 (Ill. App. 1983); *Haenel v. Epstein*, 450 N.Y.S. 2d 536 (Sup. Ct. 1982). *See also*, Pryor & Silver, *Defense Lawyers' Professional Responsibilities*, 78 Tex. L. Rev. 599 (2000); Note, *Disqualification of Corporate Counsel in Derivative Actions: Jacuzzi and the Inadequacy of Dual Representation*, 31 Hastings L.J. 347 (1979).

incompatible with the goal of limiting defendants' liability. Defendants' counsel is thus placed in an untenable position, and more often than not [counsel] will succumb to the pressure to approve any settlement between the shareholder and his individual clients."[24]

Multiple representation problems also may surface during government investigations, regulatory enforcement actions, and criminal prosecutions.[25] For example, potential and actual conflicts may occur in government investigations (such as the DOJ, EPA, FTC, SEC, etc.) when counsel for a corporation also attempts to represent some or all of the directors, officers, and employees of the company. Likewise, conflicts may arise when counsel for a broker-dealer entity also attempts to represent subordinate officers or employees such as branch managers, supervisors, or salespersons.[26]

For example, in an SEC disciplinary proceeding, *In re Merrill Lynch, Pierce, Fenner & Smith, Inc.*,[27] the SEC's Division of Enforcement formally moved to preclude Merrill Lynch's outside legal counsel from representing the firm as well as numerous employees of the firm named as respondents in the action. The SEC argued that the close relationship between counsel, a major New York City law firm, and the brokerage firm presented actual and potential conflicts of interest to the detriment of the employee-respondents. According to the SEC, for example, Merrill Lynch could attempt to defend itself by pointing to the alleged primary culpability of, and possible concealment by, some of its employees. On the other hand, the employees could try to defend themselves by blaming management.[28]

---

[24] *See In re Oracle Secs. Litig.*, 829 F. Supp. 1176, 1188 (N.D. Cal. 1993). *But see In re PSE & G Shareholder Litigation*, 801 A. 2d 295 (N.J. 2002).

[25] *See, e.g.,* G. Hazard & W. Hodes, *supra* note 9, §§ 12:14–12:20.

[26] *See* Matthews, *Effective Defense of SEC Investigations: Laying the Foundation for Successful Disposition of Subsequent Civil Administrative and Civil Proceedings*, 24 Emory L.J. 567 (1975). Mr. Matthews, a distinguished securities litigator, served as Deputy Director of the SEC's Division of Enforcement and as a partner at the prestigious firm of Wilmer, Cutler, and Pickering [known today as Wilmer Hale]. He was a superb lawyer and a wonderful man.

[27] [1973–1974 Transfer Binder] CCH Fed. Sec. L. Rep. ¶ 79,608 (ALJ 1973).

[28] *Id.* at 83,631. *See* Matthews, *supra* note 26, 24 Emory L.J. at 579.

In issuing its opinion, the administrative law judge in *Merrill Lynch* refused to preclude the law firm from representing multiple clients, stating that the SEC was unable to establish that a conflict "would necessarily occur."[29] The judge thereupon conditioned multiple representation on a procedure designed to elicit the informed consent of each employee-respondent. This included providing to each such employee a copy of the judge's order and the opportunity to read the transcript of oral arguments, briefs, and other pleadings in the case.[30]

In a more recent development, the SEC disqualified an attorney from simultaneously representing numerous persons in the same administrative enforcement proceeding.[31] Although each person consented to such multiple representation, the Commission asserted that "the right to counsel of one's choice is outweighed by the necessity of ensuring that our administrative proceeding is conducted with a scrupulous regard for the propriety and integrity of the process."[32] Hence, even though no actual conflict had yet eventuated, the SEC invoked the appearance of maintaining the integrity of its administrative process to justify disqualifying the attorney.[33]

A related issue pertaining to government investigations is determining whether separate counsel should be retained for the corporation at the outset of a government investigation. In response to this issue, a former SEC Assistant General Counsel stated that, while the attorney who is asked to represent potentially conflicting parties must obtain the consent of each affected party, "one must question whether meaningful consent by the corporation is possible when in many cases there does not exist a truly disinterested management or board of directors capable of giving such consent."[34]

---

[29] [1973–1974 Transfer Binder] CCH Fed. Sec. L. Rep. ¶ 79,608, at 83,631.

[30] *Id.* at 83,630. Matthews, *supra* note 26, 24 Emory L.J. at 579–580.

[31] *In the Matter of Blizzard and Abel,* Investment Advisers Act Release No. 2032, 2002 WL 714444 (SEC 2002).

[32] 2002 WL 714444 at *3.

[33] *Id.* at *2–3.

[34] Sonde, *The Responsibility of Professionals Under the Federal Securities Laws—Some Observations*, 68 Nw. U.L. Rev. 1, 10 (1973). *See* Anders, *Ethical*

In the context of government investigations and prosecutions, where there often exists a commonality of interest among multiple clients, counsel and such clients may consider utilizing the joint defense doctrine.[35] Generally, the joint defense doctrine preserves the confidentiality of communications, thereby enabling parties (who are represented by one attorney or who each have retained separate counsel) to exchange otherwise privileged information in the aid of a common defense, so long as they have identical or substantially similar interests.[36] Hence, use of the joint defense doctrine may allow defendants to mount a "united front" with fewer obstacles. Specifically, in order to assert the joint defense doctrine, a party must establish three elements: "(1) There must be commonality of interest; (2) the communication must be otherwise privileged; and (3) the communication must be made in furtherance of a common defense."[37]

A well-drafted joint defense agreement[38] offers a number of advantages, including: (1) facilitating the flow of information

---

Considerations for Defense Lawyers in SEC Proceedings, 48 Rev. Sec. & Comm. Reg. 77 (2015).

[35] *See, e.g., United States v. McPartlin*, 595 F.2d 1321 (7th Cir. 1979); *Continental Oil Company v. United States*, 330 F.2d 347 (9th Cir. 1964); *Ohio-Sealy Mattress Mfg. Co. v. Kaplan*, 90 F.R.D. 21, 29 (N.D. Ill. 1980); *In Matter of Grand Jury Subpoena*, 406 F. Supp. 381, 387–389 (S.D.N.Y. 1975); Steinberg & Rogers, *The Joint Defense Doctrine in Federal Securities Litigation*, 18 Sec. Reg. L.J. 339 (1991); Uelman, *The Joint Defense Privilege: Know the Risks*, 14 Litig. No. 4, at 35 (Summer 1988); Welles, *A Survey of the Attorney-Client Privilege in Joint Defense*, 35 U. Miami L. Rev. 321 (1981).

[36] *See also*, Moss & Bridge, *Can We Talk?: A "Steele-Y" Analysis of ABA Opinion 411*, 52 SMU L. Rev. 683, 683–684 (1999) (analyzing ABA Comm. on Ethics and Prof. Resp., Op. 98–411 (1998), which "addresses consultations with lawyers outside the consulting lawyer's firm who are not associated in the representation of this client on this matter" and opines that normally "a client-lawyer relationship does not arise between the consulting lawyer's client and the consulted lawyer [thereby] free[ing] [the consulted lawyer] of any ethical obligation [such as confidentiality] to the consulting lawyer's client").

[37] Steinberg & Rogers, *supra* note 35, 18 Sec. Reg. L.J. at 342. *See Bryant v. Mattel, Inc.*, 573 F. Supp. 2d 1254, 1275 (C.D. Cal. 2007); *In Matter of Grand Jury Subpoena*, 406 F. Supp. 381, 387–389 (S.D.N.Y. 1975). *See also, In re Santa Fe Int'l Corp.*, 272 F.3d 705 (5th Cir. 2001); *United States v. Zolin*, 809 F.2d 1411 (9th Cir. 1987).

[38] In order to ensure that the privilege is available, it is advisable to enter into a written agreement or understanding with co-parties and potential co-parties before communications are exchanged. Indeed, some courts have

and communication among attorneys, while ensuring that such information remains confidential under the attorney-client privilege and work product doctrine; (2) enhancing litigation efficiency, as the pertinent investigatory, pretrial, and trial tasks are divided among the various attorneys; and (3) enabling the multiple parties to mount a "united front" to the opposition. As with any situation involving multiple representation, however, asserting the joint defense doctrine raises potential conflicts of interest issues. In many joint defense efforts, for example, co-parties' interests may not be in complete harmony. Indeed, the very nature of litigation provides ample potential for breakdowns in communication among such co-parties.[39]

Moreover, when parties to a joint defense are each represented by individual counsel, a party may become privy to information through the joint defense that is adverse to the co-parties' interests, but advantageous to that party. Depending upon how the information is communicated, the joint defense privilege may preclude the party from using that information to the detriment of the co-parties. In such cases, cooperation with co-parties in order to present a united front may well impair the ability of one party's counsel to zealously represent the interests of the individual client. Similarly, when a single counsel represents several co-parties, compromises may have to be made in order to further the goals of the group as a whole. Any time counsel is faced with competing interests, the ability to zealously represent any one interest is diminished.[40]

Finally, a particularly troubling dilemma arises when a joint defense member defects and becomes a government witness. In this setting, the government and/or the targets (e.g., the defendants) may seek to disqualify the subject attorney(s).[41] In

---

implied that some type of formal agreement must exist before they will recognize the joint defense privilege. *See In re Bevill, Bresler & Schulman Asset Management Corp.*, 805 F.2d 120 (3d Cir. 1986); *United States v. Melvin*, 650 F.2d 641 (5th Cir. 1981).

[39] See Steinberg & Rogers, supra note 35, 18 Sec. Reg. L.J. at 341, 355; Capra, The Attorney-Client Privilege in Common Representations: Information-Pooling and Problems of Professional Responsibility, 1989 Trial Lawyer's Guide 20 (1989).

[40] See Steinberg & Rogers, supra note 35, 18 Sec. Reg. L.J. at 355–356.

[41] See, e.g., *United States v. Anderson*, 790 F. Supp. 231 (W.D. Wash. 1992). In that case, the government moved to disqualify defense counsel where several of the co-workers who had entered into a joint defense

such event, Model Rule 1.6, which (with certain exceptions) prohibits an attorney from revealing confidential communications, may be a cause for concern among the remaining members and their attorneys. As stated by one source:

> "[A]lthough a joint defense attorney does not have a traditional attorney-client relationship with every member of the arrangement, a duty not to reveal joint defense information or not to use such information against any member still exists. This obligation remains even if disclosure of group secrets would ultimately benefit an attorney's client. Consequently, absent other considerations, [Model] Rule 1.6 bars the attorney from cross-examining a former joint [defense] member when cross-examination would in any way reveal confidential information."[42]

In any event, it is incumbent upon counsel to disclose the potential material ramifications to his client(s) and to secure each client's informed written permission to engage in the joint defense. In situations where there is a realistic potential that the clients' interests may become adverse, separate counsel should be retained for each party.[43]

The following case illustrates a situation that should not occur—an attorney who successfully represented the plaintiffs in a litigated matter and also represented the adverse losing party in an effort to set aside that same judgment!

---

agreement with the defendant subsequently became government witnesses. The court held that the circumstances at bar did not present a disabling conflict of interest that required defense counsel's disqualification. *See also, United States v. Stepney*, 246 F. Supp. 2d 1069, 1085 (N.D. Cal. 2003) (criticizing Anderson).

[42] Forsgren, *The Outer Edge of the Envelope: Disqualification of White Collar Criminal Defense Attorneys Under the Joint Defense Doctrine*, 78 Minn. L. Rev. 1219, 1243 (1994). *See Wilson P. Abraham Constr. v. Armco Steel Corp.*, 559 F.2d 250, 253 (5th Cir. 1977); *In re Gabapentin Patent Litigation*, 407 F. Supp. 2d 607, 613–614 (D.N.J. 2005); Solovy & Byman, *Common Interest Agreements*, Nat'l L.J., May 28, 2001, at A12.

[43] *See United States v. Henke*, 222 F. 3d 633 (9th Cir. 2000); *Ohio-Sealy Mattress*, 90 F.R.D. at 29; Levenson, *The Fading Privilege*, Nat'l L.J. May 28, 2001, at A14; Steinberg & Rogers, *supra* note 35, 18 Sec. Reg. L.J. at 356.

IN RE ROSSANA
395 B.R. 697 (D. Nev. 2008)

BRUCE A. MARKEL, BANKRUPTCY JUDGE.

I. Introduction

Representing John Momot (Momot), attorney Neil Beller (Beller) moved to set aside a judgment. This was problematic because Beller represents the holders of the judgment, and represented them in execution proceedings on that judgment against Momot. This opinion deals with the consequences of this dual representation.

II. Facts

This matter began with the sale of a bar more than twenty years ago. In 1987, Momot sued Joseph Smith and Smith's brother-in-law, Joseph Rossana (Joe), in Nevada state court. Momot contended that he was entitled to a share of the proceeds of the sale of the Rum Runner Tavern; Smith and Joe disagreed. Beller represented Joe.

Momot ultimately won, and obtained a judgment of $225,779. He sought to execute on Joe's property to satisfy that judgment. Joe responded to these collection efforts in ways that were neither mild nor legal. In 1994, he was convicted of aggravated stalking of Momot, of malicious destruction of Momot's property, and of discharging a firearm from a motor vehicle at Momot's home. Although some of the convictions were later overturned, he served two years in prison for these crimes. Beller represented Joe in the criminal case as well.

While this activity was sorting itself out, Joe and his wife, Jo Ann Rossana (Jo Ann), filed bankruptcy. Beller was substituted as counsel for both Jo Ann and Joe (collectively, the Rossanas) in their bankruptcy in 1994. On May 7, 1999, on behalf of the Rossanas, Beller filed a complaint against Momot in bankruptcy court, alleging that Momot had executed on too much property when collecting on the $225,779 judgment. After trial (of which more later), the bankruptcy court agreed. On September 11, 2003, the court entered judgment in the approximate amount of $28,559 against Momot. In December of 2003, Beller garnished Momot's bank account to collect this amount. Some time after the garnishment, Joe and Jo Ann divorced. Joe later died.

There were irregularities in Momot's defense of the adversary proceeding. Momot's then-attorney testified in this proceeding that even though he entered an appearance and filed an answer for Momot, he failed to tell Momot that the adversary proceeding had started. He testified further that he did not inform Momot about the trial or that a judgment had been entered against him. This sequence of events is even stranger than it sounds: Momot is an actively practicing lawyer.

Momot testified that he first learned of the judgment when his bank account was garnished in 2003. He also testified that in the fall of 2004, he and Beller had a chance meeting, and Momot commented on the execution against his bank account. Beller and Momot both testified that at this chance encounter they discussed the trial and the fact that Momot had not attended. Momot testified that he then asked if Beller could do anything to remove the judgment. Momot testified that he was not specifically retaining Beller and that he was just discussing how to "administratively remove" the judgment.

Nothing further happened until October 29, 2007, approximately three years after the initial conversation between Beller and Momot. On that date, Beller filed a "Motion for Relief From Judgment" on behalf of Momot in this court. Although Momot testified that he did not recall reviewing the motion, Momot signed an affidavit included with it. Further, Beller stated in another affidavit included with that motion that "[f]or the purposes of this Motion for Relief from Judgment, I am counsel of record for John Momot, Esq." Later in the same affidavit, Beller made the statement "[a]s attorney for Plaintiffs/Debtors in the above entitled action."

Beller did not withdraw and has not withdrawn from his representation of the Rossannas. When asked whether he still represented the Rossanas, he replied that Joe was dead and that the matter was closed. Beller testified further that he filed the motion for Momot as "a courtesy. It is an accommodation from one lawyer to another." When asked if he had contacted Jo Ann before filing the Motion for Relief From Judgment, he replied that he had not. He did testify that he contacted her in December 2007, to which she replied in an email stating that she was out of town, that she wanted the case number, and that they could discuss it when she returned to Las Vegas. When asked why he did not contact her before he filed the motion,

Beller said, "Other than the fact that, I mean, Joe [Joseph Rossana] was old-school, Italian. I don't want to get . . . , but, but, she was always a behind-the-scenes person from the criminal matter to the bankruptcy matter. She was just there, and . . . I didn't really think about it."

On December 20, 2007, this court issued its "Order to Show Cause Why Neil J. Beller Should Not Be Sanctioned for Violating the Nevada Rules of Professional Conduct and Why This Matter Should Not Be Referred to the State Bar of Nevada Office of Bar Counsel." An evidentiary hearing on the order to show cause was held on February 5, 2008, at which time Beller formally withdrew his motion for relief from judgment. At the hearing, Beller and Momot were both represented by counsel. Beller argued that he no longer represented the Rossanas and owed no duty to them given the limited nature of his representation of Momot. Alternatively, he alleged that the Rossanas suffered no harm, or that any prejudice caused was so ephemeral that it did not constitute a violation of any of his duties as a lawyer.

Beller's legal position turns on whether he still represented the Rossanas when he undertook Momot's representation. If he did, his conduct is assessed under Rule 1.7 of the Nevada Rules of Professional Conduct; if not, the applicable rule is Rule 1.9. But first we need to decide if Beller still represented the Rossanas when he agreed to represent Momot.

Beller makes a strong case that his representation of the Rossanas was over. After the 2003 garnishment on Momot's bank account, there was apparently nothing more to do for the Rossanas, and the adversary proceeding was administratively closed. His clients divorced, and one of them died.

But Beller never filed a satisfaction of judgment (leaving open the possibility that there may be further collection activity), and administrative closure of a case has nothing to do with the parties' actions. If Beller did not represent Jo Ann Rossana in the probate of her husband's estate, it was one of the few legal actions he did not perform for the Rossanas—he had previously represented them in a civil suit, a criminal matter, and a bankruptcy. He also has never withdrawn in this case as the Rossanas' counsel of record. As the attorney-client relationship is based on the subjective belief of the client, it was

Beller's obligation to show, if he could, that his remaining client, Jo Ann Rossana, did not believe that Beller continued to represent her in this matter. He did not do so; indeed, his evidence, such as it is, shows that Jo Ann was unclear as to what Beller's continuing role was, and that she wanted further information before she would commit to any position.

III. Does Beller Currently Represent the Rossanas?

Whether a lawyer-client relationship has ended is a question of fact. Normally, when the representation has achieved its aims, it is considered terminated. Application of this test, in turn, necessarily requires an examination of the scope of the representation. When, as here, the attorney represents the client generally in many matters over a long period of time, it may be reasonable to believe that the attorney-client relationship continues unabated even though discrete projects may have reached completion. . . .

Here, the long list of diverse matters on which Beller represented the Rossanas could reasonably be seen as an undertaking of general and continuing representation, at least as to the matters actually taken on. While this position could have easily and convincingly been rebutted by a simple disclaimer in Beller's retention agreement, no such agreement was offered in evidence.

There may be other grounds to find that the representation here continued. When an attorney whose representation has terminated later "interpose[s] himself into a matter substantially related to that for which he was previously retained . . . [he] create[s] a situation in which the attorney-client relationship re-attaches." . . .

. . . As a result, Beller represented both the Rossanas and Momot—the plaintiff and defendant—in the same lawsuit.

IV. Conflict With Current Client

Not surprisingly, Nevada law does not countenance this type of joint representation. The Nevada Rules provide that an attorney may not represent a client whose interests are directly adverse to the interests of another client. . . .

As the [ALI] *Restatement* makes clear, this rule is intended to "assure clients that their lawyers will represent them with undivided loyalty," and that "[a] client is entitled to be represented by a lawyer whom the client can trust." . . .

As established above, Beller continues to represent the Rossanas. Although the attorney-client relationship between Beller and Momot is not as extensive as that between Beller and the Rossanas, the facts, including Beller's own affidavit, make clear that Beller was acting as Momot's attorney. Beller's testimony seems to be that Beller gratuitously made the motion to vacate on behalf of Momot and that there was no formal retention agreement. The attorney-client relationship is typically a contractual one based on the payment of fees in exchange for services, but this is not a condition precedent for a finding that an attorney-client relationship existed. . . . In addition, gratuitously performed legal services are sufficient to support a finding that an attorney-client relationship existed. . . .

As a consequence, despite the apparent lack of fees paid or a retention agreement, Momot was Beller's client. Beller had agreed to take steps to relieve Momot of the judgment and appeared on his behalf, creating an attorney-client relationship between them. Direct adversity is apparent on the facts of this case, and Beller has not shown the court any facts to the contrary. It is undisputed that Beller obtained a judgment against Momot on behalf of the Rossanas. It is likewise undisputed that Beller appeared on behalf of Momot and filed a motion for relief from the same judgment that he had obtained on behalf of the Rossanas. Indeed, when compared to cases in which courts have disqualified attorneys from representing a client because of direct adversity, it is obvious that the representation of Momot for the purpose of obtaining relief from the judgment against the Rossanas was directly adverse. . . .

VI. Conclusion

This court finds that Neil Beller violated the Nevada Rules of Professional Conduct, applicable in this proceeding by virtue of the local rules of this court. Specifically, Beller simultaneously represented the interests of two clients who were adverse parties in the same litigation. This is a violation of the prohibition of concurrent representation of adverse parties.

The court finds that this is an egregious violation of the Nevada Rules of Professional Conduct that fall outside all accepted norms of the legal profession. Indeed, Beller's conduct discredits the work of all attorneys before this court and in the state of Nevada by calling into question whether attorneys will faithfully and loyally serve the interests of their clients.

The following Scenario highlights many of the dilemmas that arise in the multiple representation setting.

SCENARIO

Hywell Energy, Inc. is a multinational corporation, with its headquarters in Denver, Colorado. The Company historically generated income by purchasing and selling hard assets such as pipelines. In recent years, however, the Company has generated much of its revenue from a business described as "wholesale energy operations," including the trading of natural gas, electricity, and various other futures and commodities. The Company has been very successful; for example, during the past seven years the Company's revenues have increased from $8 billion to more than $35 billion, making it one of the premier companies in the United States.

Three months ago, Hywell Energy unexpectedly restated its earnings for the past four years, reducing the amount of earnings reported by almost $350 million, or 18%. This was necessary, according to Company spokespersons, because six unconsolidated enterprises should have been consolidated in Hywell Energy's financial statements under generally accepted accounting principles (GAAP). As a result of the announcement, the securities markets questioned the credibility of the Company, causing the price of Hywell Energy's stock to drop from around $60 a share to less than $22 in just a few months. In addition, analysts began to uncover unusual descriptions of transactions that Hywell Energy and "other entities" had entered into with a "related party" that was operated by the Chief Financial Officer of Hywell Energy, Robert Cannon. These transactions—which ultimately were revealed to be limited partnerships purportedly designed to mask the Company's debt and to elevate the Company's stock price—have become the focus of investigations conducted by the U.S. Department of Justice and the Securities and Exchange Commission.

Hywell Energy has retained Bancroft & Hood, a prestigious Chicago-based law firm which has served as the Company's outside legal counsel for decades. Additionally, the Company has agreed to pay the legal fees for Bancroft & Hood to represent 27 of the Company's current and former employees. The executive officers, including the Chief Executive Officer, Harrison Dolan, the Chief Financial Officer Robert Cannon, and the Executive Vice President, Charla Brier, each has retained separate counsel.

In view of these circumstances, what potential concerns face Bancroft & Hood in representing multiple clients? Where should counsel look for guidance? What information should be disclosed to the 27 current and former employees?

Subsequently, after receiving legal advice from their respective attorneys, all the defendants decide to execute a joint defense agreement in order to mount a "united front" against the government's investigation. Thus far, the legal strategy has been successful—the government is frustrated with how little its investigation has uncovered, and it has little probative evidence to support its allegations. Consequently, in an effort to strengthen its case, the government has made it clear that leniency, including the distinct possibility of immunity, will be accorded to any of the non-executive individual targets who come forward with significant information.

Assume that one relatively high level employee (who appears credible), Harry Easterly, comes forward and agrees to testify for the government. What are the concerns? How does it affect the remaining joint defense members who are the targets of the government's investigation? Is there a way to minimize the risk for a disqualifying conflict of interest once Easterly becomes a government witness?[44]

---

[44] *See generally Foote, Joint Defense Agreements in Criminal Prosecutions: Tactical and Ethical Implications*, 12 Geo. J. Leg. Eth. 377 (1999); Schmitt & Hamburger, *Enron's Hiring of One Firm to Represent Forty Employees Raises Some Concern*, Wall St. J., Jan. 29, 2002, at A6; Wilke et al., *Two in Enron Debacle Seek Immunity Deals*, Wall St. J., Feb. 27, 2002, at A8.

SCENARIO VIII

SCREENING AND THE PERSONALLY DISQUALIFIED ATTORNEY

■ ■ ■

The practice of law is increasingly being dominated by "mega firms" with offices in many cities as well as foreign countries. Firms like Akin, Gump, Strauss, Hauer & Feld, Baker Botts, Baker and McKenzie, Foley and Lardner, Gibson, Dunn and Crutcher, Greenberg Traurig, Holland and Knight, Jones Day, Kutak Rock, Skadden Arps, Vinson & Elkins, and Weil Gotshal & Manges, to name a few, have hundreds of attorneys spread nationally and internationally.[1] Their clients, while referred to as firm clients, are often represented through a single office independent of other offices of the firm. Firms make lateral hires on a regular basis at their many different offices both within and outside of the United States. Mergers also have become a regular feature whereby smaller firms and specialized practices are being absorbed by bigger firms.[2] There is as well increasing mobility in the practice. Attorneys not only are moving from one firm to another but also from outside to inside counsel and from government service to private firm practice and vice versa. A major recurrent dilemma is conflicts of interest.

Conflicts may occur with respect to current as well as former clients. A simultaneous representation (current client) conflict arises where an attorney or a law firm represents a client with an interest directly adverse to an existing client. One scenario implicating concern in this context is when one office of a mega-firm procures a client whose interests are directly adverse to an existing client served through another office of the firm. Such a

---

[1] All these firms have offices in at least 10 major U.S. cities and many of them also have international offices. *See generally* Krishnan, *Globetrotting Law Firms*, 23 Geo. J. Leg. Eth. 103 (2010).

[2] *See* Aronson, *Elite Law Firms and Reputational Competition: Is Bigger Really Better? An International Comparison*, 40 Vand. J. Transnat'l L. 763 (2007).

situation would occur, for example, when an attorney in the Denver office of a firm is approached by a prospective client to represent it in a breach of contract suit against a "blue chip" publicly-held company, represented in securities and corporate matters through that firm's New York City office.[3]

Disqualification on grounds of successive representation is the result when an attorney represents at different times, clients with materially adverse interests in matters that are substantially related. A conflict dilemma in successive representation may arise, for instance, when a firm makes a lateral hire from another law firm or when a former government attorney moves to private practice. It is not uncommon for an attorney in government service, like the DOJ, FTC, IRS, or the SEC, to join a firm which is involved in a case or related matter in which he/she had participated in some way.[4] Also, attorneys who move from one law firm to another, may find that their "new" firms represent interests that are adverse to their former clients.

While the personal disqualification of an individual attorney is significant, a more important issue from a law firm's perspective is whether one attorney's disqualification on ethical grounds can be imputed to disqualify the firm as a whole. A key basis for such imputed disqualification is the presumption of shared confidences.[5] Under this principle, "knowledge by any member of a law firm is knowledge by all of the attorneys in the firm, partners as well as associates."[6] It is presumed that a lawyer shares client confidences with his firm colleagues. The presumption is grounded on perceptions regarding the realities of law firm practice: "Clients come and go throughout the firm's offices and documents are processed by many hands and

---

[3] *See* G. Krauss, *Partner Departures and Lateral Moves—A Legal and Ethical Guide* (2010); Leubsdorf, *Conflicts of Interest: Slicing the Hot Potato Doctrine*, 48 San Diego L. Rev. 251 (2011); Steinberg & Sharpe, *Attorney Conflicts of Interest: The Need for a Coherent Framework*, 66 Notre Dame L. Rev. 1, 34 (1990); Swisher, *The Practice and Theory of Lawyer Disqualification*, 27 Geo. J. Leg. Eth. 71 (2014).

[4] *See* Cutler, *Conflicts of Interest*, 30 Emory L.J. 1015, 1025 (1981).

[5] *See In re Columbia Valley Healthcare System, LP*, 320 S.W. 3d 819, 828 (Tex. 2010); *Kala v. Aluminum Smelting and Refining Co.*, 688 N.E. 2d 258, 265 (Ohio 1998).

[6] *Adams v. Aerojet-General Corp.*, 86 Cal. App. 4th 1324, 1333 (Cal. Ct. App. 2001).

necessarily pass before many eyes. Files and documents lie on secretaries' desks and are centrally accessible in file rooms and duplicating offices; the notes of associates are spread on library tables; computer systems bring information before many different viewers."[7] Therefore, the assumption is that information in a law firm is easily accessible even if it is not purposefully shared by attorneys among themselves. Imputed disqualification is also based on the belief that since a fee from one client generally benefits the entire firm, affiliated lawyers will tend to support violations of ethical obligations by a firm member.[8]

The vicarious disqualification rule thus has been principally adopted to protect (1) loyalty towards clients as well as (2) clients' confidences. The Model Rules, for example, generally provide that if one lawyer of a firm is disqualified from representing a client, no other lawyer of that firm can knowingly represent that client[9] unless the client gives informed consent.[10] The American Law Institute's (ALI) Restatement of the Law Governing Lawyers takes a similar approach, providing that, absent informed client consent, personal disqualification of a lawyer on conflicts grounds is imputed to lawyers affiliated with the disqualified attorney.[11]

A purported mechanism used to avoid firm disqualification is to "screen" the disqualified attorney so that no information can be exchanged between that attorney and other lawyers of the firm. This device is also referred to as the "Chinese wall" or "ethical wall." A screen or a wall is a "fictional device" used to prevent firm-wide disqualification when: (1) a member of the firm, while at a different firm (or government agency), represented a party who is an adversary of a client represented by her new firm in a substantially related matter;[12] or (2) a lawyer of the firm represents an interest adversarial to an

---

[7] C. Wolfram, *Modern Legal Ethics* 391 (1990).

[8] American Law Institute, *Restatement of the Law Governing Lawyers* § 123 cmt. (b) (2000). *See also*, G. Hazard, W. Hodes, & P. Jarvis, *The Law of Lawyering* §§ 15.01–15.18 (4th ed. 2015).

[9] Model Rules of Prof. Conduct, Rule 1.10(a).

[10] *Id*. Rule 1.10(c).

[11] ALI, *Restatement of the Law Governing Lawyers* § 123.

[12] Wozniak, *Disqualification of Member of Law Firm as Requiring Disqualification of Entire Firm—State Cases*, 6 A.L.R. 242 § 2 (1992).

existing client. The usual ways of implementing screening are "restricting a member's access to files, informing attorneys working on the case of the barrier, and excluding the disqualified member from fees generated by the representation."[13] The objective is to isolate the attorney who possesses the confidential information from all other affiliated attorneys. Some means of achieving this objective are keeping files under lock and key, color coding the pertinent files with the name of the walled attorney so that anyone allowed access is reminded of the screen, physically separating the office of the disqualified attorney from other attorneys dealing with the matter, requiring passwords for computer access to pertinent information, and the use of code names for the project.[14]

In conflict dilemmas involving simultaneous representation, courts regard representation of adverse interests by the same firm in the same litigation as "patently improper."[15] Moreover, simultaneous representation of clients having directly adverse interests even with respect to unrelated matters, without informed client consent, generally is not acceptable.[16] As stated by one court, "[a] serious effect on the attorney-client relationship may follow if a client discovers from a source other than the attorney that he is being sued in a different matter by the attorney."[17] In such circumstances, the existing client's consent after full disclosure by the subject attorney is required to avoid disqualification.[18] The Model Rules allow such representation only if each client "gives informed consent, confirmed in writing," and the attorney reasonably believes that he/she "will be able to provide competent and diligent representation to each affected client."[19]

But, will disqualification of a particular attorney be imputed to other attorneys, including other offices of the firm situated in different locales which never had any contact with the firm's

---

[13] *Id.*

[14] R. Simon, *Simon's New York Code of Professional Responsibility Annotated.*

[15] *See, e.g., People ex rel. Dept. of Corps. v. SpeeDee Oil Change Sys. Inc.,* 86 Cal. Rptr. 2d 816, 819 (Cal. 1999).

[16] *See* G. Hazard & W. Hodes, *supra* note 8, at § 15.04.

[17] *IBM v. Levin,* 579 F.2d 271, 280 (3rd Cir. 1978).

[18] *Id. See Centra, Inc. v. Estrin,* 538 F.3d 402, 419 (6th Cir. 2008).

[19] Model Rules of Prof. Conduct, Rules 1.7(b)(1), (b)(4), 1.10(c).

client? As a general principle, the same traditional doctrine of firm-wide imputation will apply irrespective of firm size or "geographical scope" of counsel.[20] This is because the rule against simultaneous adverse representation is primarily based on the principle of undivided loyalty of an attorney towards her client. Undivided loyalty helps foster "public confidence in the legal profession and the judicial process."[21] Many clients tend to identify legal representation not solely by the particular attorneys, but by the firm itself. Therefore, the duty of loyalty is extended to encompass both the lawyer and her firm. For many courts, the appearance of impropriety is also a key concern.[22] It appears improper if an attorney in the firm is representing an existing client's adversary, even if the matter is unrelated. Therefore, none of the attorneys in the firm, even if they had no contact with the existing client and are in a different locale, can represent interests directly adverse to that client even in matters unrelated to the area of representation.

Courts also reason that an adversarial posture towards an existing client may impact the "independent judgment" of the lawyer towards that client.[23] A lawyer may be influenced by a client's importance (such as a blue-chip publicly held company that generates lucrative revenues for the firm) and thereby advance its interests at the cost of the smaller client.[24] Further, the breach of the lawyer's duty of loyalty may have adverse effects on the United States' legal system in which "opposing attorneys, within the bounds of legal and ethical norms, will engage in a zealous, uninhibited presentation of their client's position."[25] Divided loyalties "impair a lawyer's representation" and adversely impact the adversarial nature of the system.[26] In view of the foregoing principles, courts generally have not thus

---

[20] *Westinghouse Electric Corp. v. Kerr-McGee Corp.*, 580 F.2d 1311, 1318 (7th Cir. 1978).

[21] *People ex rel. Dept. of Corps. v. SpeeDee Oil Change Sys. Inc.*, 86 Cal. Rptr. 2d 816, 824 (Cal. App. 1999).

[22] *Levin,* 579 F.2d at 283; *State ex rel. Bluestone Coal Corporation v. Mazzone,* 697 S.E. 2d 740, 749–750 (W. Va. Sup. Ct. App. 2010). *See* Rotunda, *Alleged Conflicts of Interest Because of the "Appearance of Impropriety,"* 33 Hofstra L. Rev. 1141 (2005).

[23] *Levin,* 579 F. 2d at 280.

[24] C. Wolfram, *supra* note 7, at 349.

[25] Steinberg & Sharpe, *supra* note 3, 66 Notre Dame L. Rev. at 33.

[26] *Id.*

far permitted screening to avert firm-wide disqualification in simultaneous representation cases.[27] However, a client's informed consent based on adequate disclosure frequently will eliminate the conflict dilemma in cases of simultaneous adverse representation.[28] This issue arises with some frequency with respect to advance waivers of conflicts of interest. A decision addressing this subject is contained later in this Scenario.

With respect to successive representation situations, attorney loyalty and protecting clients' confidences are key concerns.[29] The relationship between an attorney and his client is premised on the duty of undivided loyalty and confidentiality towards a client.[30] These duties continue even after representation has been completed and regardless whether an attorney moves to a new employer.[31]

Duties toward a former client are underscored by the Model Rules. These rules prohibit, absent informed client consent, a lawyer who represented a former client in a matter from subsequently representing another person "in the same or a substantially related matter in which that person's interests are materially adverse to the interests of the former client."[32] Even if the lawyer herself did not personally represent the subject

---

[27] *See, e.g., Westinghouse Electric Corp. v. Kerr-McGee Corp.*, 580 F.2d 1311, 1321 (7th Cir. 1978); *In re Cendant Corp. Securities Litigation*, 124 F. Supp. 2d 235, 247 (D.N.J. 2000). *But see Boston Scientific Corporation v. Johnson & Johnson, Inc.*, 647 F. Supp. 2d 369, 374 (D. Del. 2009) (declining to disqualify law firm where "the law firm's concurrent representations were in unrelated matters, were being done out of different offices in different cities, and were being done with an ethical wall in place between the two matters").

[28] C. Wolfram, *supra* note 7, at 352. The issue of client "informed consent" also is discussed in Scenario VII. *See generally* DiLernia, *Advance Waivers of Conflicts of Interest in Large Law Firm Practice*, 22 Geo. J. Leg. Eth. 97 (2009); Painter, *Advance Waiver of Conflicts*, 13 Geo. J. Leg. Eth. 289 (2000); Zacharias, *Waiving Conflicts of Interest*, 108 Yale L.J. 407 (1998).

[29] *Kassis v. Teacher's Ins. & Annuity Ass'n*, 93 N.Y.2d 611, 616 (N.Y. 1999).

[30] Beck, *Legal Malpractice in Texas*, 50 Baylor L. Rev. 547, 608 (1998).

[31] *See People ex rel. Dept. of Corps. v. SpeeDee Oil Change Sys. Inc.*, 86 Cal. Rptr. 2d 816, 825 (Cal. App. 1999).

[32] Model Rules of Prof. Conduct, Rule 1.9(a). *See id.* Rules 1.9(b), (c), 1.10. *See generally* Aronson, *Conflict of Interest*, 52 Wash. L. Rev. 807 (1977); Wolfram, *Former Client Conflicts*, 10 Geo. J. Leg. Eth. 677 (1997); *Developments in the Law-Conflicts of Interest in the Legal Profession*, 94 Harv. L. Rev. 1244 (1981).

client but her former firm had, upon moving to a new firm, she
cannot represent a new client materially adverse to the interests
of the former firm's client in the same or a substantially related
matter if she had acquired confidential information about that
client "that is material to the matter."[33] However, if the lawyer's
participation was of a "peripheral nature," a number of courts
allow the lawyer to rebut the presumption that she had acquired
"material" confidential information.[34] With respect to whether
the suspect attorney possesses confidential information, it will
be sufficient if the attorney simply had the opportunity (in terms
of her involvement with the representation) to acquire
information pertinent to the current representation.[35] Such
cases will be fact-intensive. But generally, if the lawyer's
participation involved discovery, reviewing pleadings, drafting
motions, conferences with the client and the like, she will be
deemed to have received confidential information.[36]

As in simultaneous adverse representation, in cases of
successive representation, disqualification of one lawyer has
traditionally led to disqualification of the entire firm.[37] Vicarious
disqualification in subsequent representation therefore "protects
client confidences from misuse in substantially related and
adverse litigation, frees the former client from any anxiety that
matters disclosed to an attorney will subsequently be used
against it in related litigation and provides a clear and readily
administered test encouraging self-enforcement among members
of the legal profession."[38]

Like simultaneous representation, there is a presumption
that confidences are shared among lawyers (and other personnel
such as paralegals) of a law firm. The methodology in successive
representation matters involves a two-step process. In general,

---

[33] Model Rule 1.9(b).

[34] *See, e.g., Silver Chrysler Plymouth, Inc. v. Chrysler Motors Corp.*, 518
F.2d 751, 756–757 (2d Cir. 1975).

[35] *See* G. Hazard & W. Hodes, *supra* note 8, at §§ 15.11–15.12. *See also,
Proeducation International, Inc. v. Mindprint*, 587 F.3d 296, 299–304 (5th
Cir. 2009); *Schwed v. General Elec. Co.*, 990 F. Supp. 113, 116 (N.D.N.Y.
1998).

[36] *See generally Kassis*, 93 N.Y. 2d 611 (N.Y. 1999); *Schwed*, 990 F. Supp.
113 (N.D.N.Y. 1998).

[37] *See, e.g., Flatt v. Superior Ct.*, 36 Cal. Rptr. 2d 537, 541 (Cal. App.
1991).

[38] *Kassis*, 93 N.Y. 2d at 616.

before considering a motion of firm-wide imputed disqualification, courts first determine whether the circumstances require disqualification of the individual attorney. Personal disqualification is based on the scope of the attorney's activities in the prior representation as well as application of the "substantial relationship" test.[39]

The "substantial relationship" test seeks to determine the similarities in the issues and contexts implicated with respect to the current and the former representations. The standard historically has been defined as follows:

> "[T]he former client need show no more than that the matters embraced within the pending suit wherein his former attorney appears on behalf of his adversary are substantially related to the matters or cause of action wherein the attorney previously represented him, the former client. The Court will assume that during the course of the former representation confidences were disclosed to the attorney bearing on the subject matter of the representation. It will not inquire into their nature and extent."[40]

Only after the attorney is determined to be disqualified, does the question of her law firm's disqualification arise. Traditionally, disqualification of the attorney on grounds of "substantial relationship" results in automatic disqualification of the firm.[41] However, several courts have reformulated the rigid test of "substantial relationship" and have allowed counsel to rebut the presumption by showing that the attorney was not in a position to have obtained confidential information.[42] For example, if the lawyer had performed only routine and

---

[39] *See* Hagan & Kaufman, *The Chinese Wall: A Limited Remedy for Conflicts of Interest*, C641 ALI–ABA 187, 217 (1991).

[40] *T.C. Theatre Corp. v. Warner Bros. Pictures*, 113 F. Supp. 265, 268 (E.D.N.Y. 1953).

[41] *See In re Marriage of Zimmerman*, 16 Cal. App. 4th 556, 563 (Cal. Ct. App. 1993) (quoting *Rosenfeld Construction Co. v. Superior Ct.*, 235 Cal. App. 3d 566, 575 (Cal. Ct. App. 1991)).

[42] G. Hazard & W. Hodes, *supra* note 8, at § 15.12. *See also, Nissan Motor Corp. v. Orozco*, 595 So. 2d 240 (Fla. Dist. Ct. App. 1992); *In re Marriage of Zimmerman*, 16 Cal. App. 4th 556 (Ct. App. 1993) (although the court determined that the former and current representations were substantially similar, it held that disqualification was not warranted where the contact of the attorney was "brief and insubstantial").

peripheral functions (such as conducting solely legal research) and could not have acquired confidential information, neither the individual attorney nor the law firm will be disqualified.[43]

But if the "substantial relationship" test is satisfied and the attorney is determined to have had access to confidential information based on the nature of his involvement in the prior case, the traditional view is that the law firm will be disqualified. This presumption of shared confidences is usually regarded as irrebuttable.[44] Indeed, this irrebuttable presumption has been extended by some courts to paralegals and secretaries.[45] However, given the frequent lateral movement of attorneys between law firms and the mega-size of national law firms today, this approach is being relaxed.

For example, in such cases, the Model Rules today permit timely and effective screening to avert firm-wide disqualification when a personally disqualified private attorney moves from one firm to another.[46] Likewise, the ALI Restatement of the Law Governing Lawyers allows screening of private attorneys if timely and adequate notice is provided to all subject clients (former as well as current) and the confidential information

---

[43] *See Nissan Motor Corp.*, 595 So. 2d at 243.

[44] *See, e.g., State v. Ehless*, 631 N.W. 2d 471, 482 (Neb. 2001).

[45] *See In re American Home Products Corp.*, 985 S.W. 2d 68, 74 (Tex. 1998), *citing, Phoenix Founders, Inc. v. Marshall*, 887 S.W. 2d 831, 834 (Tex. 1994).

[46] Model Rules of Prof. Conduct, Rule 1.10(a). *See* G. Hazard & W. Hodes, *supra* note 8, at §§ 15.11–15.16. Hence, under Rule 1.10(a), in successive representation situations, firm-wide disqualification may be averted if:

"(i)   the disqualified lawyer is timely screened from any participation in the matter and is apportioned no part of the fee therefore;

(ii)   written notice is promptly given to any affected former client to enable the former client to ascertain compliance with the provisions of this Rule, which shall include a description of the screening procedures employed; a statement of the firm's and of the screened lawyer's compliance with these Rules; a statement that review may be available before a tribunal; and an agreement by the firm to respond promptly to any written inquiries or objections by the former client about the screening procedures; and

(iii) certifications of compliance with these Rules and with the screening procedures are provided to the former client by the screened lawyer and by a partner of the firm, at reasonable intervals upon the former client's written request and upon termination of the screening procedures."

possessed by the subject attorney is unlikely to be important in the subsequent matter.[47]

Nonetheless, a number of the state ethical codes reject the use of screening to avoid vicarious law firm disqualification. These state ethical codes deem the sharing of confidences among law firm attorneys as an irrebuttable presumption, which cannot be overridden by screening when a private lawyer is concerned.[48] New York, for example, does not permit a law firm, absent informed client consent, to escape imputed disqualification.[49] In New York, even a well-constructed screening mechanism is not enough to avoid law firm disqualification if a former client objects and the personally disqualified attorney possesses the former client's confidences.[50] According to one authority, "as of now, it will be a rare case where a court will deny a motion to disqualify a law firm simply because the firm has established a screen around a personally disqualified attorney and small firms stand virtually no chance because the lawyers in small firms tend to be collegial, frequently discussing their cases with each other and sharing confidential information and strategy."[51]

Some courts that reject screening as rebutting the presumption of shared confidences believe that public suspicion

---

[47] ALI, *Restatement of the Law Governing Lawyers* § 124(2). A number of states permit the use of screening to avert law firm disqualification in circumstances similar to those set forth by the ALI. *See, e.g.,* sources cited in note 69 *infra.*

[48] *See, e.g., Roberts v. Hutchins,* 572 So. 2d 1231 (Ala. 1990) (under local rules of professional conduct, screening not available to attorneys moving between private law firms). *Accord, Edward J. De Bartolo Corp. v. Petrin,* 516 So. 2d 6 (Fla. Dist. Ct. App. 1987); *Weglarz v. Bruck,* 470 N.E.2d 21 (Ill. App. Ct. 1984); *Monroe v. City of Topeka,* 988 P.2d 288 (Kan. 1999); *State ex rel. Freezer Services, Inc. v. Mullen,* 458 N.W. 2d 245 (Neb. 1990); *Kassis v. Teacher's Ins. & Annuity Ass'n,* 93 N.Y. 2d 611 (N.Y. 1999); *Kala v. Aluminium Smelting and Refining Co.,* 688 N.E. 2d 258 (Ohio 1998); *Petroleum Wholesale, Inc. v. Marshall,* 751 S.W. 2d 295, 300 (Tex. App. 1988).

[49] N.Y. Rules of Prof. Conduct, Rule 1.10; R. Simon, *supra* note 14, at 377. *See Kassis v. Teacher's Ins. & Annuity Ass'n,* 93 N.Y. 2d 611 (N.Y. 1999) (stating, however, that screening mechanism should be set up when the attorney possesses no material confidential information to remove even the appearance of impropriety).

[50] *See* R. Simon, *supra* note 14, at 377, *citing, Kassis,* 93 N.Y.2d 611 (N.Y. 1999).

[51] R. Simon, *supra* note 14, at 347.

of the legal profession outweighs the interest of a party in obtaining the counsel of his choice.[52] These courts reason that when the case involves a private attorney with actual knowledge of a former client's confidences, "such an appearance of impropriety arises that not even an effective Chinese wall can allay public suspicion."[53]

Irrespective that numerous state ethical codes and courts currently do not allow screening in the private attorney setting, the situation is rapidly changing. For over two decades, a number of federal courts have allowed counsel to rebut this presumption.[54] The modern day practice of law has led to the growing belief that a non-rebuttable presumption in the successive representation context is out of touch with reality.[55] Attorneys no longer stay with one firm throughout their entire careers. In such a mobile practice, automatic disqualification would cast immense hardship on "the lawyer, the firm and the firm's clients."[56] Costs associated with disqualification are also formidable. Not only does the firm lose a prospective client but the client too has to bear the expense of finding alternate counsel.[57] Automatic disqualification is also disfavored because it makes law firms hesitant to hire lawyers trying to move to other firms.[58] These lawyers "would find themselves cast adrift as 'Typhoid Marys' and clients would find their choice of counsel substantially diminished."[59] Further, a strict rule favoring vicarious disqualification leads to abuse as it is often used as a litigation tactic seeking to deny an opposing party its counsel of choice.[60] Further, it may be asserted that the growth of the "mega-firm" has undermined the presumption of shared

[52] *See, e.g., Petroleum Wholesale, Inc.* v. *Marshall*, 751 S.W. 2d 295, 297 (Tex. App. 1988).

[53] *Id.* at 300.

[54] *See, e.g., Manning v. Waring, Cox, James, Sklar & Allen*, 849 F.2d 222, 225 (6th Cir. 1988); *Schiessle v. Stephens*, 717 F.2d 417, 421 (7th Cir. 1983).

[55] *See Adams v. Aerojet Gen. Corp.*, 86 Cal. App. 4th 1324, 1336 (Cal. Ct. App. 2001).

[56] *In re County of Los Angeles*, 223 F.3d 990, 996 (9th Cir. 2000).

[57] *Adams v. Aerojet Gen. Corp.*, 86 Cal. App. 4th at 1339.

[58] *In re County of Los Angeles*, 223 F.3d at 996.

[59] *Id.*

[60] *See Manning v. Waring, Cox, James, Sklar & Allen*, 849 F.2d 222, 224 (6th Cir. 1988) ("Unquestionably, the ability to deny one's opponent the services of capable counsel is a potent weapon.").

confidences.[61] Confidences and information are more likely to be shared in a small firm rather than lawyers practicing in different cities in a mega-firm.[62] Due to such changing realities of law practice, a change in the direction of the courts is being noticed. As the Ohio Supreme Court reasoned, "[u]ltimately, one must have faith in the integrity of members of the legal profession to honor their professional oath to uphold the Code of Professional Responsibility, safeguarded by the precautions required to rebut the presumption of shared confidences."[63]

The factors that courts have considered in determining the efficacy of a screening quarantine are: "(1) the size of the firm;[64] (2) the extent of departmentalization within the firm; (3) prohibitions against discussion of the action with the new member; and (4) exclusion of the new member from the relevant files, participation in the action, and sharing in firm earnings from the action."[65] Further, the wall must be timely built and effectively implemented.[66] To be timely, the wall must be constructed as soon as the potential for conflict becomes known.[67] But under certain circumstances, an ethical wall cannot provide an effective screen, no matter how timely and well constructed it is. This may happen when the size of the firm

---

[61] *See* Lenhardt, *Ethical Screens in the Modern Age,* 50 Santa Clara L. Rev. 1345, 1346 (2010).

[62] Steinberg & Sharpe, *supra* note 3, 66 Notre Dame L. Rev. at 13 ("It is quite different to irrebuttably presume that a lawyer in the Chicago office of a 500-lawyer firm obtained confidential information about a client represented by a lawyer in the firm's New York Office.").

[63] *Kala v. Aluminum Smelting and Refining Co.,* 688 N.E. 2d 258, 265 (Ohio 1998). *See also, Clinard v. Blackwood,* 46 S.W. 3d 177 (Tenn. 2001).

[64] *Solow v. Grace & Co.,* 83 N.Y. 2d 303, 313 (N.Y. 1994) ("In firms characterized by informality, disqualification will be imposed as a matter of law without a hearing.").

[65] *Petroleum Wholesale, Inc. v. Marshall,* 751 S.W. 2d 295, 297 (Tex. App. 1998). *See Norfolk Southern Railway Company v. Reading Blue Mountain & Northern Railroad Company,* 397 F. Supp. 2d 551, 553–556 (M.D. Pa. 2005).

[66] *See* Hagan & Kaufman, *supra* note 39, at 223.

[67] *Id. See LaSalle National Bank v. County of Lake,* 703 F.2d 252, 259 (7th Cir. 1983) (a wall built months after conflict became apparent does not rebut the presumption); *Intelli-Check, Inc. v. Tricom Card Technologies, Inc.,* 2008 WL 4682433, at *4–5 (E.D.N.Y. 2008) (finding that firm's timely implementation of effective screen averted firm-wide disqualification).

is so small that an effective screen is particularly difficult to implement.[68]

Nonetheless, as a general proposition, several courts and states (in their respective Model Rules of Professional Conduct) have become more receptive to the propriety of screening to avert firm-wide disqualification.[69] For example, numerous federal courts have held that if a screen is timely and effectively implemented, it can rebut the presumption of shared confidences in successive representation matters.[70] These courts recognize that firm-wide automatic disqualification is a drastic measure and should be imposed only when circumstances indicate that no feasible alternative exists for protecting client confidences.[71] When appropriate, therefore, institutional

---

[68] *See Cheng v. GAF Corp.*, 631 F.2d 1052, 1058 (2d Cir. 1980) (the firm was too small for a screening mechanism to be effective); R. Simon, *supra* note 14, at 377. *But see Essex Equity Holdings USA, LLC v. Lehman Brothers, Inc.*, 2010 WL 2331407, at *9–10 (N.Y. Sup. Ct. 2010) (no per se rule preventing small firm from using screening mechanisms).

[69] *See, e.g., In re County of Los Angeles*, 223 F.3d 990 (9th Cir. 2000); *Manning v. Waring, Cox, James, Sklar & Allen*, 849 F.2d 222 (6th Cir. 1988); *Schiessle v. Stephens*, 717 F.2d 417, 421 (7th Cir. 1983); Rule 1.10(c) of the Indiana Rules of Prof. Conduct; Rule 1.10(b) of the Michigan Rules of Prof. Conduct; Rule 1.10(c) of the North Carolina Rules of Prof. Conduct; Rule 1.10(c) of the Oregon Rules of Prof. Conduct; Rule 1.10(b) of the Pennsylvania Rules of Prof. Conduct. For example, the Pennsylvania provision states:

"When a lawyer becomes associated with a firm, the firm may not knowingly represent a person in the same or a substantially related matter in which that lawyer, or a firm with which the lawyer was associated, had previously represented a client whose interests are materially adverse to that person and about whom the lawyer had acquired information protected by Rules 1.6 and 1.9(b) that is material to the matter unless:

(1) the disqualified lawyer is screened from any participation in the matter and is apportioned no part of the fee therefrom; and

(2) written notice is promptly given to the appropriate client to enable it to ascertain compliance with the provisions of this rule."

Penn. Rules of Prof. Conduct, Rule 1.10(b).

[70] *See, e.g., In re County of Los Angeles*, 223 F.3d at 996.

[71] *See Schiessle v. Stephens*, 717 F.2d at 420, *quoting, Freeman v. Chicago Musical Instrument Co.*, 689 F.2d 715, 721 (7th Cir. 1982). *See generally* Bateman, *Return to the Ethics As a Standard for Attorney Disqualification*, 33 Duquesne L. Rev. 249 (1995); Penegar, *The Loss of Innocence: A Brief History of Law Firm Disqualification in the Courts*, 8 Geo. J. Leg. Eth. 831 (1995); Reich, Vernick & Horn, *Screening Mechanisms: A Broader Application?*, 72 Temple L. Rev. 1023 (1999); Rotunda, *Conflicts Problems*

screening mechanisms can be implemented to effectively insulate the disqualified attorney from the rest of the firm.

By comparison, when the conflict of interest dilemma concerns a former government attorney, the courts and ethical rules traditionally have been more flexible. In the case of a personally disqualified government attorney who has moved to private practice, disqualification of the firm can be avoided by timely and effectively screening the particular lawyer.[72] The personally disqualified lawyer must not receive any part of the fee from the client and written notice must be provided to the appropriate government agency.[73] The rationale is that if strict firm-wide disqualification were to be applied to former government lawyers, the potential impact on the government and attorneys it seeks to recruit would be too severe.[74] Since the government's sphere of representation involves all private citizens and organizations, disallowing screening, proponents claim, will adversely impact the government's efforts to attract adept attorneys to government service.[75] Automatic firm-wide vicarious disqualification thus would cause qualified attorneys not to seek government jobs due to fear that government service would cause them to be shunned by prospective private employers.[76]

As discussed earlier in this Scenario, scores of law firms in this country have hundreds of attorneys. Firms having 200 or more lawyers are common. Nonetheless, the general principle prevails, based in part on agency law principles, that knowledge

---

When Representing Members of Corporate Families, 72 Notre Dame L. Rev. 655 (1997).

[72] *See* Model Rules of Prof. Conduct, Rule 1.11.

[73] *Id.*

[74] *Id.* cmt. 4.

[75] *Id. See Armstrong v. McAlpin*, 625 F.2d 433, 443 (2d Cir. 1980) (en banc). *See generally* Morgan, *Appropriate Limits on Participation by a Former Agency Official in Matters Before an Agency*, 1980 Duke L.J. 14 (1980); Mundheim, *Conflict of Interest and the Former Government Employee: Rethinking the Revolving Door*, 14 Creighton L. Rev. 707 (1981).

[76] With the current depressed employment situation for attorneys, this rationale may be challenged. *See generally* U.S. Bureau of Labor Statistics, *Occupational Outlook Handbook—Lawyers*, at www.bls.gov/oco/ocos053.htm (2010–2011 edition).

by any attorney or other agent of the law firm is attributable to the principal—namely, the firm itself. Although not a "conflicts" case, the decision that follows illustrates the monetary liability exposure that may be incurred when there is inadequate dissemination of significant information to all of the law firm's attorneys who are working on matters for that client.

CROMEANS V. MORGAN KEEGAN & CO., INC.
69 F. Supp. 3d 934 (W.D. Mo. 2014)

NANETTE K. LAUGHREY, DISTRICT JUDGE.

The Court previously granted partial summary judgment in favor of Defendant Armstrong Teasdale, LLP on Plaintiff John Cromeans' claims for legal malpractice and negligent misrepresentation. Cromeans filed a motion to vacate the order which the Court denied. Upon further consideration, the Court grants the motion to vacate, in part. It finds that summary judgment should be granted on the malpractice claims, but should not be granted on Cromeans' negligent misrepresentation claim.

I. Discussion

A. Legal Malpractice

In granting summary judgment to Armstrong Teasdale on the legal malpractice claim, the Court recognized that an attorney-client relationship must ordinarily exist before a plaintiff can recover for legal malpractice against an attorney. But this element of a legal malpractice claim may be satisfied if a non-client plaintiff can show that the attorney performed services specifically intended by a client to benefit the plaintiff. . . . If specific intent is established, a six-factor balancing test is then used to determine, as a separate matter, the question of legal duty of attorneys to non-clients. Because Cromeans' evidentiary submissions failed to show that Morgan Keegan specifically intended Armstrong Teasdale's services to benefit the bond purchasers, the Court granted summary judgment to Armstrong Teasdale on the legal malpractice claim.

Therefore, the Court denies Cromeans' motion to vacate the grant of summary judgment in favor of Armstrong Teasdale on the legal malpractice claim.

B. Negligent Misrepresentation

Justifiable reliance is a necessary element of all negligent misrepresentation claims. In granting summary judgment to Armstrong Teasdale on Cromeans' negligent misrepresentation claim, the Court found that Cromeans could not prove reasonable reliance. Because Morgan Keegan did not hire Armstrong Teasdale to investigate the facts contained in the offering statement and Armstrong Teasdale disclaimed any responsibility for the accuracy of those facts, the Court concluded that justifiable reliance could not be shown. When making its decision, however, the Court overlooked evidence that Armstrong Teasdale made an affirmative misstatement of fact when it said "no facts have come to our attention which lead us to believe that the Official Statement contains" misrepresentations or omitted material facts.

In his motion to vacate, Cromeans cites evidence that Armstrong Teasdale had a contract with the Missouri Department of Economic Development (DED) to assist DED in attracting Chinese businesses to Missouri. When DED wanted a background check on a Chinese company, Mamtek, it contacted Armstrong Teasdale's agent, Mr. Li, to obtain whatever information he could about Mamtek. Mr. Li is a non-lawyer based in China, who was retained by Armstrong Teasdale to fulfill Armstrong Teasdale's contract with DED. Mr. Li made a phone call and did an internet search. In April 2010, Mr. Li reported to DED and to Maria Desloge, who was Armstrong Teasdale's Associate Director of the China Trade and Investment Office, that Mamtek's plant in Fujian Province, China, never started to manufacture, and that it could not because it did not meet the "zoning" requirements for that location. The offering statement, however, stated that the plant was operational.

Citing the [ALI] Restatement (Second) of Torts, § 552, Cromeans argues that Armstrong Teasdale is liable to the bond purchasers because Armstrong Teasdale knew that some statements in the offering statement were false. Section 552 provides, in relevant part:

(1) One who, in the course of his business, profession or employment, or in any other transaction in which he has a pecuniary interest, supplies false information

for the guidance of others in their business transactions, is subject to liability for pecuniary loss caused to them by their justifiable reliance upon the information, if he fails to exercise reasonable care or competence in obtaining or communicating the information.

(2) Except as stated in Subsection (3), the liability stated in Subsection (1) is limited to loss suffered

(a) by the person or one of a limited group of persons for whose benefit and guidance he intends to supply the information or knows that the recipient intends to supply it, and

(b) through reliance upon it in a transaction that he intends the information to influence or knows that the recipient so intends or in a substantially similar transaction. . . .

The national trend is to recognize a cause of action by non-clients for negligent misrepresentations by professionals, including lawyers, if the requirements of § 552 of the Restatement are satisfied. . . .

Having concluded that Missouri will recognize Cromeans' negligent misrepresentation claim, the Court turns to the additional arguments made by Armstrong Teasdale as to why summary judgment should be granted on that claim. Armstrong Teasdale argues that Edward Li's information should not be attributable to it because Mr. Li was not an employee of Armstrong Teasdale. It also argues that Mr. Li's knowledge should not be imputed to the Armstrong Teasdale lawyer who actually prepared the offering statement because that lawyer did not have the information, and to impute the information to that lawyer would violate well-established principles of confidentiality.

Under Missouri law, a corporate entity "can obtain knowledge only through its agents and, under the well-established rules of agency, the knowledge of agents obtained in the course of their employment is imputed to the corporation." . . . Therefore, the fact that the lawyer making the false statement did not know it was false does not show that Armstrong Teasdale lacked knowledge of the false statement.

Armstrong Teasdale also suggests that Mr. Li's knowledge could not be shared within the firm because of professional rules of confidentiality, and therefore, his knowledge should not be imputed to the lawyer who prepared the offering statement that contained the false information. This argument is unpersuasive because the information Mr. Li gathered was publicly available. Information available to the public is not subject to non-disclosure rules. Further, Mr. Li is not an attorney and never provided legal services to DED. And he did provide the information to Maria Desloge, an Armstrong Teasdale employee.

In summary, there is evidence that Armstrong Teasdale, in the course of its professional duties, supplied information that it knew to be false to Morgan Keegan, knowing that Morgan Keegan intended to supply it to potential bond purchasers. Further, Cromeans arguably relied on that information and suffered loss as a result. This is sufficient to make a submissible claim for negligent misrepresentation under § 552. While Armstrong Teasdale disclaimed any responsibility for checking the accuracy of the facts, it could not with impunity include facts in the offering statement that it knew to be false, particularly in light of its affirmative statement that it knew of no facts contrary to the offering statement.

In view of the above, the order granting summary judgment to Armstrong Teasdale on the negligent misrepresentation claim was in error and is vacated.

With increasing frequency, law firms have their clients sign advance waivers to avert disqualification if a conflict of interest should arise.[77] The following decision addresses this timely subject.

---

[77] For law review articles addressing this subject, see the sources cited in note 28 *supra*.

GALDERMA LABORATORIES, L.P. v. ACTAVIS MID ATLANTIC LLC

927 F. Supp. 2d 390 (N.D. Tex. 2013)

ED KINKEADE, DISTRICT JUDGE.

Before the Court is Plaintiffs Galderma Laboratories, L.P., Galderma S.A., and Galderma Research & Development, S.N.C.'s (collectively "Galderma") Motion to Disqualify Vinson & Elkins, LLP. . . . The Court denies Galderma's Motion because Galderma gave informed consent to Vinson & Elkins's ("V & E") representation of clients directly adverse to Galderma in matters that are not substantially related to V & E's representation of Galderma.

I. *Factual Background*

Galderma is a worldwide leader in the research, development, and manufacturing of branded dermatological products. Galderma is headquartered in Fort Worth where it employs approximately 240 people. Galderma and its affiliates have operations around the world, employing thousands of people and reporting worldwide sales of 1.4 billion euros for the year 2011 alone.

As a complex, global company, Galderma routinely encounters legal issues and the legal system. Galderma has its own legal department to address these issues. The legal department is headed by its Vice President and General Counsel, Quinton Cassady. Mr. Cassady is a lawyer who has practiced law for over 20 years and has been general counsel for Galderma for over 10 of those years. In addition to an in-house legal department, Galderma, through Mr. Cassady, frequently engages outside counsel to assist with a wide range of issues. Over the past 10 years, Galderma has been represented by large law firms including DLA Piper, Paul Hastings, and Vinson & Elkins, LLP ("V & E"). Galderma also engages smaller law firms as needed.

In 2003, Galderma and V & E began its attorney-client relationship. V & E sent Galderma an engagement letter. As part of the engagement letter, V & E sought Galderma's consent to broadly waive future conflicts of interest, subject to specific limitations identified in the engagement letter. The waiver contained in the engagement letter is as follows:

We understand and agree that this is not an exclusive agreement, and you are free to retain any other counsel of your choosing. We recognize that we shall be disqualified from representing any other client with interest materially and directly adverse to yours (i) in any matter which is substantially related to our representation of you and (ii) with respect to any matter where there is a reasonable probability that confidential information you furnished to us could be used to your disadvantage. You understand and agree that, with those exceptions, we are free to represent other clients, including clients whose interests may conflict with yours in litigation, business transactions, or other legal matters. You agree that our representing you in this matter will not prevent or disqualify us from representing clients adverse to you in other matters and that you consent in advance to our undertaking such adverse representations.

On behalf of Galderma, Mr. Cassady signed that he understood and, on behalf of Galderma, agreed to the terms and conditions of engaging V & E, including the waiver of future conflicts of interest.

Beginning in 2003, Galderma engaged V & E for legal advice relating to employee benefit plans, Galderma's 401(k) plan, health care benefit programs, employment issues, and other issues relating to the administration of such programs. V & E continued to advise Galderma on employment and benefits issues into July of 2012.

In June 2012, while V & E was advising Galderma on employment issues, Galderma represented by DLA Piper and Munck Wilson Mandala, filed this intellectual property lawsuit against Actavis Mid Atlantic, LLC ("Actavis"). At that time, V & E had already represented various Actavis entities in intellectual property matters for six years. Without any additional communication to Galderma, V & E began working on this matter for Actavis, and in July 2012, V & E filed Actavis's answer and counterclaims.

In July 2012, Galderma received a copy of Actavis's answer and counterclaims, and became aware that V & E was representing Actavis. After brief discussions in late July between Mr. Cassady and V & E, Galderma asked V & E to withdraw from representing Actavis. On August 6, 2012, V & E

chose to terminate its attorney-client relationship with
Galderma rather than Actavis. On that same day, V & E stated
that it would not withdraw from representing Actavis, because
Galderma had consented to V & E representing adverse parties
in litigation when it signed the waiver of future conflicts in the
2003 engagement letter. Galderma then brought this motion to
disqualify.

II. Galderma's Motion to Disqualify

Galderma now moves to disqualify V & E from representing
Actavis in the underlying patent litigation. The briefing of the
parties has been wide-ranging, but at oral arguments, counsel
acknowledged that the crux of the issue is this: whether or not
Galderma, a sophisticated client, represented by in-house
counsel gave informed consent when it agreed to a general,
open-ended waiver of future conflicts of interest in V & E's 2003
engagement letter. Galderma argues that its consent was not
"informed consent" when its own, in-house lawyer signed the
agreement on its behalf because V & E did not advise Galderma
of any specifics with regards to what future conflicts Galderma
may be waiving. V & E argues that in this case, because
Galderma is a highly sophisticated client who is a regular user
of legal services and was represented by its own counsel, the
waiver language is reasonably adequate to advise Galderma of
the material risks of waiving future conflicts, despite being
general and open-ended.

A. Legal Framework for Resolving Ethics Questions

Fifth Circuit precedent requires the court to consider several
relevant ethical standards in determining whether there has
been an ethical violation. Disqualification cases are guided by
state and national ethical standards adopted by the Fifth
Circuit. In the Fifth Circuit, the source for the standards of the
profession has been the canons of ethics developed by the
American Bar Association. Additionally, consideration of the
Texas Disciplinary Rules of Professional Conduct is also
necessary, because they govern attorneys practicing in Texas
generally. The Court also considers, when applicable, local rules
promulgated by the local court itself. . . .

When a client hires multiple firms, that creates inadvertent
problems for the ethical system in at least two ways. One is
when the client hires every large and small firm possible to

prevent any local firm from being on the other side. The second problem happens in cases such as this, where a client hires a firm for work that is important, but small in size compared to some unrelated large matters. The ABA recognized this problem may occur:

> When corporate clients with multiple operating divisions hire tens if not hundreds of law firms, the idea that, for example, a corporation in Miami retaining the Florida office of a national law firm to negotiate a lease should preclude that firm's New York office from taking an adverse position in a totally unrelated commercial dispute against another division of the same corporation strikes some as placing unreasonable limitations on the opportunities of both clients and lawyers. . . .

Sophisticated clients can retain their adversary's counsel of choice in unrelated matters while attempting to invalidate prospective waivers of future conflicts when that counsel later becomes adverse to them. Large firms would never be able to take on small, specialized matters for a client unless the firms could reasonably protect against this potential abuse by preserving their ability to practice in other areas where the client has chosen to retain different counsel.

B. Ethical Standards for Waiver of Future Conflicts

With the ABA canons of ethics as a guide, informed by state and local rules, the Court considers the ethical standards relevant to this specific case.

As a general rule, a lawyer is not allowed to sue his own client, which he concurrently represents in other matters. This holding mirrors the position of the ABA Model Rules of Professional Conduct ("Model Rules"), which provide that, "[e]xcept as provided in paragraph (b) a lawyer shall not represent a client if the representation involves a concurrent conflict of interest." Rule 1.7 creates an exception:

> Notwithstanding the existence of a concurrent conflict of interest under paragraph (a), a lawyer may represent a client if:
>
> (1) The lawyer reasonably believes that the lawyer will be able to provide competent and diligent representation to each affected client;

(2) the representation is not prohibited by law;

(3) the representation does not involve the assertion of a claim by one client against another client represented by the lawyer in the same litigation or other proceeding before a tribunal; and

(4) each affected client gives informed consent, confirmed in writing.

"Informed consent" denotes the agreement by a person to a proposed course of conduct after the lawyer has communicated adequate information and explanation about the material risks of and reasonably available alternatives to the proposed course of conduct. . . .

Under the Model Rules, a client's waiver of future conflicts is valid when the client gives informed consent. Clearly, all clients, even the most sophisticated, must give informed consent. What disclosure from an attorney is reasonably adequate to allow for informed consent for a particular client is not clear. The Model Rules, the Comments to the Model Rules, and the Formal Opinions of the ABA's Committee on Ethics and Professional Responsibility outline a number of factors for courts to consider in determining whether a client has given informed consent to waive future conflicts of interest.

1. ABA Model Rules and Applicable Comments

One source for determining how to apply the Model Rules is the comments to the Model Rules. The comments do not add obligations to the Model Rules but provide guidance for practicing in compliance with the Rules. The text of each Rule is authoritative, but the Comments are intended as guides to interpretation. . . .

The Comments to Rule 1.7, governing current client conflicts, recognize that a lawyer may properly request a client to waive future conflicts, subject to the test in Rule 1.7(b). The effectiveness of the waiver is generally determined by the extent to which the client reasonably understands the material risk that the waiver entails.

When dealing with a waiver of future conflicts, a specific waiver of a particular type of conflict has the greatest likelihood of being effective. A general and open-ended waiver will ordinarily be ineffective, because the client will likely not have understood the material risks involved. Consent using a general or open-ended waiver is not per se ineffective, but considering the entire spectrum of clients, a general and open-ended waiver is likely to be ineffective because the vast majority of clients are not in a position to understand the material risks from the open-ended language of the waiver itself.

The same comment highlights that consent to a general, open-ended waiver is more likely to be effective when dealing with a narrow set of circumstances. If the client is an experienced user of the legal services involved and is reasonably informed regarding the risk that a conflict may arise, that consent is more likely to be effective. The consent is particularly likely to be effective when the client is independently represented by other counsel in giving consent and the consent is limited to future conflicts unrelated to the subject of the representation.

The comments to Rule 1.0, which defines "informed consent," mirror the comments to Rule 1.7. For consent to be "informed," the lawyer must take reasonable steps to ensure that the client or other person possesses information reasonably adequate to make an informed decision. Ordinarily, this requires communication that includes a disclosure of the facts and circumstances giving rise to the situation, any explanation reasonably necessary to inform the client or other person of the material advantages and disadvantages of the proposed course of conduct and a discussion of the client's or other person's options and alternatives. The more experienced the client is in legal matters generally and in making decisions of the type involved, the less information and explanation is needed for a client's consent to be informed. When dealing with a client who is independently represented by other counsel in giving the consent, generally the client should be assumed to have given informed consent. Just like Rule 1.7, Rule 1.0 shows there is a vast difference in what type of disclosure is necessary to ensure that a client has reasonably adequate information to make an informed decision, depending on the sophistication of the client and, importantly, whether or not the client is represented by an independent lawyer.

2. ABA Committee on Ethics and Professional Responsibility Formal Ethics Opinions

The ABA's Standing Committee on Ethics and Professional Responsibility has also issued a formal ethics opinion dealing expressly with informed consent to future conflicts. ABA Comm. On Ethics & Prof'l Responsibility, Formal Op, 05–436 (2005) [hereinafter ABA Formal Op. 05–436]. As amended in February 2002, Rule 1.7 permits a lawyer to obtain effective informed consent to a wider range of future conflicts than would have been possible under the Model Rules prior to their amendment. Prior to the 2002 Amendment of the Model Rules, informed consent was limited to circumstances in which the lawyer was able to and did identify the potential party or class of parties that may be represented in the future matter. . . . Additionally, informed consent may have been limited further by the need to identify the nature of the likely future matter. Relying on Comment 22, the Committee opined that, following the amendment, open-ended, general informed consent was likely to be valid if the client is an experienced user of legal services. The opinion gave significant weight to the sophistication of the client and its use of independent counsel, factors which previously had not been relevant to informed consent. . . .

C. Burden of Proof

On a motion to disqualify, the movant bears the ultimate burden of proof. Galderma must establish that there is a conflict of interest under the applicable ethics standards and if so, that disqualification is the proper remedy. . . . V & E does not dispute the concurrent representation of Galderma and Actavis establishes a conflict of interest under the Model Rules. V & E argues that Galderma gave informed consent for V & E to represent clients adverse to it in litigation, which waives any right to claim a conflict of interest. Absent informed consent, there is no question that V & E's contemporaneous representation of Actavis and Galderma is a current client conflict on an unrelated matter. . . .

With regards to allocating the burden of proof, the issue of "informed consent" is similar to the issue of exceptional circumstances. . . . On the issue of exceptional circumstances, . . . it would be the attorney's burden to show a reason why the court should allow the otherwise impermissible dual representation. . . . Because, absent informed consent, there is no question that V & E's contemporaneous representation of Actavis and Galderma is a current client conflict on an unrelated matter, Galderma need prove nothing more to establish a violation of Model Rule 1.7. V & E has raised the issue of informed consent in response to the otherwise established violation. Because V & E has raised the issue in its defense, the Court concludes that V & E has the burden to show that Galderma gave informed consent. . . .

D.   Whether or Not Galderma Gave Informed Consent to the Waiver of Future Conflicts

To meet its burden of showing informed consent, V & E must show that it provided reasonably adequate information for Galderma to understand the material risks of waiving future conflicts of interest. Two related questions in this test form the analysis. The first question is whether the information disclosed is reasonably adequate for a client to form informed consent. If the waiver does, the second question is, whether or not the disclosure is reasonably adequate for the particular client involved in this case. The focus of the first question is on what information is being disclosed, and the focus of the second question is on circumstances pertaining to the client.

1.   Whether V & E's Disclosure Is Reasonably Adequate for a Client to Form Informed Consent

Rule 1.0 provides three basic factors to help determine whether a disclosure is reasonably adequate to allow for informed consent. Rule 1.0(e) identifies that informed consent is characterized by: 1) agreement to a proposed course of conduct, 2) after the lawyer has communicated adequate information and explanation about the material risks, and 3) the lawyer has proposed reasonably available alternatives to the proposed course of conduct. The language of the agreement is a primary source for determining whether or not a particular client's consent is informed.

The waiver language at issue in this case is found in V & E's 2003 engagement letter. First, the 2003 engagement letter identifies a course of conduct with regard to concurrent conflicts of interest. Second, the engagement letter includes an explanation of the material risk in waiving future conflicts of interest. Third, the letter explains an alternative course of conduct for Galderma. All of these favor a finding that Galderma's agreement manifested informed consent.

The Court concludes that the waiver in the 2003 engagement letter is reasonably adequate to allow clients in some circumstances to understand the material risk of waiving future conflicts of interest. The language discloses a course of conduct for determining when V & E will be disqualified, explains the material risk that V & E may be directly adverse to the client, and explains an alternative, that the client need not hire V & E if it does not wish to consent. The Court must next examine Galdermas' sophistication and whether Galderma was independently represented in the waiver to determine whether or not the disclosure provided was reasonably adequate to allow Galderma to understand the material risks of waiving future conflicts.

2. Whether V & E's Disclosure Is Reasonably Adequate for Galderma to Form Informed Consent

For the general, open-ended waiver to be valid in this case, V & E must still establish that the disclosure was reasonably adequate to allow Galderma to understand the material risks involved. The communication necessary to obtain informed consent varies with the situation involved. The principal considerations at this point in the analysis are the sophistication of the parties and whether the client was represented by counsel independent of the law firm seeking the waiver. . . .

a. The Client's Sophistication

The parties have disagreed sharply as to whether or not the client's sophistication is relevant to resolving this issue. Galderma argues that the sophistication of the client is not relevant, whereas V & E argues that a client's sophistication is a critical factor.

The Comments to the Model Rules and the ABA Committee on Ethics Opinions state that client sophistication is indeed relevant. A lawyer need not inform a client of facts or implications already known to the client. . . . Thus, the client's existing knowledge affects whether the disclosure in a case is reasonably adequate. Additionally, a client is also sophisticated when "the client . . . is experienced in legal matters generally and in making decisions of the type involved." Normally, such persons need less information and explanation than others. The comments to Model Rule 1.7, specifically dealing with conflicts of interest, also consider the knowledge and experience of the client in determining whether or not a client's consent is effective. . . .

Galderma is a highly sophisticated client. Galderma describes itself as one of the world's leading dermatology companies. In 2011, Galderma and its affiliates reported worldwide sales of 1.4 billion euros, which is approximately 1.87 billion dollars. Galderma is involved in extensive research as part of its normal operations, having filed approximately 5,500 patent applications and patents. Galderma operates worldwide with either R & D centers or manufacturing centers in France, Sweden, Canada, Brazil, Japan, and the United States.

Galderma is also sophisticated in its legal experience. Galderma is presently involved in approximately a dozen different lawsuits, many involving large, complex patent disputes. Galderma litigates in state and federal courts across the country, including Texas, New York, Massachusetts, Florida, Georgia, Illinois, Wisconsin, and Delaware. In doing so, Galderma routinely retains different, large law firms to advise the corporation on various matters across the country including, DLA Piper, Paul Hastings, and V & E. Galderma is experienced in retaining large, national law firms and has signed waivers of future conflicts as part of engaging a national law firm on at least two other occasions, including as recently as February of 2012. Quinton Cassady, who signed the 2003 V & E engagement letter, is the same person who signed engagement letters with DLA Piper which also contained waivers of future conflicts. In one case, Mr. Cassady even initialed the future conflicts waiver portion of an engagement letter. The record in this case demonstrates that Galderma is a client who is highly sophisticated in both legal matters generally and in making decisions to retain large, national firms. This level of sophistication weighs in favor of finding informed consent in this case.

b. *Independent Counsel*

Another related, but different factor the Court considers is whether the client is represented by independent counsel. A client represented by independent counsel needs less information and explanation than others for its consent to be informed. . . . For the purposes of determining informed consent, the effect is the same whether that independent lawyer is inside the client's organization or is other, outside counsel. The importance of this factor is obvious. The ultimate test for determining whether a client gave informed consent is whether the disclosure is reasonably adequate to allow a client to understand the material risks involved. When the client has the benefit of its own lawyer, who is bound by and familiar with the same ethical obligations of the lawyers seeking a waiver, less disclosure is needed to reveal to the independent counsel and its client the consequences of agreeing to the proposed waiver of future conflicts. Another lawyer, who is familiar with the ethical requirements of practicing law, is inherently more informed than even the most sophisticated lay person. . . .

Galderma has its own legal department. Galderma has a general counsel with over 20 years of experience practicing law, who is a member of both the Texas state bar and the federal bar. Galderma relies on its general counsel, Mr. Cassady, and the corporate legal department to give competent legal advice pertaining to complex legal matters. Mr. Cassady, as an inside counsel, is [a] lawyer *independent* from V & E, advising Galderma on whether or not Galderma should give its consent. . . .

Mr. Cassady claims now that he did not intend to consent to V & E representing a generic drug manufacturer when he signed the 2003 engagement letter. The language in the Model Rules is clear; informed consent turns on an objective standard of reasonable disclosure and reasonable understanding. . . . [W]hen a sophisticated party is represented by independent counsel, a general, open-ended waiver is still likely to be reasonably adequate disclosure.

3. Whether Galderma Gave Informed Consent to the Waiver of Future Conflicts of Interest

V & E's disclosure is general and open-ended. In many cases, and for many clients, the disclosure in this case would likely not be reasonably adequate to allow a client to make an informed decision. Even though general, the disclosure language does lay out a course of action for when V & E would be disqualified for a conflict of interest and when not. The disclosure warns in plain language that Galderma's consent means V & E may appear directly adverse to Galderma in litigation, the very risk of which Galderma now claims they were not made aware. Galderma is a sophisticated client who has experience engaging multiple large law firms and has twice signed similar waiver provisions with at least one other law firm it has hired. Finally, having the benefit of its own independent counsel to advise Galderma on what the language meant, Galderma, through its own counsel, chose to sign the engagement letter which included the waiver of future conflicts.

Given the 2002 amendment to the Model Rules on informed consent and waivers of future conflicts, the authority related to those changes, and the evidence in this case, the Court concludes that Galderma gave informed consent to V & E's representation of clients directly adverse to Galderma in substantially unrelated litigation. Because V & E's representation of Actavis falls within the scope of that informed consent, V & E is not disqualified from representing Actavis.

III. Conclusion

Galderma gave informed consent for V & E to represent other clients in litigation directly adverse to Galderma, subject to the limitations specifically identified in the waiver language. V & E's representation of Actavis falls within the scope of that informed consent. Therefore, V & E's representation of Actavis is not a violation of ethical standards, and disqualification is not warranted.

The following Scenario illustrates a common dilemma faced by attorneys and law firms in these times of lawyer mobility and mega-firms.

SCENARIO

Alexandra Franco graduated from the University of Missouri-Columbia School of Law in 2013.[78] After graduation, she joined the St. Louis law firm of Delaney Gibbs & Showater, L.L.C. as an Associate in the firm's real estate section. In the Spring of 2014, Franco worked on the sale of real estate—a

---

[78] Of course, the narrative as set forth in this Scenario, like the other Scenarios in this text, is fictitious.

shopping center—from her firm's client Fendum Associates L.P. to Luger Properties, Inc. As the junior lawyer on the transaction, Franco conducted legal research, wrote a legal memorandum on a zoning-related issue to the firm's partner (Teresa Fielding) working on the transaction, drafted some of the minor closing documents, and met with the two general partners of Fendum Associates L.P. on one twenty minute occasion when Fielding was also present. The transaction timely closed without undue complication.

One year later, Franco elected to leave Delaney Gibbs & Showater to join another St. Louis law firm, Olendar & Shawnessey, P.C., as an Associate. A $20,000 signing bonus, $10,000 increase in annual salary and the opportunity to have more "hands-on" experience are the key inducements. After joining Olendar & Shawnessey, Franco learns that the firm's client Luger Properties, Inc., has sued Fendum Associates L.P. in Missouri state court alleging breach of contract, misrepresentation, and fraud in the real estate shopping center transaction that Franco had worked on while at Delaney Gibbs & Showater.

Upon discovering Franco's prior representation of Fendum Associates L.P., Olendar & Shawnessey promptly "screens" her from all contact with the subject litigation. Instructions are sent to all attorneys and employees of the firm that absolutely no communication should be made to Franco regarding this matter. Franco's office located in the firm's real estate section is in the same building, three floors above the litigation section's offices.

Shortly thereafter, Delaney Gibbs & Showater, on behalf of its client Fendum Associates L.P., files a motion to disqualify the Olendar & Shawnessey firm in the subject litigation. Should the law firm be disqualified under applicable ethical standards? What are the policies implicated?

Should there be a different result if Franco's prior employment had been with a government agency? Suppose, for example, that prior to being an Associate at Delaney Gibbs & Showater, Franco was a staff attorney in the Missouri Attorney General's Department. She participated actively in a staff investigation that focused on suspicious real estate dealings by Fendum Associates L.P. After the investigation was completed, Franco joins Delaney Gibbs & Showater as an Associate. Six months later, the State of Missouri institutes an action alleging fraud against Fendum Associates L.P. Assuming that Franco is effectively and promptly "screened," should Delaney Gibbs & Showater be disqualified from representing Fendum Associates L.P. in this litigation?

SCENARIO IX

BUSINESS ATTORNEY AS LITIGATOR IN CORPORATE SETTINGS

■ ■ ■

In the popular culture view of the American legal system, an attorney is seen as an aggressive advocate, using every conceivable tactic to benefit his client. While those involved in the legal profession realize that this pop-culture view of an attorney is limited to some extent by legal ethics and rules of conduct, there is some underlying truth to the zealous advocate persona. In fact, this "truth" is incorporated in the "zeal in advocacy" terminology used in the American Bar Association's (ABA) Model Rules of Professional Conduct.[1]

The Model Rules give guidance to the attorney with respect to how to zealously, yet ethically, represent a client. After all, an attorney has duties both to the client and the court—private and public duties if you will.[2] The foundation of a lawyer's duties to a client is encapsulated in Model Rules 1.1 and 1.3. Rule 1.1 provides that "[a] lawyer shall provide competent representation to a client" and competence requires "the legal knowledge, skill, thoroughness, and preparation reasonably necessary for the representation."[3] Furthermore, Rule 1.3 provides that "[a] lawyer shall act with reasonable diligence and promptness in representing a client."[4] The lawyer should "take whatever lawful and ethical measures are required to vindicate a client's cause" acting "with commitment and dedication to the interests of the

---

[1] Comment 1 to Rule 1.3 of the Model Rules of Professional Conduct states in part: "A lawyer should pursue a matter on behalf of a client despite opposition, obstruction or personal inconvenience to the lawyer, and take whatever lawful and ethical measures are required to vindicate a client's cause or endeavor. A lawyer must also act . . . with zeal in advocacy upon the client's behalf."

[2] *See* Wendel, *Rediscovering Discovery Ethics*, 79 Marq. L. Rev. 895, 899 (1996).

[3] Model Rule 1.1.

[4] Model Rule 1.1.

client and with zeal in advocacy upon the client's behalf."[5] However, as a modest check on the potentially overzealous advocate who may be tempted to use abusive litigation tactics, a Comment to Model Rule 1.3 provides that the "lawyer is not bound . . . to press for every advantage that might be realized for a client."[6]

On the other side of the equation, the attorney has responsibilities as an officer of the court and representative of the public interest. The basis for this "public duty" is a lawyer's duty to "make reasonable efforts to expedite litigation consistent with the interests of the client" which includes avoiding the use of dilatory practices.[7] Practices that are done merely to frustrate the opposing party's attempt to seek redress are generally not considered reasonable.[8] Two significant areas of abusive litigation tactics are the filing of frivolous claims and abuse of the discovery process.

With respect to the first area, two main regulatory sources have developed to deal with the subject of frivolous filings. First, Rule 3.1 of the Model Rules provides that an attorney may not assert a claim, argument, or defense unless there exists "a basis in law and fact . . . that is not frivolous" or "a good faith argument for an extension, modification, or reversal of existing law."[9] The second source is based on Rule 11 of the Federal Rules of Civil Procedure (FRCP).[10] While FRCP Rule 11 applies

---

[5] *Id.* Rule 1.3 cmt. 1.

[6] Id.

[7] Id. Rule 3.2 & cmt. 1.

[8] Id. Comment 1 states in part:

"Nor will a failure to expedite be reasonable if done for the purpose of frustrating an opposing party's attempt to obtain rightful redress or repose. It is not a justification that similar conduct is often tolerated by the bench and bar. The question is whether a competent lawyer acting in good faith would regard the course of action as having some substantial purpose other than delay."

For a recent case abroad involving attorney misconduct, see *Boreh v. Republic of Djibouti,* [2015] EWHC 769 (Comm) (Queen's Bench 2015) (submission of false affidavits by legal counsel).

[9] See Model Rule 3.1.

[10] FRCP Rule 11(b) states:

"By presenting to the court (whether by signing, filing, submitting, or later advocating) a pleading, written motion, or other paper, an

only to proceedings in federal court, many states have adopted comparable provisions.[11] Therefore, both the rules of civil procedure and the rules of professional conduct within a jurisdiction often are relevant to the issue of frivolous filings.[12]

At their heart, both FRCP 11 and Model Rule 3.1 require that an attorney's assertions and arguments have a basis in law and fact that is not frivolous or that make a non-frivolous argument for a modification of the existing law.[13] A non-frivolous basis in law or fact has not been precisely defined but it is based on the concept that the claim as filed must allege a

---

attorney or unrepresented party is certifying that to the best of the person's knowledge, information, and belief, formed after an inquiry reasonable under the circumstances,—

(1) it is not being presented for any improper purpose, such as to harass or to cause unnecessary delay or needless increase in the cost of litigation;

(2) the claims, defenses, and other legal contentions therein are warranted by existing law or by a nonfrivolous argument for the extension, modification, or reversal of existing law or the establishment of new law;

(3) the allegations and other factual contentions have evidentiary support or, if specifically so identified, are likely to have evidentiary support after a reasonable opportunity for further investigation or discovery; and

(4) the denials of factual contentions are warranted on the evidence or, if specifically so identified, are reasonably based on a lack of information or belief."

[11] Crystal, *Limitations on Zealous Representation in an Adversarial System*, 32 Wake Forest L. Rev. 671, 679 (1997). Note that administrative agencies may discipline litigation attorneys based on unethical or improper professional conduct. Such misconduct encompasses suborning perjury, document destruction, and obstructing the government investigation. *See* Hill, *Divide and Conquer: SEC Discipline of Litigation Attorneys,* 22 Geo. J. Leg. Eth. 373, 376–377 (2009).

[12] Note that there are a number of other statutes that take aim at frivolous or vexatious litigation, including but not limited to 15 U.S.C. '77z–1 (enacted as part of the Private Securities Litigation Act, requiring the court to make findings whether each attorney complied with FRCP Rule 11(b) and to assess appropriate sanctions for violation thereof); 28 U.S.C. '1927 (authorizing sanctions against an attorney "who so multiplies the proceedings in any case unreasonably and vexatiously"); 28 U.S.C. '1912 and Fed. R. App. Proc. Rule 38 (frivolous appeals); and Model Rules of Prof. Conduct Rule 3.4(d) (discovery). For additional discussion regarding federal and state statutory responses to vexatious litigation, *see* Schiller & Wertkin, *Frivolous Filings and Vexatious Litigation*, 14 Geo. J. Legal Ethics 909 (2001).

[13] *See* FRCP Rule 11(b)(2) and Model Rule 3.1.

set of facts that, under the settled law of the jurisdiction, will provide a chance of success for the filing party to prevail on the issue.[14] When a clear reading of the law shows that a plaintiff lacks standing or that no remedy is available, then this rule has likely been violated. For example, a situation which would almost certainly provide no chance for success is a clear case of res judicata or collateral estoppel.[15]

Nonetheless, both Model Rule 3.1 and FRCP 11 take into account the harried pace of a litigator's schedule, particularly at the early stages of a lawsuit. First, they both provide leeway for an attorney to escape a non-meritorious filing violation due to that the facts have not been fully developed prior to filing. Commentary to Rule 3.1, for example, provides that a filing "is not frivolous merely because the facts have not first been fully substantiated or because the lawyer expects to develop vital evidence only by discovery."[16] This principle is coupled, however, with counsel's duty to undertake a reasonable inquiry.[17] Hence, a poorly conceived legal theory, coupled with a complete failure to investigate, will subject an attorney to possible sanctions.[18]

---

[14] *See* Crystal, *supra* note 11, 32 Wake Forest L. Rev. at 681. Professor Crystal argues that the appropriate measure for a "chance of success" should be somewhere between a de minimus chance of success and a substantial chance of success. Toward the upper end of this spectrum, a substantial chance of success, he defines "as a probability of at least a twenty-five percent chance of success." At the lower end (a de minimus chance), he quotes private correspondence between Judge Frank Easterbrook, currently on the U.S. Court of Appeals, and Professor Sanford Levinson: "99 of 100 practicing lawyers would be 99% sure that the position is untenable, and the other 1% would be 60% sure it's untenable." Levinson, *Frivolous Cases: Do Lawyers Know Anything At All?*, 24 Osgoode Hall L.J. 353, 375 (1987) (quoting letter of January 29, 1986 written by Judge Easterbrook to Professor Levinson).

[15] *See In re Watson*, 121 P.3d 982, 986 (Kan. 2005) (lawyer violated Kansas Rule of Professional Conduct 3.1 when he filed a case based on the same legal theories that had been advanced and dismissed in a previous filing).

[16] Model Rule 3.1 cmt. 2. *See* FRCP Rule 11(b)(3), quoted in note 10 *supra*.

[17] Model Rule 3.1 cmt 2. As the Commentary to Rule 3.1 recognizes, attorneys representing criminal defendants are given more leeway "in presenting a claim or defense that otherwise would be prohibited by this Rule." *Id*. cmt. 3.

[18] *See Jones v. Illinois Central Railway Company*, 617 F.3d 843, 856 (6th Cir. 2010) (affirming attorney sanctions where counsel improperly failed to investigate pertinent facts); *Thunberg v. Strause*, 682 A.2d 295, 299–302 (Pa.

But how much investigation or inquiry is reasonable? Courts will assess what a reasonable, similarly-situated attorney would have done, looking to factors such as how much time was available for the attorney to conduct her inquiry, to what extent the attorney relied on her client's statements, whether the attorney took over a case from another attorney, how susceptible the underlying facts are to discovery, and the complexity of the factual and legal issues.[19] For instance, in *CTC Imports*, an attorney faced sanctions for filing a complaint seeking the seizure of a Nigerian oil tanker docked in Pennsylvania.[20] As it turned out, the client's ownership documents for the tanker were forged.[21] The *client* knew of this forgery *prior to* the filing of the seizure suit but failed to relay this information to the attorney.[22] The court, in overturning the attorney's sanctions, reasoned that because the attorney had only a 24-hour period within which to seek the seizure of the tanker, he was reasonable in relying on his client's initial assertion of ownership and had not failed in his duty to investigate.[23]

1996) (Plaintiff's attorney in car crash suit advanced a "failure to avoid" theory asserting that defendant's use of a cell phone while driving caused him to negligently fail to avoid the plaintiff's car as it came over a median into defendant's lane of traffic and crashed head-on into defendant's car. Plaintiff's attorney admitted that over a two year period between the accident and the filing of the suit, he did no investigation other than to talk to the plaintiff and read the police report. Interestingly, in this case, the court entered the judgment only against the plaintiff, even though it was the attorney who proposed the questionable "failure to avoid" theory.).

[19] *CTC Imports & Exports v. Nigerian Petroleum Corp.*, 951 F.2d 573, 578 (3d Cir. 1991), *cert. denied,* 504 U.S. 914 (1992). *See also, Sanchez v. Liberty Lloyds*, 672 So. 2d 268, 272 (La. Ct. App. 1996) (Attorney for car crash defendant's insurance company was sanctioned for answering a plaintiff's interrogatories with a general denial, where simply talking to the insured party would have shown that the defendant was responsible for the accident. The appellate court overturned the sanctions based on three key considerations. First, the attorney was dealing with a heavy volume of case files. Secondly, by the time he examined the insured's case file, his client insurance company was in danger of losing contribution from a co-plead defendant. Lastly, the general denial was not harassing in that it did not cause any delay or increase the cost of litigation.).

[20] *CTC Imports*, 951 F.2d at 575.

[21] *Id.* at 578.

[22] *Id.*

[23] *Id.* at 579.

However, it is not proper for an attorney to continue an action after she has learned that it has no merit. This can have serious ramifications, as seen in the disbarment case of an attorney who practiced in Missouri and Kansas.[24] The subject lawyer was charged by the Missouri Chief Disciplinary Counsel on four counts of sanctionable misconduct.[25] One of these counts involved wrongful discharge claims and slander claims filed against General Motors (GM) on behalf of two former GM employees in a federal court.[26] Even though the attorney knew that the employees had signed documents releasing GM from employment-related claims, she filed suit without ever looking at the documents.[27] For the same clients, the attorney also advanced a slander claim against GM even though the only witness stated in an affidavit that GM had never spoken to her regarding the employees.[28] In the federal sanctions action, the court found that this lack of a basis in law and fact for the claims, combined with a complete failure to investigate, showed that the claims were filed for improper purposes.[29] Not only did the lawyer fail to withdraw the cases, but she pushed forward and "papered" General Motors with voluminous discovery requests.[30] The attorney's actions in this case not only resulted in a $50,000 monetary sanction imposed by the federal court but also contributed to her disbarment.[31]

A proper course of action in such a situation would be to terminate the case once it is sufficiently clear that the claims are not factually supported. Arguably, this is the policy behind the safe-harbor provision in FRCP 11, which provides 21 days for an attorney to withdraw or amend a pleading upon receiving notification that sanctions will be sought.[32] This pattern of file-

---

[24] *In re Caranchini*, 956 S.W.2d 910 (Mo. 1997).

[25] *Id.* at 911.

[26] *Id.* at 915 (referring to the court's findings in the underlying federal sanctions proceeding in *White v. General Motors Corp.*, 126 F.R.D. 563 (Kan. 1989)).

[27] *White*, 126 F.R.D. at 565–566.

[28] *Id.*

[29] *Id.* at 566–567.

[30] *Id.*

[31] *Caranchini*, 956 S.W.2d at 915–919.

[32] *See* FRCP Rule 11(c)(1)(A). *But see* Brown, *Ending Illegitimate Advocacy: Reinvigorating Rule 11 Through Enhancement of the Ethical Duty*

investigate-dismiss is seen in *Lawyer Disciplinary Board v. Neely*.[33] In this case, an attorney initially was admonished by the state disciplinary board for filing a non-meritorious claim under the West Virginia Rules of Professional Conduct.[34] In the underlying claim, the attorney filed intentional battery and infliction of emotional distress counts on the client's behalf against a childcare provider.[35] The claims were based on allegations that an autistic child had been left alone in a dark room on multiple occasions for many hours at a time, when in actuality, the client knew of a single instance which lasted a few minutes.[36] When interviews with additional employees of the childcare provider exposed the allegations as overstated, the claims were dismissed.[37] The appellate court reversed the disciplinary board's decision, finding that the attorney did a reasonable post-filing investigation and took proper action to dismiss the claim once the true facts were uncovered.[38]

Another possible "escape" for the allegedly non-meritorious filing is the opportunity for the attorney to present a "good-faith" or "nonfrivolous" argument for an extension, reversal, or modification of the law.[39] In the case of *In re Boone*, the attorney filed a wrongful termination suit on his client's behalf under the American with Disabilities Act (ADA).[40] However, his client was fired prior to the effective date of the ADA; therefore, there was purportedly no factual and legal basis for recovery.[41] Nonetheless, the attorney argued that the suit arose under a continued course of conduct which gave rise to a "quasi-retroactive" theory of recovery.[42] The Kansas Supreme Court viewed this reasoning as a good-faith argument for an extension

---

to Report, 62 Ohio St. L.J. 1555 (2001) (proposing measures to curtail the abuse of the 21–day "safe harbor" provision).

[33] 528 S.E.2d 468 (W. Va. 1998).

[34] *Id.* at 471.

[35] *Id.*

[36] *Id.*

[37] *Id.* at 473–474.

[38] Id. at 474.

[39] Model Rule 3.1 provides that the argument must be made in "good faith." FRCP 11(b)(2) provides that the argument must be "nonfrivolous."

[40] *In re Boone*, 7 P.3d 270 (Kan. 2000).

[41] *Id.* at 280.

[42] *Id.* at 282.

of the law, and therefore cleared attorney Boone of the alleged violation.[43]

Interestingly, in the *Boone* case, the Kansas court applied an objective standard to the question of whether the change-of-law argument was made in good-faith, following the objective standard used in FRCP 11 cases.[44] Arguably, however, when the drafters of the Model Rules used the phrase "good faith argument," they intended that a subjective standard should apply.[45] When the Rules were amended in 2002, the drafters decided not to change the language, reasoning that the states that had adopted the Model Rules were applying the proper standard.[46] Nonetheless, as states adopt versions of the amended Model Rules, they may follow the lead of Kansas as well as FRCP 11 and substitute an objective standard.

A more recent and higher profile case shows the complexity of identifying what is a reasonable argument for a modification of the law, particularly in view of the complex body of statutory law in the United States. *Merrill Lynch, Pierce, Fenner & Smith, Inc. v. Dabit* involved a class action suit brought in state court alleging, among other things, that Merrill Lynch clients suffered investment losses when they relied on overly optimistic and fraudulent research opinions issued by the investment firm's analysts in deciding to retain their stock holdings during the market downturn of the late 1990s.[47] During the pendency of the action, Merrill Lynch had successfully blocked the case from proceeding by relying on two interrelated arguments. First, the U. S. Supreme Court's decision in *Blue Chip Stamps v. Manor Drug Stores* limited standing of private claimants in suits alleging federal securities laws violations under Section 10(b) of the Securities Exchange Act to actual purchasers or sellers of

[43] *Id.*

[44] *Id.* at 281. *See Business Guides, Inc. v. Chromatic Communications Enterprises, Inc.,* 498 U.S. 533, 551 (1991).

[45] Love, *The Revised ABA Model Rules of Professional Conduct: Summary of the Work of Ethics 2000,* 15 Geo. J. Leg. Eth. 441, 464 (2002) ("Ethics 2000"). Ms. Love's interpretation of the drafters' intent is pertinent since she was a member of the Ethics 2000 Commission.

[46] *Id. But see Lawyer Disciplinary Board v. Neely,* 528 S.E. 2d 468, 473 (W. Va. 1998) ("With the adoption of the Rules of Professional Conduct, and more specifically Rule 3.1, an objective standard was established to determine the propriety of pleadings and other court papers.").

[47] 547 U.S. 71 (2006).

the subject security.[48] Second, with certain exceptions not here relevant, the Securities Litigation Uniform Standards Act of 1998 (SLUSA) prohibits class action lawsuits brought under *state law* involving a nationally traded security[49] that "alleg[e] a misrepresentation or omission of a material fact in connection with the purchase or sale of [such] security."[50] The first limitation precluded the plaintiff class from bringing a suit under federal law for the alleged fraud since the class members were "holders" and not purchasers or sellers of the subject securities; the second limitation arguably preempted the class' ability to bring a state law fraud claim on the basis that the alleged fraud implicated the purchase or sale of a nationally traded security. In an effort to steer clear of these limitations and to keep the state courthouse doors open to the class action, the plaintiff class was sought to be defined to exclude those Merrill Lynch clients who had purchased or sold the securities in question during the applicable time period of the suit, thereby seeking to avoid the "purchase or sale" language of the governing statutes.[51] Nonetheless, the U.S. Supreme Court rejected the plaintiffs' argument, interpreting the "purchase or sale" language of SLUSA to extend the preemption of state law class actions in this context to holders (namely, to those who held, rather than sold, their securities allegedly due to knowingly false rosy opinions).[52] The Court relied heavily on the

---

[48] 421 U.S. 723, 755 (1975). Section 10(b) provides: "It shall be unlawful for any person . . . [t]o use or employ, in connection with the purchase or sale of any security registered on a national securities exchange or any security not so registered . . . any manipulative or deceptive device or contrivance in contravention of such rules and regulations as the Commission may prescribe as necessary or appropriate in the public interest or for the protection of investors." *See generally* M. Steinberg, *Securities Regulation* 463–623 (6th ed. 2013).

[49] Under SLUSA, a nationally traded security includes, for example, a security listed on the New York Stock Exchange or traded on the NASDAQ National Market System (NMS). Exceptions to SLUSA, for example, include individual actions, derivative suits and class actions implicating tender offers, mergers, going-private transactions, and the exercise of appraisal rights.

[50] 15 U.S.C. § 78bb(f)(1).

[51] *Dabit*, 547 U.S. at 76.

[52] *Id.* at 89.

desire of Congress, in enacting SLUSA, to reduce "wasteful, duplicative litigation."[53]

Turning to a second major area of litigation abuse—discovery abuse—ABA Model Rule 3.4(d) enumerates two categories of discovery process violation: making frivolous discovery requests and failing to make reasonable efforts to respond to the opposition's lawful discovery requests.[54]

In most jurisdictions, the rules of procedure provide ample guidance to theoretically curb an attorney's vexatious use of discovery. For instance, under the Federal Rules of Civil Procedure, litigants are required to make extensive initial disclosures,[55] follow a discovery plan developed under the guidance of the court,[56] and adhere to specific limits with regard to each discovery mechanism.[57] In states that follow the FRCP model of controlled discovery, the days of thousand question interrogatories (absent a court-approved plan to set aside these limits) are infrequent.[58]

However, even within these specific limits, a litigant may seek discovery of matters that are remotely relevant to the claim or defense of either party, so long as the requests are not unreasonably cumulative, duplicative, or burdensome.[59] Combining this broad and liberal definition of what material is discoverable[60] with the possibility of expansive requests for

---

[53] *Id.* at 86.

[54] Rule 3.4(d) of the Model Rules provides that an attorney "shall not . . . in pretrial procedure, make a frivolous discovery request or fail to make reasonably diligent effort to comply with a legally proper discovery request by an opposing party."

[55] *See* FRCP Rule 26(a)(1).

[56] *Id.* Rule 26(f).

[57] FRCP Rules 28 to 32 define rules and limits for depositions of a party or third persons; Rule 33 applies to written interrogatories; Rule 34 applies to production of documents; Rule 35 applies to physical or mental examinations; and Rule 36 applies to requests for admissions.

[58] *See Vendola Corp. v. Hershey Chocolate Corp.*, 1 F.R.D. 359 (S.D.N.Y. 1949) (plaintiff served interrogatories with more than 1,100 questions for defendant chocolate companies).

[59] *See* FRCP Rules 26(b)(1); 26(b)(2)(i); 26(b)(2)(iii).

[60] The discussion of the scope of discoverable material is a book unto itself. It should be sufficient for the purposes of this discussion to point out that while the amendments to Rule 26(b) in 2000 narrowed the scope by changing the outer bounds of discoverable material from any "subject matter involved in the pending action" to any material "relevant to the claim or

document production, there is still an avenue for overwhelming an opponent with discovery paperwork. This concern for discovery abuse was part of the rationale invoked by then-Justice Rehnquist in limiting standing in Section 10(b) securities fraud actions:[61]

> "The prospect of extensive deposition of the defendant's officers and associates, and the concomitant opportunity for extensive discovery of business documents, is a common occurrence in this and similar types of litigation. To the extent that this process eventually produces relevant evidence which is useful in determining the merits of the claims asserted by the parties, it bears the imprimatur of those Rules and of the many cases liberally interpreting them. But to the extent that it permits a plaintiff with a largely groundless claim to simply take up the time of a number of other people, with the right to do so representing an in terrorem increment of the settlement value, rather than a reasonably founded hope that the process will reveal relevant evidence, it is a social cost rather than a benefit."[62]

Conflicts over the propriety of discovery tactics usually ripen into dispute upon the failure of one party to adequately respond to the discovery requests of another. While discovery violations are often characterized by a continual and repeated failure to follow the discovery-related orders of the court[63] or egregious

---

defense of any party," the realm of discoverable material is still much broader than what would be admissible at trial under a jurisdiction's rules of evidence. *See* Gensler, *Some Thoughts on the Lawyer's E-volving Duties in Discovery,* 36 N. Ky. L. Rev. 521 (2009); Thornburg, *Giving the "Haves" a Little More: Considering the 1998 Discovery Proposals,* 52 SMU L. Rev. 229, 238 (1999).

[61] *Blue Chip Stamps v. Manor Drug Stores,* 421 U.S. 723 (1975).

[62] *Id.* at 741.

[63] *See In re Seroquel Products Liability Litigation,* 244 F.R.D. 650, 666 (M.D. Fla. 2007) (finding sanctions warranted based on company's failure timely to produce reasonably accessible e-documents); *In re Boone,* 7 P.3d 270, 283 (Kan. 2000) (The subject attorney was given two-years suspended probation for repeatedly failing to meet discovery deadlines, failing to request additional time, and failing to fax documents to opposing attorney after stating that he would do so.).

behavior during the deposition process,[64] there are still gray zones of the discovery process where the potential for abuse may be difficult to discern.[65] One example of this area of confusion is the case of *Washington State Physicians Insurance Exchange & Association v. Fisons Corporation (Fisons)*.[66]

The dispute in *Fisons* was related to a medical products liability suit.[67] Fisons Corporation made two medications for

---

[64] The following example illustrates egregious, yet unpunished, disrespect of another party in *Paramount Communications v. QVC Network*, 637 A.2d 34, 53–54 (Del. 1994):

> "MR. JOHNSTON [to Mr. Joe Jamail's client]: Okay. Do you have any idea why Mr. Oresman was calling that material to your attention?
>
> MR. JAMAIL: Don't answer that. How would he know what was going on in Mr. Oresman's mind? Don't answer it. Go on to your next question.
>
> MR. JOHNSTON: No, Joe–
>
> MR. JAMAIL: He's not going to answer that. Certify it. I'm going to shut it down if you don't go to your next question.
>
> MR. JOHNSTON: No. Joe, Joe–
>
> MR. JAMAIL: Don't "Joe" me, a_____. You can ask some questions, but get off of that. I'm tired of you. You could gag a maggot off a meat wagon. Now, we've helped you every way we can.
>
> MR. JOHNSTON: Let's just take it easy.
>
> MR. JAMAIL: No, we're not going to take it easy. Get done with this.
>
> MR. JOHNSTON: We will go on to the next question.
>
> MR. JAMAIL: Do it now.
>
> MR. JOHNSTON: We will go on to the next question. We're not trying to excite anyone.
>
> MR. JAMAIL: Come on. Quit talking. Ask the question. Nobody wants to socialize with you.
>
> MR. JOHNSTON: I'm not trying to socialize. We'll go on to another question. We're continuing the deposition.
>
> MR. JAMAIL: Well, go on and shut up."

In 1987, the Texas Supreme Court adopted "The Texas Lawyer's Creed—A Mandate for Professionalism," which augments the Texas Disciplinary Rules of Professional Conduct. The Creed includes provisions defining appropriate attorney conduct. These provisions include:

> "I will not quarrel over matters of form or style.
>
> I will avoid disparaging personal remarks or acrimony towards opposing counsel.
>
> I will abstain from any allusions to personal peculiarities or idiosyncrasies of opposing counsel."

[65] *See* Wendel, *supra* note 2, 79 Marq. L. Rev. at 907.

[66] 858 P.2d 1054 (Wash. 1993).

[67] *Id.* at 1054.

opening children's bronchial passageways—Intal and Somophyllin Oral Liquid (the medication which caused the injury).[68] After taking the Somophyllin liquid, a two-year old child suffered brain damage due to high levels of theophylline (the primary drug in the Somophyllin medication). The prescribing doctor, who was a co-defendant in the products liability case, settled with the child's family before the trial began.[69] After settling, the doctor discovered that Fisons had failed to disclose two "smoking gun" documents which would have cleared the doctor from liability.[70] The doctor subsequently brought a motion for sanctions against Fisons for abusing the discovery process.[71] The documents, which were contained within Fisons' Intal product files rather than its Somophyllin product files, demonstrated the potential for Somophyllin to cause dangerous levels of theophyllin toxicity within children.[72] During discovery, Fisons routinely resisted discovery requests for documents relating to Intal and medications other than Somophyllin, arguing that such discovery requests were overly broad.[73] Fisons' legal counsel defended their actions by arguing that they were ethically required to construe the discovery requests as narrowly as possible, thereby invoking the zealous advocate rationale.[74] The court rejected this argument, reasoning that under the attorneys' interpretation no conceivable request could have uncovered the relevant documents,[75] hence constituting abuse of the discovery process.[76]

---

[68] *Id.* at 1080.

[69] *Id.* at 1074.

[70] *Id.*

[71] *Id.*

[72] *Id.* at 1080 (Fisons Corporation's Intal marketing manager evidently used the information about the theophylline toxicity danger associated with Somophyllin in his efforts to market Intal as an alternative medication.).

[73] *Id.*

[74] *Id.* at 1083.

[75] *Id.*

[76] *Id.* The Washington Supreme Court upheld an award against Fisons Corporation of over $1 million for damage to the doctor's reputation and $450,000 in attorney's fees. In addition, the Court remanded the case to the trial court for a determination of appropriate sanctions for the discovery abuses. See id. at 1059–1060, 1085. Bogle & Gates, the firm representing Fisons Corporation, agreed to pay a $325,000 fine and make a public admission of its mistake. Zitrin & Langford, *The Moral Compass: Calculated*

Effectively, the court rejected the reasoning that zealous advocacy warrants the use of vexatious and dilatory discovery practices.[77] The *Fisons* decision illustrates how some courts will not allow attorneys to justify vexatious discovery practices by standing behind the "zeal in advocacy" language of Model Rule 1.3.[78]

While an attorney should be aware of the rules that govern her conduct in the litigation context (and the corresponding threat of sanctions or disciplinary proceedings), her client may not share the same enthusiasm for abiding by these rules. After all, it is the client's money and perhaps livelihood at stake in the litigation; therefore, the client may feel that she should call all the shots. Model Rule 1.2 seeks to address this tension by clarifying the division of decisionmaking power between an attorney and her client.

ABA Model Rule 1.2(a) provides that "a lawyer shall abide by a client's decisions concerning the objectives of representation and, as required by Rule 1.4, shall consult with the client as to the means by which they are to be pursued."[79] The drafters of

---

Malfeasance, Law News Network (May 7, 1999), available at http://www.law. com.

[77] *Fisons*, 858 P.2d at 1085. *See Thomas E. Hoar, Inc. v. Sara Lee Corp.*, 900 F.2d 522, 528 (2d Cir. 1990) (In a breach of contract case, plaintiff and counsel were sanctioned multiple times for a total of more than $35,000 for failure to comply with court-prescribed discovery process and opposing counsel's legitimate discovery requests. The court emphatically rejected the attorney's contention that his ethical duty to zealously represent his client required the vexatious discovery practices.).

[78] Model Rule 1.3 cmt. 1.

[79] Model Rules of Prof. Conduct, Rule 1.2(a) states: "Subject to paragraphs (c) and (d), a lawyer shall abide by a client's decisions concerning the objectives of representation and, as required by Rule 1.4, shall consult with the client as to the means by which they are to be pursued. A lawyer may take such action on behalf of the client as is impliedly authorized to carry out the representation. A lawyer shall abide by a client's decision whether to settle a matter. . . ." Comment 1 to Model Rule 1.2 states: "With respect to the means by which the client's objectives are to be pursued, the lawyer shall consult with the client as required by Rule 1.4(a)(2) and may take such action as is impliedly authorized to carry out the representation." Model Rule 1.4(a)(2) requires counsel to "reasonably consult with the client about the means by which the client's objectives are to be accomplished." Comment 3 to Model Rule 1.4 provides that determining what is reasonable consultation will depend on "the importance of the action under consideration and the feasibility of consulting with the client."

the Model Rules thus were attempting to make a clear distinction between the objectives and the means of the representation, leaving the former decisions wholly within the client's domain and the latter a matter of consultation between client and counsel.[80] Because the tactics and strategies used to pursue litigation can dramatically affect a client's substantive rights, in practice the distinction is not precise.[81] The attorney's tactical decisions can result in significant harm to the client.[82] Furthermore, the U. S. Supreme Court has held that parties, in addition to attorneys, can be subject to Rule 11 sanctions.[83] This decision recognizes the client's interest and responsibilities with respect to the strategies and tactics being employed in litigation.[84]

Further adding to the confusion is the language that was added to the Model Rules in 2002 pursuant to recommendation of the American Bar Association's Ethics 2000 Commission ("Commission").[85] The 2002 amendments include that "a lawyer may take such action on behalf of the client as is impliedly authorized to carry out the representation."[86] This addition seems to reinforce that an attorney may make tactical decisions unilaterally, without consulting with the client, so long as the attorney has *implied* authority to do so. While this language invokes agency principles for resolving attorney-client decisionmaking dilemmas and thereby may decrease the clarity of the rule, the Commission sought to clarify this possible confusion by adding Comment 2 to Rule 1.2.[87] Comment 2 suggests that both the attorney and client defer to the knowledge of the other in negotiating the boundaries of decisionmaking authority.[88] But the Comment expressly stopped

---

[80] *See* Barker & Cosentino, *Current Developments 2002–2003: Who's in Charge Here? The Ethics 2000 Approach to Resolving Lawyer-Client Conflicts,* 16 Geo. J. Legal Ethics 505, 507 (2003).

[81] *Id.*

[82] *See Fisons*, 858 P.2d at 1059–1060, 1085.

[83] *Business Guides, Inc. v. Chromatic Communications Enterprises*, 498 U.S. 533 (1991).

[84] *Id.* at 545.

[85] Love, *supra* note 45, 15 Geo. J. Leg. Eth. at 447.

[86] Model Rule 1.2(a).

[87] *See* Barker & Cosentino, *supra* note 80, 16 Geo. J. Leg. Eth. at 512.

[88] Model Rule 1.2 cmt. 2 states: "Clients normally defer to the special knowledge and skill of their lawyer with respect to the means to be used to

short of suggesting a resolution to such conflicts,[89] relying instead on the liberal withdrawal and dismissal rules of Rule 1.16.[90]

If an attorney and his client truly reach an impasse regarding their differences of opinion with respect to the decisions made in the litigation context, either the client or attorney may terminate the relationship.[91] In a civil context, the client has a virtually unchecked ability to discharge her attorney.[92] The attorney in the civil context also has broad discretion in withdrawing from representation, subject to some limitations.[93] To begin with, Model Rule 1.16(b)(1) allows an attorney to withdraw if such withdrawal has no "material adverse effect on the interests of the client."[94] However, even if the client suffers a material adverse effect, the attorney may still have grounds for withdrawal. These grounds include the client's failure to pay for the attorney's services,[95] the client's creation of an unreasonable financial burden on the attorney,[96] the client's insistence on taking action with respect to which the attorney "has a fundamental disagreement,"[97] or if "other good cause for withdrawal exists."[98]

---

accomplish their objectives, particularly with respect to technical, legal and tactical matters. Conversely, lawyers usually defer to the client regarding such questions as the expense to be incurred and concern for third persons who might be adversely affected."

[89] Comment 2 goes on to state: "Because of the varied nature of the matters about which a lawyer and client might disagree . . . this Rule does not prescribe how such disagreements are to be resolved."

[90] Comment 2 continues: "If such efforts are unavailing and the lawyer has a fundamental disagreement with the client, the lawyer may withdraw from the representation. See Rule 1.16(b)(4). Conversely, the client may resolve the disagreement by discharging the lawyer. See Rule 1.16(a)(3)."

[91]   Model Rule 1.16(a)(3), (b)(1), (b)(4), (b)(7), (c).

[92]   Rule 1.16 cmt. 4 states: "A client has a right to discharge a lawyer at any time, with or without cause, subject to liability for payment for the lawyer's services."

[93]   Model Rule 1.16(b) deals with permissive withdrawal of an attorney from representation.

[94]   *Id.* Rule 1.16(b)(1).

[95]   *Id.* Rule 1.16(b)(5).

[96]   *Id.* Rule 1.16(b)(6).

[97]   *Id.* Rule 1.16(b)(4).

[98]   *Id.* Rule 1.16(b)(7).

Accordingly, when the *disagreement* is the grounds for attorney withdrawal, Model Rule 1.16(b)(4) dictates that the attorney may withdraw if "the client insists on taking action that the lawyer considers repugnant or with which the lawyer has a fundamental disagreement."[99] The 2002 amendments to Rule 1.16(b)(4) highlight that this last cause for withdrawal is intended to be read narrowly. Under the previous rule, the attorney could withdraw if she found the client's actions "repugnant or imprudent." The term "imprudent" has been replaced by the phrase "with which the lawyer has a fundamental disagreement." The concepts of "repugnancy" and "fundamental disagreement" both suggest severe discord between the client and counsel.[100] Furthermore, the client must "insist" on a course of action. The mere suggestion of a particular course of action is insufficient to give rise to the lawyer's withdrawal under Rule 1.16(b)(4).[101]

Where the continued representation of a client will result in a violation of a law or a violation of the rules of professional conduct, the attorney is required to withdraw from representation.[102] Thus, the Model Rules distinguish between a situation requiring withdrawal and one giving the attorney the option of withdrawing.[103] For instance, in *Disciplinary Board v. Edwardson*, the North Dakota Supreme Court affirmed sanctions against an attorney for failing to withdraw from representing a client whom the attorney knew had falsified

---

[99]   *Id.* Rule 1.16(b)(4).

[100]   *See* Markovits, *Further Thoughts About Ethics from the Lawyer's Point of View*, 16 Yale J.L. & Human. 85, 103 (2004).

[101]   Nonetheless, depending on the circumstances, the client's conduct may give rise to "other good cause for [the attorney's] withdrawal." Rule 1.16(b)(7). Note that Comment 2 of Rule 1.16 provides: "A lawyer ordinarily must decline or withdraw from representation if the client demands that the lawyer engage in conduct that is illegal or violates the Rules of Professional Conduct or other law. The lawyer is not obliged to decline or withdraw simply because the client suggests such a course of conduct. . . ."

[102]   *See* Rule 1.16(a)(1) (generally, requiring counsel to withdraw from representation of a client "if the representation will result in violation of the rules of professional conduct or other law").

[103]   *Compare* Model Rule 1.16(a)(1) *with* Model Rule 1.16(b)(2) which states that "a lawyer *may* withdraw from representing a client if the client persists in a course of action involving the lawyer's services that the lawyer reasonably believes is criminal or fraudulent."

discovery responses.[104] The court ruled that since the attorney admitted that she knew the client had lied, she was obligated, under North Dakota Rule of Professional Conduct 1.16(a), "to remove herself from the situation to the least detriment of her client."[105]

Hence, the propriety of an attorney's withdrawal may come down to several key questions. First, is the client's suggested course of improper action avoidable or is the client insisting that his demands be followed? Secondly, does the attorney believe that the course of conduct will result in a legal or ethical violation or can such a violation be avoided? Thirdly, even if a violation can be avoided, is the strategy or tactic urged by the client nonetheless so offensive to the attorney's sensibilities that it rises to the level of repugnancy or fundamental disagreement?

The following decision provides a relatively recent example addressing misconduct in the context of discovery production.

KAYNE V. GRANDE HOLDINGS LIMITED
198 Cal. App. 4th 1470 (2011)

ARMSTRONG, J.

The Grande Holdings Limited ("Grande") appeals an order granting the motion of plaintiffs Fred Kayne, et al. ("plaintiffs") for discovery sanctions in the amount of $74,809. Finding no error, we affirm.

FACTUAL AND PROCEDURAL BACKGROUND

Plaintiffs filed a lawsuit in the United States District Court for the Central District of California . . . in which they alleged that MTC Electronics Technologies Co., Ltd. [MTC], Grande's subsidiary, and others violated federal and state laws by failing to disclose material facts in connection with plaintiffs' purchase of MTC securities, among other things. In December 2005, plaintiffs obtained a "net default Partial Final Judgment" in favor of plaintiffs and against MTC in the amount of

---

[104]   647 N.W.2d 126 (N.D. 2002).

[105]   *Id.* at 131. *See In re Hopkins,* 687 A.2d 938 (D.C. 1996) (declining to sanction attorney for failing to withdraw when counsel suspected that her client might engage in illegal conduct).

$37,562,122. In this lawsuit, plaintiffs seek to enforce this judgment, less the amount of certain settlements, against Grande. Plaintiffs allege that MTC, which ceased doing business in 2003, was Grande's alter ego, and that Grande misused or converted MTC's assets over a period of several years before leaving it a judgment-proof shell.

Plaintiffs sought document discovery from Grande in March 2007. Grande responded solely by objecting. Plaintiffs filed a motion to compel on July 2, 2007. The motion was continued, and after Grande's demurrer was overruled, the parties reached an agreement pursuant to which plaintiffs would narrow the request and Grande would produce documents. . . .

Grande produced over 30,000 pages of documents in three tranches. . . . Plaintiffs complained that all but 28 pages were documents which Grande knew plaintiffs already had as a result of discovery demands in other lawsuits against Grande and MTC. Plaintiffs also asserted that entire categories of documents, such as MTC's internal financial and accounting records, or Grande's own ledgers, journals and bank records reflecting transactions with MTC, were not produced. In a series of meet-and-confer sessions, plaintiffs requested, among other things, that Grande describe its search efforts in response to plaintiffs' discovery request.

On March 5, 2009, after Grande neither produced additional documents nor provided an explanation of its efforts to locate the requested documents, plaintiffs filed a motion to enforce the discovery order. While the motion was pending, Grande represented that it would comply with the discovery order and produce additional documents which it had located. In reliance on that representation, plaintiffs agreed to take the motion to enforce off calendar.

Grande thereafter produced approximately 60,000 additional pages of MTC documents in April and May of 2009, which it stated it had only recently uncovered. These consisted of approximately 5,000 pages of a partial computerized general ledger, as well as 55,000 pages of MTC financial, accounting, banking and transaction records, which plaintiffs described as being in complete disorder. When Grande refused plaintiffs' request to label the documents in accordance with [California law], plaintiffs hired three attorneys to organize the documents by category and date, so that they could use them to prepare for upcoming depositions of Grande witnesses.

In August 2009, plaintiffs filed a motion to enforce the discovery order. Plaintiffs sought $74,809 in sanctions . . ., claiming that Grande employed a discovery method in a manner or to an extent that caused undue burden and expense. Grande opposed the motion, claiming it had fully discharged its obligations under the discovery statutes, because the documents were produced in the same state that they had been found by Grande, in plastic bags in a file cabinet in office space which MTC once leased from Grande (and which Grande occupied after MTC's demise). . . .

At a hearing on December 3, 2009, the trial court granted plaintiffs' motion in part, and continued the sanctions motion . . . in order to give Grande an opportunity to provide evidence of the manner in which MTC's documents were kept by Grande between March 2007, when plaintiffs served their discovery request, and their production in 2009.

On January 15, 2010, Grande served the declarations of Bianca Leung, MTC's former controller and a 16-year "Grande Group" employee, and Felicity Porter, Grande's *in-house counsel* (emphasis supplied). These declarations did not, however, provide evidence of when and how Grande "discovered" the documents in storage, or how they had been kept while in Grande's possession and control. Neither declarant had any personal knowledge as to the condition in which the documents were found, or had any explanation for the disorganized condition in which they were produced.

The trial court conducted a hearing on the sanctions motion on March 30, 2010. Initially, the court noted that Grande had been in litigation concerning its alter ego liability for the obligations of MTC since 1998, and since December 15, 2000, was on notice that, if and when plaintiffs received a judgment in their litigation against MTC, they intended to sue Grande on an alter ego theory. The trial court further stated: "I specified in the [December 3, 2009] order that I was ordering defendant to file a client declaration by a person with knowledge regarding the manner in which the documents were kept in March 2007. . . . That is a very specific order, especially given the extremely unusual document production here. On the bell curve of document productions, this one is very near the end of the bell curve. Grande has proffered no satisfactory explanation under oath by a person with knowledge as to why the documents were produced in the fashion that the plaintiffs said they were produced." The trial court ordered Grande to pay the sums plaintiffs incurred to organize the documents, as a sanction for willful abuse of discovery procedure and failure to comply with [California law].

DISCUSSION

Grande challenges the sanctions order. . . . It claims that the trial court abused its discretion in sanctioning Grande for failure to organize the MTC documents, because, as the producer of third-party documents, it had no duty to do so under the discovery statutes. . . .

Grande states that "plaintiffs argued that Grande's 'strategy' of producing documents in a shuffled order has severely prejudiced plaintiffs' ability to adequately prepare for upcoming depositions. However, plaintiffs offered no evidence that Grande did anything to cause MTC's documents to be produced to plaintiffs in a disorganized fashion, let alone as part of a litigation 'strategy.' "

Grande's entire argument is based on the assumption that Grande found the documents at issue in a disordered condition and produced them to plaintiffs in that same disordered condition. Thus, Grande argues that "even if the trial court found that the documents should have been produced in a different order, sanctions are unwarranted because Grande was substantially justified in producing the documents as they were found." In response to the trial court request that Grande provide the declaration of a person with personal knowledge of this alleged fact, Grande offered two declarations of Grande employees with no knowledge of the condition of the documents at the time Grande first obtained possession of them. Thus, there is no evidence in the record that Grande found the documents in a disordered condition. While Grande sought to place the burden of coming forward with this evidence on plaintiffs, the trial court reasonably determined that Grande was the only party who could provide any evidence at all concerning the state of the documents in its possession, custody and control. Because Grande produced no admissible evidence on the subject, the trial court concluded that Grande was responsible for the disordered state of the documents, and acted well within its discretion in ordering Grande to bear the costs of organizing the documents.

As the trial court recounted, Grande had been less than forthcoming in its discovery responses over a period of years. Indeed, the documents here at issue were produced after Grande had represented that it had fully complied with plaintiffs' discovery requests, and only a short time before plaintiffs were scheduled to take the depositions of representatives of Grande and MTC, in preparation for trial. . . .

In sum, plaintiffs incurred substantial costs in organizing the documents which Grande produced in contravention of the requirements of [California law], thereby employing a discovery method in such a manner as to cause undue burden and expense to plaintiffs. . . .

The judgment is affirmed.

SCENARIO

Perry Alesi is a partner for the law firm of Chelsea McBride & Contreras, P.C. which serves as legal counsel for Smithson & Smithson ("S & S"), a leading pharmaceutical giant. Fees paid by S & S to the law firm last year exceeded $2,500,000, making S & S one of the firm's five largest clients. For the last several years, and at the insistence of Jeb Chamel, the CEO of S & S, Alesi has been the "lead chair" on all significant S & S litigation. One of the key products made by S & S is an over-the-counter headache remedy, known as Headache-Away. S & S makes two versions of this pill—one is regular strength sold as "Original Headache-Away," and the other is for sufferers of migraines sold as "Headache-Away for Migraines." The key difference between the two pills is the addition of caffeine to "Headache-Away for Migraines"; the box clearly identifies the migraine version by stating that the product contains caffeine and is for migraines. Outside that difference, the two medications look almost identical on the shelf.

One afternoon, Harry Healy ran into the local pharmacy suffering from a bad headache. Harry suffers from an allergy to caffeine, and any introduction of caffeine into his system is sure

to cause physical problems, possibly even death. In his haste
and desire to get rid of the pain, Healy grabbed a bottle of pills
off the shelf and took several. Shortly thereafter, while waiting
in line to pay, Healy had a heart attack and collapsed.
Thankfully, Healy survived the heart attack, but has now
brought a product liability suit against S & S alleging that the
packaging for the Headache-Away products was deceptive and
that S & S provided inadequate warnings of the potential
serious reactions.

Concerned with the possibility that Healy's action will
initiate an onslaught of product liability suits, Chamel directs
Alesi to "bring all your dogs to the fight." He directs Alesi to
deny all of the charges and assert a comparative negligence
defense against Harry Healy. While Alesi has some doubt
whether Healy's conduct, short of a fundamental misuse of the
product, has any bearing on the case, Chamel is adamant that
the store clerk, who threw away the pills after the paramedics
carted Healy away, can be convinced to testify that Healy spent
several minutes studying the packages before he chose one off
the shelf, opened it, and popped the pills. In addition, Chamel
wants to overwhelm the solo practitioner who has taken Healy's
case by taking every conceivable step to deluge her with "paper"
and motions in order to induce a modest settlement and/or
prolong the litigation. Chamel also has been adamant about
resisting all discovery requests and moving for sanctions against
Healy's attorney whenever arguably plausible. Moreover,
Chamel directs Alesi to interview everyone remotely tied to the
incident in the store and to interview anyone (friends, co-
workers, relatives) who can conceivably give insight into Healy's
background.

Alesi is concerned that these tactics and strategies may push
the envelope of appropriate litigation tactics but does not want
to risk losing one of his firm's biggest clients. What are Alesi's
alternatives, from both a practical and ethical perspective?

SCENARIO X

LAWYERS TAKING EQUITY INTERESTS IN THEIR CLIENTS

■ ■ ■

Although far less common than during the "high-tech" boom, corporate attorneys may accept equity interests in their clients, in addition to or in lieu of cash compensation.[1] These arrangements create potential conflicts of interest and implicate significant professional and ethical issues. An attorney's personal stake in a client could potentially cloud that attorney's professional and independent judgment. Rather than objectively counseling what is best for that particular client, the attorney could become influenced by what is best for his/her own pocketbook. The American Bar Association (ABA) has opined that while such fee arrangements are not per se unethical, they do constitute business transactions, and must therefore meet certain standards.[2] Among these governing standards are Rules

---

[1] *See* Dzienkowski & Peroni, *The Decline in Lawyer Independence: Lawyer Equity Investments in Clients,* 81 Tex. L. Rev. 405 (2002); Klein, *No Fool For A Client: The Finance and Incentives Behind Stock-Based Compensation For Corporate Attorneys*, 1999 Colum. Bus. L. Rev. 329 (1999); McAlpine, *Getting a Piece of the Action: Should Lawyers Be Allowed to Invest in Their Clients' Stock?,* 47 UCLA L. Rev. 549 (1999); Puri, *Taking Stock of Taking Stock*, 87 Cornell L. Rev. 99 (2001).

Note that ordinary fee agreements between the attorney and client should not be deemed business transactions. *See* American Law Institute, *Restatement of the Law Governing Lawyers* § 126, cmt. A (2000).

[2] *See* Model Rules of Prof. Conduct, Rule 1.8 cmt. 1; American Bar Association, *Acquiring Ownership In A Client In Connection With Legal Services*, ABA Formal Op. 00–418 (2000).

The question arises how expansive Rule 1.8 (i.e., an attorney entering into a business transaction with a client) should be interpreted. For example, should the rule apply to inside counsel whose compensation consists of several components, including cash salary, cash bonus, vacation leave, deferred cash compensation, health and disability insurance and stock benefits? It may be posited that, under custom and practice, such a multi-faceted employment agreement between the corporate client and the in-house lawyer is a routine employment transaction that should not be defined as a "business transaction" within the scope of the Model Rules. *See* C. Wolfram,

1.5,[3] 1.7,[4] and 1.8[5] of the Model Rules of Professional Conduct.

Modern Legal Ethics 482 (1986) (stating that Rule 1.8 should not apply in situations where the client's bargaining leverage is the same or greater than the attorney's bargaining power). *But see* Moore, *Conflicts of Interest for In-House Counsel: Issues Emerging from the Expanding Role of the Attorney-Employee,* 39 So. Tex. L. Rev. 497, 539 (1998) (asserting that such arrangements where an attorney-employee receives stock benefits as part of her employment arrangement is a business transaction under Model Rule 1.8 even though "[t]hese lawyers are rarely at an advantage in dealing with their employers").

[3] Model Rule 1.5(a) provides:

"A lawyer shall not make an agreement for, charge, or collect an unreasonable fee or an unreasonable amount for expenses. The factors to be considered in determining the reasonableness of a fee include the following:

(1) the time and labor required, the novelty and difficulty of the question involved, and the skill requisite to perform the legal service properly;

(2) the likelihood, if apparent to the client, that the acceptance of the particular employment will preclude other employment by the lawyer;

(3) the fee customarily charged in the locality for similar legal services;

(4) the amount involved and the results obtained;

(5) the time limitations imposed by the client or by the circumstances;

(6) the nature and length of the professional relationship with the client;

(7) the experience, reputation, and ability of the lawyer or lawyers performing the services; and

(8) whether the fee is fixed or contingent."

[4] Model Rule 1.7 (Conflict of Interest: Current Clients) generally precludes an attorney from representing a client if such representation implicates "a concurrent conflict of interest." A client may waive the conflict if such client "gives informed consent, confirmed in writing," and the attorney reasonably believes that "competent and diligent representation" can be rendered to such client.

[5] Model Rule 1.8(a) provides:

"(a) A lawyer shall not enter into a business transaction with a client or knowingly acquire an ownership, possessory, security or other pecuniary interest adverse to a client unless:

(1) the transaction and terms on which the lawyer acquires the interest are fair and reasonable to the client and are fully disclosed and transmitted in writing in a manner that can be reasonably understood by the client;

Rule 1.5 essentially provides that an attorney's fees must be reasonable.[6] In a traditional fee arrangement, reasonableness can be generally assessed by comparing the overall compensation received by the attorney to the total number of hours billed and the complexity of the issues involved. In an equity compensation structure, however, reasonableness becomes more elusive. First, one must decide at what point reasonableness is to be ascertained. This determination is complicated by the fact that in an equity compensation arrangement the lawyer and client agree upon an amount that may fluctuate significantly after the agreement is executed. Subsequent fluctuations in the value of the company in which the attorney owns an equity interest can significantly impact this compensation amount. Thus, what appears to be reasonable compensation at first, suddenly may seem outrageous a short time later.[7]

For example, a law firm agrees to represent a corporate client as general outside counsel for a one-year period in exchange for a 5% equity interest in the corporation. As of the date of the agreement, this 5% equates to 1000 shares of the corporation's outstanding stock that is valued at $50 per share, resulting in contemplated compensation of $50,000. Ten months later the Company encounters financial difficulty whereby its stock is valued at $15 per share. Consequently, the law firm's compensation, which was originally $50,000, is now only $15,000. Or, in the converse, assume the Company "goes public,"

---

(2) the client is advised in writing of the desirability of seeking and is given a reasonable opportunity to seek the advice of independent legal counsel on the transaction; and

(3) the client gives informed consent, in writing signed by the client, to the essential terms of the transaction and the lawyer's role in the transaction, including whether the lawyer is representing the client in the transaction."

[6]   *See* Model Rule 1.5(a), note 3 *supra*.

[7]   *See* G. Hazard, W. Hodes, & P. Jarvis, *The Law of Lawyering* § 13.07 (4th ed. 2015); McAlpine, *supra* note 1, 47 UCLA L. Rev. at 586–587. *See also*, ABA Formal Opinion No. 00–418, *supra* note 2, at n. 14 (citing Utah Ethics Advisory Committee Opinion 98–13, 1998 WL 863904 (1998), for the principle that "in addition to factors enumerated in [Model] Rule 1.5(a), the lawyer also should consider in determining the reasonableness of a fee when accepting client stock: (i) the liquidity of the stock, (ii) whether and when it can be expected to be publicly traded, (iii) any restrictions on its transfer, and (iv) its presently anticipated value. . . .").

with a ten to one stock split, and its initial public offering (IPO) is priced at $20 per share. The law firm's compensation is now $200,000, (10,000 shares at $20 per share) or $150,000 more than the amount initially agreed upon between the law firm and the client.

These situations demonstrate some potential obstacles to the traditional determinations of reasonableness with respect to attorneys' fees. Model Rule 1.5 provides little guidance when attempting to determine the point in time when the reasonableness assessment is to be made.[8] However, ascertaining reasonableness at any time other than when the agreement between the client and attorney is made seems misplaced. Under this view, a review of the lawyer's fee is appropriate only at the time it is agreed upon between the lawyer and the client. In the example above, the agreement contemplated $50,000 in compensation to counsel. Whether that constitutes a reasonable fee should be determined at the time of the agreement. Thus, this approach posits that it is irrelevant for Model Rule 1.5 purposes that the fee may subsequently experience significant fluctuations.[9]

The ABA's opinion on this subject seems to concur, stating: "For purposes of judging the fairness and reasonableness of the transaction and its terms, the Committee's opinion is that when assessing the reasonableness of a contingent fee, only the circumstances reasonably ascertainable at the time of the transaction should be considered."[10] In such a situation, it is counsel's responsibility to disclose to the client in writing the essential terms and reasonably foreseeable consequences of the stock compensation agreement.[11]

Model Rule 1.7 serves as the general prohibition on lawyers engaging in conflicts of interest within the scope of their client representations. A lawyer with an equity interest in a client

---

[8] Model Rule 1.5 does list certain factors that are to be taken into consideration in assessing the reasonableness of an attorney's fee. *See* Model Rule 1.5(a) in note 3 *supra*. These factors as well as the Comments to Rule 1.5 do not, however, provide any guidance with respect to when the fee reasonableness assessment is to be made.

[9] *See* Klein, *supra* note 1, 1999 Colum. Bus. Law. Rev. at 336.

[10] ABA Formal Opinion No. 00–418, note 2 *supra*.

[11] *Id. See* Model Rule 1.8(a) & cmts. 1–3. *See* Klein, *supra* note 1, 1999 Colum. Bus. Law. Rev. at 336.

could render legal services with less than the requisite independence of judgment with respect to that client, since the lawyer now has a personal interest at stake. According to Rule 1.7(a)(2), the lawyer normally may not represent the client "if there is a significant risk that the representation of [that] client will be materially limited by . . . a personal interest of the lawyer."[12] Nonetheless, even if counsel's representation of a client may be materially limited by such lawyer's personal interest, so long as the attorney "reasonably believes that the lawyer will be able to provide competent and diligent representation to [the] client" and the "client gives informed consent, confirmed in writing," the lawyer may undertake the representation.[13] Thus, the challenging inquiry is: when does the lawyer's ability to represent the client become materially limited by the lawyer's pecuniary ownership (e.g., stock) interest in the client so that, even with informed client consent, the lawyer will be disabled from rendering competent and diligent representation?[14]

When responding to this inquiry, counsel must focus on the general conflict of interest provisions in Model Rule 1.7, the reasonableness of attorney fee provisions in Rule 1.5, and the criteria for entering into a business transaction with a client set forth in Rule 1.8(a). The commentary to Rule 1.8 makes clear that equity-based (e.g., stock) attorney-client compensation arrangements are business transactions that trigger the

---

[12] Moreover, Model Rule 1.8 cmt. 3 provides:

"The risk to the client is greatest . . . when the lawyer's financial interest otherwise poses a significant risk that the lawyer's representation of the client will be materially limited by the lawyer's financial interest in the transaction. Here the lawyer's role requires that the lawyer must comply, not only with the requirements of paragraph (a) [of Rule 1.8], but also with the requirements of Rule 1.7. Under Rule [1.7], the lawyer must disclose the risks associated with the lawyer's dual role as both legal adviser and participant in the transaction, such as the risk that the lawyer will structure the transaction or give legal advice in a way that favors the lawyer's interests at the expense of the client. Moreover, the lawyer must obtain the client's informed consent. In some cases, the lawyer's interest may be such that Rule 1.7 will preclude the lawyer from seeking the client's consent to the transaction."

[13] *Id.* Model Rule 1.7(a), 1.7(b)(1), (b)(4).

[14] *See* McAlpine, *supra* note 1, 47 UCLA L. Rev. at 583; Puri, *supra* note 1, 87 Cornell L. Rev. at 140–144.

requirements of that Rule.[15] Generally, Rule 1.8(a) requires that: first, prior to agreeing to equity-based compensation, the lawyer must ensure that the transaction and terms of the arrangement are fair and reasonable to the client, and have been fully disclosed in an understandable manner to the client in writing;[16] second, the lawyer must inform the client in writing of the benefits of seeking the advice of independent legal counsel and such client must be provided with a reasonable opportunity to seek such advice;[17] and third, the client must give informed consent in writing to the essential terms of the agreement as well as to the attorney's role with respect thereto.[18]

The prevalence of equity compensation during the 1990s was largely a result of the rise in start-up companies dominating the high-tech sector.[19] These innovative companies oftentimes do not have the cash on hand to afford quality legal services. What they do offer, however, is the opportunity for a law firm to become an early stage investor. This usually allows the firm (or the individual attorneys) to purchase the company's stock at an attractive price. If and when the company goes public, the law firm theoretically has an unlimited upside potential payoff. On the other hand, because many of these companies "go broke" (such as during the "dot-com bust"), the law firm also faces considerable downside exposure. Indeed, due to this downside exposure, a number of law firms that took stock in their clients as payment for legal fees suffered financial hardship when the stock diminished in value or became worthless.[20]

From the company's perspective, having the law firm take an equity interest provides congruent goal alliance.[21] With the amount of the law firm's fee largely dependent on the success of the company's stock offering, counsel has additional incentive to

---

[15] *See* Model Rule 1.8 cmt. 1; ABA Formal Opinion No. 00–418, note 2 *supra*.

[16] Model Rule 1.8(a)(1). *See* C. Wolfram, *supra* note 2, at § 8.11.

[17] Model Rule 1.8(a)(2).

[18] *Id*. Model Rule 1.8(a)(3).

[19] *See* McAlpine, *supra* note 1, 47 UCLA L. Rev. at 550–558.

[20] *Id*. at 577–582. *See* Klein, *supra* note 1, 1999 Colum. Bus. L. Rev. at 352; Puri, *supra* note 1, 87 Cornell L. Rev. at 114; Sandburg, *Brobeck to End Turmoil By Going Out of Business,* Nat. L.J., Feb. 3, 2003, at A15.

[21] *See* McAlpine *supra* note 1, 47 UCLA L. Rev. at 572; Puri, *supra* note 1, 87 Cornell L. Rev. at 140.

ensure that the offering is a success. Furthermore, the law firm's financial stake in the company may have a positive signaling effect in the venture capital and institutional investor markets.[22] Presumably, a large, prestigious law firm would not invest in a start-up company unless the company was bound for success. Thus, the law firm's equity investment sends a signal to the marketplace that the company's stock is a good investment.[23] Not surprisingly, if the price of the company's stock subsequently diminishes in value or, even worse, if the company declares bankruptcy, legal counsel, who invested in the company's securities and cashed-out prior to the debacle, may become targets for disgruntled investors and regulators.

The following Scenario highlights many of the ethical issues that may arise when the client pays its attorneys' fees in stock (or other equity securities such as limited partnership interests) rather than cash.

SCENARIO

Super Hi-Tech, Inc. is a California based technology company that is just getting off the ground. Willard Wendell, the company's founder and CEO, decides that it is time to retain legal counsel to assist the Company in moving forward. Wendell wants a mid to large size law firm that is known not only for its quality reputation, but also for its ability to attract high dollar venture capitalists and, eventually, institutional investors. While Super Hi-Tech is currently a privately-held corporation, Wendell has big plans for the future, and dreams of dollar signs if an initial public offering (IPO) of the Company's stock is successful.

Danielle Danford is a third year corporate associate with Connor, Chui, & Cohen (CCC), a prestigious Los Angeles based law firm. Wendell and Danford went to the same small liberal arts college and, at an alumni function, Danford heard of Wendell's rumored success in the technology industry. As a third

---

[22] *See* Klein *supra* note 1, 1999 Colum. Bus. L. Rev. at 346.

[23] *See* McAlpine, *supra* note 1, 47 UCLA L. Rev. at 572–574; Puri, *supra* note 1, 87 Cornell L. Rev. at 104–106. *But see* Sandburg, *supra* note 20, at A15.

year associate, Danford is beginning to feel pressure to start bringing in her own clients.

Shortly thereafter, remembering what she heard about Wendell, Danford decides to contact him. The call could not have come at a better time. Wendell is ready to retain Danford's law firm immediately. The problem is that the retainer for Danford's law firm is $25,000, and Super Hi-Tech has about $12,000 in the bank. After learning more about Super Hi-Tech, Danford becomes enthused about the Company and its conceptual products. She meets with the law firm partner in charge of CCC's Corporate Section, George Henderson, and relays the good news. Not surprisingly, Henderson is less than thrilled about Super Hi-Tech's inability to cover the initial retainer. Danford suggests that in lieu of the retainer, the firm accept as compensation Super Hi-Tech stock. Being envious of some of his acquaintances in other law firms who have made "fortunes" taking stock as fees, Henderson agrees to explore the possibility.

Subsequently, Super Hi-Tech and Connor, Chiu & Cohen agree that CCC will serve as the Company's corporate counsel, will advise it through the process of venture financing, provide contacts to potential investors, and ultimately help take the Company public. In return, Super Hi-Tech will compensate the firm $50,000 in stock, up front, and then another $300,000 in stock immediately prior to the initial public offering (IPO).

Super Hi-Tech enjoys huge success. Its products are market blockbusters. The venture capitalists are fighting for a piece of the action, and Wendell, CCC, and the investment bankers realize the time has come to take the Company public. Henderson, Danford, and their team begin the necessary steps, including performing due diligence. Before they are even near completion, however, the market window ripens and analysts predict that this will be the last wave of high-tech IPO success for quite a while. Henderson asks Danford repeatedly why the due diligence is taking so long. Against her better judgment, Danford expedites the process in order to get the deal to market while the market window is still promising. As a result of cursory due diligence, the CCC due diligence team fails to verify the existence of significant "contracts" between Super Hi-Tech and three of its customers. The IPO raises over $350 million, and things could not look better. The Company has raised impressive capital, the law firm's investment looks golden,

Wendell is a multi-millionaire, and Danford is soon promoted to partner.

Then the technology market heads south, and things begin to unravel. In addition to a sour market, Super Hi-Tech just realized that the product, on which it had pinned much of its future hopes, is a flop. A dejected Wendell calls Danford to discuss the current situation. Wendell wants to know how to inform Super Hi-Tech's shareholders and the investing public of the failed product that the Company has spent the last ten months touting. Normally, CCC advises clients having such a material adverse development to promptly issue a press release.

Before Danford can explain this course of action to Wendell, he tells her that he has some seriously bad news. Danford wonders what could possibly be worse than what she has already heard. Wendell explains that perceived contracts between Super Hi-Tech and three major customers amounting to 12% of the Company's revenues, as set forth in the IPO Prospectus, in fact never existed. Danford feels her stomach crawl into her throat as she wonders about the contents of her malpractice insurance policy.

Shortly thereafter, you are retained as legal counsel by Connor, Chiu & Cohen to assess the firm's compliance with ethical standards and the risk of liability should lawsuits be brought.

SCENARIO XI

INSIDE COUNSEL

■ ■ ■

The role of inside counsel[1] has changed dramatically in the last three decades. As Irving Shapiro, former general counsel of DuPont, remarked:

> "In the past, businessmen wore blinders. After hours, they would run to their club, play golf with other businessmen, have a martini—and that was about it. . . . In a world where government simply took taxes from you and did not interfere with your operations, maybe that idea was sensible. In today's world, it is not."[2]

H.J. Aibel, then chief legal officer of ITT, upon reflecting on the status of inside counsel in the times of yesteryear, commented that "then the generally accepted wisdom [was] that jobs in corporate law departments were for second raters, or lawyers who had failed to make partner at some of the better firms."[3] Today, however, the responsibility and prestige of inside counsel have increased dramatically.[4] Indeed, the issues facing

---

[1] Inside counsel is generally defined as attorneys employed full-time by corporations. See generally M. Steinberg & S. Yeager, *Inside Counsel—Practices, Strategies, and Insights* (2015); E. Veasey & C. Di Guglielmo, *Indispensable Counsel—The Chief Legal Officer in the New Reality* (2012).

[2] Loeb, *The Corporate Chiefs' New Class*, Time, Apr. 14, 1980, at 87 (quoting Irving Shapiro).

[3] Aibel, *Corporate Counsel and Business Ethics: A Personal Review*, 59 Mo. L. Rev. 427, 427 (1994).

[4] Williams, *The Role of Inside Counsel in Corporate Accountability*, [1979–1980 Transfer Binder] CCH Fed. Sec. L. Rep. ¶ 82,318, at 82,369 (1979). See Symposium, *The Changing Role and Nature of In-House and General Counsel*, 2012 Wis. L. Rev. No. 2 (2012); Daly, *The Cultural, Ethical and Legal Challenges in Lawyering for a Global Organization: The Role of the General Counsel*, 46 Emory L.J. 1057 (1997); Duggin, *The Pivotal Role of the General Counsel in Promoting Corporate Integrity and Professional Responsibility*, 51 St. Louis U.L.J. 989 (2007); Hackett, *Corporate Counsel and the Evolution of Practical Ethical Navigation: An Overview of the Changing Dynamics of Professional Responsibility for In-House Practice*, 25 Geo. J. Leg. Eth. 317 (2012); Nishizawa, *Ethical Conflicts Facing In-House*

in-house attorneys have become as multifaceted and challenging as those arising in law firms. Inside counsel now plays an active role in shaping corporate events, in assessing corporate policies, and in establishing the tone and standard for corporate conduct.[5] Today, for example, there are many corporate legal departments with hundreds of in-house attorneys.

As a full-time employee of his own client, in-house counsel faces the unique situation of being "wedded" to his client. As such, inside counsel is likely to encounter difficult questions of professional independence.[6] For example, when outside counsel has a "difficult" client (such as one that fails to timely pay its bills or one that engages in improper conduct), the attorney may "walk" from that client.[7] Although the attorney certainly may miss the revenues that the client otherwise would have generated, she normally has the economic leeway to resign from the engagement. However, when inside counsel's client is unduly "difficult" or behaves improperly, counsel must either tolerate such conduct or find another job. Hence, being in-house counsel makes separation and divorce far more onerous.

On the other hand, inside counsel's "marital" relationship to his client has key attributes. One particularly attractive one, for example, is that inside counsel is very much at the center of the key legal functions of the enterprise, including that of corporate law compliance. Moreover, inside counsel in many corporations are involved in business strategy. As a result, she has the financial acumen to understand the benefits and risks of a prospective venture and has the opportunity to communicate with management regarding the economic aspects of a

---

Counsel: Dealing with Recent Trends and an Opportunity for Positive Change, 20 Geo. J. Leg. Eth. 849 (2007); Schwarcz, *To Make or to Buy: In-House Lawyering and Value Creation,* 33 J. Corp. L. 497 (2008). But *see* Aman, *A Desire to Move Up, But No Place to Go,* Nat. L.J., Nov. 21, 2005, at 9 (reporting that a national survey indicates that inside attorneys perceive there is little opportunity for advancement within their corporations).

[5] See M. Steinberg, *Corporate Internal Affairs: A Corporate and Securities Law Perspective* 251 (1983). *See also,* Steinberg & Yeager, note 1 *supra;* Williams, note 4 *supra.*

[6] See DeMott, *The Discrete Roles of General Counsel,* 74 Fordham L. Rev. 955, 956 (2005).

[7] See generally Model Rules of Prof. Conduct, Rule 1.16 & cmts.; Hemmer, *Resignation of Corporate Counsel: Fulfillment or Abdication of Duty?,* 39 Hastings L.J. 641 (1988).

contemplated "deal." In these functions, inside counsel seeks to be perceived within the enterprise as a "can do yes person," while retaining the leverage to effectively say "no" when appropriate.[8]

H.J. Aibel, while discussing his experience as corporate counsel for ITT, elaborated upon this view:

> "Early involvement of the lawyer often depends upon the prior establishment of a reputation for being a 'team player,' a 'can do lawyer'. . . . Although it is not easy for inside counsel to bring to the attention of the corporation's Board of Directors situations in which senior management is failing to take appropriate action, in the end, his or her career may depend upon doing so."[9]

As the following discussion illustrates, in-house counsel often confront many challenging issues, such as: (1) client identification and loyalty; (2) the general duty to inquire when offering advice; (3) the obligation to take appropriate action when a corporate fraud or crime is discovered; (4) liability arising under applicable laws; and (5) the implementation of law compliance policies.

The first area of concern facing in-house counsel involves client identification. Stated succinctly, who is inside counsel's client? According to both the American Bar Association (ABA) Model Code of Professional Responsibility (Model Code) and the Model Rules of Professional Conduct (Model Rules), the client is the corporate entity. For example, The Model Code provides that:

> "A lawyer employed or retained by a corporation or similar entity owes his allegiance to the entity and not to a stockholder, director, officer, employee, representative, or other person connected with the entity. In advising the entity, a lawyer should keep paramount its interests

---

[8] *See* Creedon, *Lawyer and Executive—The Role of the General Counsel*, 39 Bus. Law. 25 (1983); *How Agile is Your Legal Department?*, Corp. Legal Times, Aug. 1995, at 1, 5 (quoting statements by McDonald's Corp. assistant general counsel Ira S. Feldman that "[a]ll of the lawyers at McDonald's become intimately involved on the business side" and that "lawyer[s] . . . wear two hats: a business hat as well as [a] legal hat").

[9] Aibel, *supra* note 3, 59 Mo. L. Rev. at 431.

and his professional judgment should not be influenced by the personal desires of any person or organization."[10]

Similarly, ABA Model Rule 1.13(a) provides that "[a] lawyer employed or retained by an organization represents the organization acting through its duly authorized constituents."[11] The American Law Institute's Restatement of the Law Governing Lawyers likewise states that "the lawyer represents the interests of the organization as defined by its responsible agents acting pursuant to the organization's decision-making procedures."[12]

The seeming simplicity of these rules often breaks down in practice, however, because the organizational entity can "speak" and make decisions only through its "authorized constituents," including the corporation's directors, officers, employees, and shareholders.[13] Due to the close working relationship that develops between in-house counsel and corporate executives, counsel may be forced to choose between her obligations to the corporate client and conflicting orders given by a superior; in other words, counsel may be faced with following an executive officer's directions or being fired from her only client.[14] To alleviate this dilemma, the general perception is that, so long as the board of directors and senior management are acting in a lawful manner, inside counsel may look to these constituents as the "spokespersons" for the corporate entity.[15] In this regard, if practicable, the inside general counsel should meet with the independent directors (or the lead independent director) in executive session on a regular basis to address pertinent issues.[16]

---

[10] *See* Model Code of Prof. Responsibility EC 5–18.

[11] *See* Model Rules of Prof. Conduct, Rule 1.13(a).

[12] *See* ALI, *Restatement of the Law Governing Lawyers* § 96(1)(a) (2000). *Accord,* Report of the New York City Bar Association Task Force on the Lawyer's Role in Corporate Governance, 62 Bus. Law. 427, 481 (2007).

[13] *See* Olson, *The Potential Liabilities Faced by In-House Counsel*, 7 U. Miami Bus. L. Rev. 1 (1998).

[14] *Id.* at 5. *See* Steinberg, *The Role of Inside Counsel in the 1990s: A View From Outside*, 49 SMU L. Rev. 483 (1996).

[15] *See* Taylor, *The Role of Corporate Counsel*, 32 Rutgers L. Rev. 237, 241–245 (1979).

[16] *See* NYC Bar Association Task Force Report, *supra* note 12, 62 Bus. Law. at 487. *See generally* Ferrara & Wolkinson, *Managing Corporate Crisis: A Brief Case Study*, 48 Rev. Sec. & Comm. Reg. 71 (2015).

In certain situations, however, the perception that the lawyer may rely on a company's management or board of directors may prove problematic.[17] For instance, the Fifth Circuit in *Garner v. Wolfinbarger*,[18] in determining whether a corporation could invoke the attorney-client privilege to preclude shareholders in a derivative suit from obtaining requested documents, stated:

> "[I]t must be borne in mind that management does not manage for itself and that the beneficiaries of its action are the stockholders. Conceptualistic phrases describing the corporation as an entity separate from its stockholders are not useful tools of analysis. They serve only to obscure the fact that management has duties which run to the benefit ultimately of the stockholders. . . . There may be situations in which the corporate entity or its management, or both, have interests adverse to those of some or all stockholders. But when all is said and done management is not managing for itself."[19]

Additional concerns may arise from counsel's duty to inquire when offering advice. Generally, inside counsel regularly provides advice to employees and management concerning law compliance and consults with management as to what steps to take when possible violations are uncovered. In this context, the question arises as to whether counsel should accept the facts as they are presented or, alternatively, whether she has a duty to inquire. Not surprisingly, the facts and circumstances of a particular situation will determine the proper course of action.[20]

Particularly when "red flags" are raised, inside counsel should be cautious when advising on the basis of facts furnished

---

[17] Taylor, *supra* note 15, 32 Rutgers L. Rev. at 241–245.

[18] 430 F.2d 1093 (5th Cir. 1970).

[19] *Id.* at 1101. *See* Cooper, *An Uncertain Privilege: Reexamining Garner v. Wolfinbarger and Its Effect on Attorney-Client Privilege*, 35 Cardozo L. Rev. 1217 (2014). Another issue related to client identification is whether in-house counsel may represent corporate constituents in addition to the corporate entity. Although the organization is technically the counsel's client, dual representation is generally allowed pursuant to Model Rule 1.7. *See also, infra* notes 28–31 and accompanying text. This issue is also addressed in Scenarios IV, VII herein.

[20] *See* Ferrara & Steinberg, *The Role of Inside Counsel in the Corporate Accountability Process*, 4 Corp. L. Rev. 3, 12 (1981); Williams, note 4 *supra*.

by a corporate manager with whom he deals. In other words, certain circumstances should call for a duty to inquire. If in-house counsel conducts the necessary inquiry and renders advice accordingly, it normally is implemented. However, in instances where such advice is disregarded and the situation at hand involves a crime or fraud likely to result in substantial harm to the business enterprise, counsel must take affirmative action. In such situations, as set forth in Model Rule 1.13, "the lawyer shall refer the matter to higher authority in the organization, including, if warranted by the circumstances, to the highest authority [i.e., the corporation's board of directors] that can act on behalf of the organization as determined by applicable law."[21] If the board of directors insists upon action that constitutes a clear violation of law and that is likely to cause substantial injury to the corporation, the attorney would be prudent to resign.[22] Additionally, the ABA Model Rules, the SEC Standards of Conduct for Attorneys, and many state ethical rules permit counsel to disclose the corporate client's illegality to a shareholder or to a third party, such as a government regulatory authority (e.g., the DOJ, SEC, EPA, FTC) under certain circumstances.[23]

It should be noted that resignation in such circumstances certainly is a drastic step, resulting in loss of employment, but nonetheless may be required under the ethical standards discussed above. Proceedings against attorneys brought by the

---

[21] Model Rules of Prof. Conduct, Rule 1.13(b). Pursuant to the Sarbanes-Oxley Act of 2002 (SOX), the SEC by rule must:

> "(1) requir[e] [a subject] attorney to report evidence of a material violation of securities law or breach of fiduciary duty or similar violation by the company or any agent thereof, to the chief legal counsel or the chief executive officer of the company (or the equivalent thereof); and

> (2) if the counsel or officer does not appropriately respond to the evidence (adopting, as necessary, appropriate remedial measures or sanctions with respect to the violation), requir[e] [such] attorney to report the evidence to the audit committee of the board of directors of the issuer or to another committee of the board of directors comprised solely of directors not employed directly or indirectly by the issuer, or to the board of directors."

This statute and the SEC Standards of Conduct for Attorneys, implemented pursuant to SOX's directive, are discussed in Scenario II herein.

[22] *See* Model Rule 1.16(a)(1).

[23] *See id.* Rule 1.13(c); discussion in Scenario II herein.

Securities and Exchange Commission (SEC) illustrate this dilemma. As the SEC pointed out, inside counsel may be charged with both ethical and supervisory responsibilities under the federal securities laws. In such circumstances, in-house counsel cannot simply advise senior management and then decline to ascertain whether such advice is being implemented. Rather, counsel must remain alert to developments and, if corrective measures are not taken, must climb the corporate ladder. If the ultimate decision-maker embodying the corporate client—the board of directors—fails to take appropriate action, counsel's practical recourse is resignation.[24]

In sum, inside counsel must be careful not to become a participant in the client's illegality.[25] Generally, provided that the client listens in good faith to the advice given, counsel should not be obligated to resign when a legitimate question exists regarding the legality of corporate conduct. In such circumstances, inside counsel's "energies should be channeled into advising and prompting corporate management and the board of directors to engage in conduct that is both legal and ethical."[26]

Another troubling issue arises when inside counsel learns that a corporate employee has allegedly violated the law. In this context, counsel may give the employee "quasi-Miranda" warnings to the effect that:

> "(a) [counsel's] role is to represent the organization; (b) an actual or potential conflict of interest may exist between the organization and the individual; (c) [counsel] cannot represent the individual; (d) their conversation may not be confidential and any

---

[24] *See In re Gutfreund*, [1992 Transfer Binder] CCH Fed. Sec. L. Rep. ¶ 85,067 (SEC 1992); *In re Carter*, [1981 Transfer Binder] CCH Fed. Sec. L. Rep. ¶ 82,847 (SEC 1981).

[25] *See, e.g., SEC v. National Student Mktg. Corp.*, 457 F. Supp. 682 (D.D.C. 1978); Callcott & Slonecker, *A Review of SEC Actions Against Lawyers*, 42 Rev. Sec. & Comm. Reg. 71 (2009).

[26] Ferrara & Steinberg, *supra* note 20, at 22. *See* M. Steinberg & R. Ferrara, *Securities Practice: Federal and State Enforcement* §§ 4:27–4:28 (2d ed. 2001 & 2016 supp.); Millstein, *The Professional Board*, 50 Bus. Law. 1427, 1431 (1995) ("Lawyers ... understand that in most circumstances they render advice, and that taking or leaving that advice is the client's role. The limit is when the lawyer's professional responsibilities require him or her to act when the advice is ignored.").

information the individual provides may be used against [such individual]; and (e) he [or she] may wish to retain independent counsel."[27]

A number of inside counsel, however, argue against conveying these warnings to a suspected erring employee, reasoning that so doing is not in the corporation's interest.[28] On the other hand, the prevailing approach posits that failure to provide these warnings may subject counsel to increased liability exposure, particularly where the employee has a reasonable belief that counsel is personally representing the employee. For example, according to Model Rule 1.13(f), counsel has the responsibility of explaining to a non-client constituent the identity of her client (namely, that she represents the corporation) when such counsel knows or reasonably should know that the corporation's interests are adverse to those of such non-client constituent. Counsel also may be obligated to expressly communicate to the non-client that she does not represent such individual.[29] Failure to provide such disclosure may subject the attorney to liability for failure to warn.[30] Moreover, in certain jurisdictions—if the employee reasonably believes that the corporation's lawyer represents the employee personally—an attorney-client relationship may be implicated, thereby signifying that such communications between counsel and the employee may be deemed confidential.[31]

---

[27] Martin, *When Corporate Counsel Get Caught in the Middle*, Cal. Law., Dec. 1989, at 75. See Scenario IV herein.

[28] *See, e.g.,* Aibel, *supra* note 3, 59 Mo. L. Rev. at 438–439.

[29] *See* Model Rules of Prof. Conduct, Rule 1.13(f).

[30] *See Parker v. Carnahan*, 772 S.W. 2d 151, 157 (Tex. App.1989) (stating that "an attorney can be held negligent where he fails to advise a party that he is not representing him . . . where the circumstances lead the party to believe that the attorney is representing him"); Scenario IV herein.

[31] *See, e.g., Westinghouse Elec. Corp. v. Kerr-McGee Corp.*, 580 F.2d 1311 (7th Cir. 1978). *Cf. United States v. Ruehle*, 583 F.3d 600, 609 (9th Cir. 2009) (stating that employee-interviewee's statements made to corporate counsel during an internal investigation interview not within the attorney-client privilege due to that the "statements made to the [attorneys] were not made in confidence but rather for the purpose of disclosure to outside auditors"); *In re Grand Jury Subpoena Under Seal*, 415 F. 3d 333 (4th Cir. 2005) (concluding that employee interviewed in internal investigation did not have an attorney-client relationship with legal counsel who was conducting the interview). For further discussion, *see* Scenario IV herein.

In addition to the issues arising from in-house counsel's unique employment relationship, counsel also should be aware of potential liability concerns under common and statutory (e.g., securities) law. Indeed, securities laws claims, as well as malpractice, negligent misrepresentation, aiding and abetting, and breach of fiduciary duty allegations may be of significant concern, due to in-house counsel's principal involvement in drafting key corporate documents (such as transactional documents, corporate filings, lending agreements, and legal opinions).[32] Consistent with the scope of the engagement, counsel should seek to ensure that the information which she uses to draft the documents is correct. In certain situations, this objective may signify that counsel has an affirmative duty of inquiry.[33] For example, in *FDIC v. O'Melveny & Myers*,[34] a case involving counsel who had prepared securities offering documents and who had relied solely on information provided by the client company's internal participants, the Ninth Circuit held that under the circumstances presented securities counsel was to have made a reasonable, independent investigation in order to detect and correct materially false or misleading statements.[35]

It is also important to consider in-house counsel's role within the boardroom. Generally, it is essential for counsel to comprehend the business dynamics of the enterprise and possess the acumen to understand the economics of the transaction or other matter being considered.[36] Counsel's role also encompasses the implementation of internal governance procedures to reduce

---

[32] *See generally* M. Steinberg, *Attorney Liability After Sarbanes-Oxley* (2015); Webb et al., *Understanding and Avoiding Corporate and Executive Criminal Liability*, 49 Bus. Law. 617 (1994).

[33] Olson, *supra* note 13, 7 U. Miami Bus. L. Rev. at 4 (quoting Snow, et. al, *Defending Securities Class Actions*, C123 A.L.I.–A.B.A. Course of Study, June 2, 1995, at 710). In-house counsel may have a greater duty to inquire than outside counsel because in-house counsel have greater access to corporate information. *Id.*

[34] 969 F.2d 744 (9th Cir. 1992), *rev'd on other grounds*, 512 U.S. 79 (1994).

[35] *See* 969 F.2d at 748–749. *See also,* Olson, *supra* note 13, 7 U. Miami Bus. L.Rev. at 32.

[36] *See* Creedon, *Lawyer and Executive—The Role of the General Counsel*, 39 Bus. Law. 25 (1983)*; How Agile is Your Legal Department?*, Corp. Legal Times, No. 45, Aug. 1995, at 40. *See generally* Symposium, *Business Lawyering and Value Creation for Clients*, 74 Or. L. Rev. No. 1 (1995).

the threat of subsequent litigation. In this regard, the business judgment rule serves as an impressive shield to deflect otherwise successful challenges to board action.[37]

In this context, process is key. If the board abides by an acceptable procedural framework, courts will be reluctant to second-guess a deliberative decision reached in good faith by a reasonably informed board.[38] Hence, inside counsel's role here is to guide the board through this process, building a fortress that will protect the decision from successful attack.

In conflict of interest transactions,[39] such as interested director transactions with a controlling shareholder, parent-subsidiary mergers, and leveraged buy-outs engineered by incumbent management, even more attention to process frequently will be necessitated. In such situations, establishment of a committee comprised of the disinterested directors may be called for, as well as appointment of special counsel for the committee.[40] As decisions such as *Weinberger v. UOP, Inc.*[41] demonstrate, deficiency in process accompanied by

---

[37] Stated succinctly, the business judgment rule has four components. First, the board of directors must focus on the issue and make a deliberative decision. Second, the board's decision must be adequately informed (with gross negligence being the applicable standard). In this regard, the board should be provided with adequate information, including pertinent reports, appraisals, and other material documents central to the transaction or other matter at issue. Once having such information before it, the board should take the time necessary to reach an informed decision. Third, directors making the board's determination must be disinterested, signifying that they are not engaged in self-dealing, do not have a disproportionate financial stake in the transaction, and are not under the control or domination of a director who has such a disabling conflict of interest. Last, the decision must have a rational basis or, stated differently, must be made without gross negligence. *See, e.g., Aronson v. Lewis*, 473 A.2d 805, 812 (Del. 1984); American Law Institute, *Principles of Corporate Governance: Analysis and Recommendations* § 4.01 (1994).

[38] *See* ALI, *Principles of Corporate Governance, supra* note 37, § 4.01 & cmts. *See also, In re Walt Disney Company Derivative Litigation*, 906 A.2d 27 (Del. 2006).

[39] In conflict of interest transactions, the intrinsic fairness test generally is the applicable standard. *See, e.g., Schlensky v. South Parkway Building Corp.*, 166 N.E. 2d 793 (Ill. 1960).

[40] *See, e.g., Rosenblatt v. Getty Oil Co.*, 493 A.2d 929 (Del. 1985); *Weinberger v. UOP, Inc.*, 457 A.2d 701, 709 n.7 (Del. 1983); Scenario V herein.

[41] 457 A.2d 701 (Del. 1983).

the specter of overreaching by the control group heightens the risk that the transaction (or its terms) will be successfully challenged. To allay this prospect, participation by reasonably informed outside directors who have sufficient leverage to negotiate with the control group in an effective manner will dissuade a court from upsetting the subject transaction.[42] Playing a key role in this setting, inside counsel orchestrates the process in such a manner as to hopefully further the best interests of the corporation, shareholders, and other affected constituencies.[43]

Inside counsel also plays a pivotal role in the practice of preventive law by establishing an effective and operational law compliance program for the subject corporation. In corporations with multifaceted operations, law compliance programs may cover such diverse areas as antitrust, environmental policies, employment and hiring practices, and securities.[44] When rendering advice with respect to law compliance, counsel may consider the following:

1. Although no system is "bullet-proof," the corporation should keep in mind that, if a violation were to occur, it would have the burden of showing that its law compliance program (Program) is reasonably effective.

2. The subject corporation's board of directors should adopt the Program, and the Program should be administered under the board's supervision as an integral part of its monitoring function. On a

---

[42] *See Kahn v. M&F Worldwide Corp.*, 88 A.3d 635 (Del. 2014); M. Steinberg, *Securities Regulation: Liabilities and Remedies* § 15.04 (2015).

[43] With respect to the interests of other constituencies, *see, e.g., Symposium, Corporate Malaise—Stakeholder Statutes: Cause or Cure?*, 21 Stetson L. Rev. No. 1 (1991). *See also,* Veasey & Brown, *An Overview of the General Counsel's Decision Making on Dispute-Resolution Strategies in Complex Business Transactions*, 70 Bus. Law. 407 (2015); Scenario V herein.

[44] American Bar Association, *Corporate Director's Guidebook—Sixth Edition*, 66 Bus. Law. 975, 999–1000 (2011). *See* Gruner, *General Counsel in an Era of Compliance Programs and Self-Policing*, 46 Emory L.J. 1113 (1997); Fiorelli & Tracey, *Why Comply? Organization Guidelines Offer a Safer Harbor in the Storm*, 32 J. Corp. L. 467 (2007); Steinberg & Fletcher, *Compliance Programs for Insider Trading*, 47 SMU L. Rev. 1783 (1994); Stucke, *In Search of Effective Ethics & Compliance Programs*, 39 J. Corp. L. 769 (2014).

periodic basis, the board should review the Program for possible revision.

3. The Program's scope should reflect the nature of the enterprise's business and the legal issues such enterprise realistically may face. Given the economic practicalities involved and with the proviso that the law must be obeyed, an objective cost/benefit analysis normally is appropriate. Certainly, an enterprise engaged in several different businesses with operations abroad should be expected to develop a more extensive program than one with purely local operations specializing in a particular product market.

4. The Program (such as a Code of Conduct) should be disseminated to and understood by all affected company personnel.

5. To integrate the Program into the corporation's culture and to help ensure continued personnel compliance, educational seminars should be conducted on a periodic basis. Moreover, consideration should be given to the question whether affected personnel should be required to certify annually that they have complied with the applicable Code(s) of Conduct.

6. The Program should be effectively administered. In this regard, the enterprise should not adopt any non-essential aspect of a prospective Program that it cannot feasibly implement. For example, a corporation's failure to obtain annual compliance certificates from a significant number of affected personnel may prove more harmful when such a component is contained in the corporation's Program.

7. The Program should be subject to adequate enforcement, such as spot checks, board of director (or delegated committee) review, "whistleblower" procedures, and the taking of meaningful

disciplinary action against those who fail to comply.[45]

In sum, inside counsel's role in helping to administer and oversee an enterprise's law compliance program is critical and may help reduce the risk of significant liability exposure.

The following case provides an example of the type of legal advice rendered by in-house counsel to her client. Such advice, as held by the U.S. Court of Appeals, is protected under the attorney-client privilege.

EXXON MOBIL CORPORATION V. HILL
751 F.3d 379 (5th Cir. 2014)

JERRY E. SMITH, CIRCUIT JUDGE:

Exxon Mobil Corporation ("Exxon Mobil") appeals a judgment that dismissed its intervention based on the district court's ruling that a memorandum prepared by Exxon Mobil's in-house counsel was ineligible for the protections of the attorney-client privilege. Concluding that the memorandum is privileged, we vacate and remand.

In the late 1980s, Exxon Mobil was negotiating with another company ("ITCO") over a proposed contract under which ITCO would clean and store oilfield production tubulars for Exxon Mobil. The parties knew that some of the tubulars had accumulated scale, some of which was contaminated with "naturally occurring radioactive material" or "NORM." ITCO had created a new device designed to contain any dust generated by cleaning NORM-contaminated scale from the tubulars. As part of its due diligence, Exxon Mobil sent an industrial

---

[45] Steinberg, 19 Sec. Reg. L. J. 323 (1992); Aibel, *supra* note 3, at 59 Mo. L. Rev. at 435–439; Pitt & Groskaufmanis, *Minimizing Corporate Civil and Criminal Liability: A Second Look at Corporate Codes of Conduct*, 78 Geo. L.J. 1559 (1990). Note that the federal criminal sentencing guidelines deem a subject company's establishment and implementation of a reasonably effective law compliance program to be a mitigating factor in the assessment of an appropriate sentence. *See* United States Sentencing Commission, U.S. Sentencing Guidelines Manual §§ 8B2.1, 8C2.5. While the guidelines were declared unconstitutional in *Blakely v. Washington*, 542 U.S. 296 (2004), they nonetheless continue to be persuasive with the federal courts.

hygienist, Lindsey Booher, to conduct tests designed to reveal whether the device would work as intended. Booher wrote a confidential report to Exxon Mobil employee John Guidry containing the results of his test, including four tables, numbered I through IV, showing the air-sampling data.

During their negotiations, ITCO asked Guidry for Booher's test results. Guidry, in turn, sought advice from Rosemary Stein, an in-house lawyer for Exxon Mobil, on how to respond. Stein suggested that Guidry disclose only Table IV, because it contained the only data that ITCO specifically had requested, and that Guidry remove the caption "Table IV" so as not to flag the existence of other tables. According to the defendants, the "withheld data confirms much higher levels of radiation" than what Table IV suggested. Stein also drafted a suggested response to accompany the table, including a disclaimer of any warranty as to the data's accuracy and a statement that the data was created solely for Exxon Mobil's internal use.

Stein's advice was recorded in a memorandum dated July 22, 1988. Now referred to by the parties as the "Stein Memo," it is the epicenter of the fight on appeal.

Various persons, in the ensuing years, have sued Exxon Mobil, ITCO, or both alleging exposure to NORM at ITCO's pipe yard. In 2008, in the course of discovery, Exxon Mobil accidentally produced a number of allegedly privileged documents, including the Stein Memo. Months later, Exxon Mobil discovered the inadvertent production. Pursuant to Louisiana Code of Civil Procedure article 1424(D) (a claw-back provision), its counsel sent a letter to plaintiffs' attorney Timothy Falcon informing him of the error and demanding a return of the production. Although he returned the CDs and made no objection to Exxon Mobil's assertion of privilege, Falcon kept a copy of the Stein Memo and distributed it to other plaintiffs' attorneys, who in turn attempted to use it in other cases.

[Plaintiff's] counsel . . . filed the Stein Memo into the record as part of a fight over expert testimony. . . .

. . . Exxon Mobil moved to enforce its attorney-client privilege over the Stein Memo, to have the memorandum stricken from the record, and to compel [Plaintiff's] attorneys to destroy or return all copies to Exxon Mobil. The district court denied the motion and entered final judgment dismissing Exxon Mobil's intervention. The basis for its holding was that the advice in the Stein Memo was primarily *business* advice rather than *legal* advice.

II.

In this diversity case, Louisiana provides the applicable law of privilege. The Louisiana attorney-client privilege, codified in Article 506 of the Louisiana Code of Evidence, provides that "[a] client has a privilege to refuse to disclose, and to prevent another person from disclosing, a confidential communication, whether oral, written, or otherwise, *made for the purpose of facilitating the rendition of professional legal services to the client.*" . . . The Code then provides a number of exceptions and definitions, but the parties agree that the beginning and end of this case is the "made for the purpose of facilitating the rendition of professional legal services" language in article 506.

The Stein Memo reflects the advice by in-house counsel concerning disclosure of certain data during contract negotiations. Context here is key: The document was prepared during contract negotiations in which both sides were assisted by legal counsel. The negotiations, according to the record, involved a number of legal issues, including indemnity for downstream tort claims, storage and handling of nuclear residue, licensure, trade secrets, and other issues.

Disclosure of material facts is a universal concern in contract law. When ITCO requested internal data prepared by and on behalf of Exxon Mobil, it is no surprise that Exxon Mobil would seek advice from its attorney as to how to respond. All of this is to say that the context in which the Stein memo was produced—even before we say anything of the memorandum itself—strongly suggests that Exxon Mobil was approaching its in-house counsel for just the sort of lawyerly thing one would expect of an in-house lawyer: advice on transactional matters. Though we recognize that in-house counsel can often play a variety of roles within an organization, this record is devoid of any indication that Stein was providing business advice divorced from its legal implications.

Especially when viewed in context, the Stein Memo cannot be mistaken for anything other than legal advice. Stein drafted a proposed response to ITCO in which she included elaborate language disclaiming liability for any reliance ITCO may have on the data, stating that the data was prepared for Exxon Mobil's own internal use and disclaiming any warranty as to the accuracy of the test results. The manifest purpose of the draft was to deal with what would be the obvious reason Exxon Mobil would seek its lawyers' advice in the first place, namely to deal with any legal liability that may stem from under-disclosure of data, hedged against any liability that may occur from any implied warranties during complex negotiations.

. . . The judgment of dismissal is vacated and remanded for whatever appropriate actions the district court may elect to take in light of our determination that the Stein Memo is protected by the attorney-client privilege.

The following Scenario highlights the difficult challenges that inside counsel may have to confront.

SCENARIO

Sylvia Gladstone, who recently left her job at a mid-size law firm in Baltimore Maryland, is offered a position as the sole in-house attorney for Nuval Atlantic Resources, Inc. (Nuval), an Alexandria Virginia-based company traded on the NASDAQ National Market System (NMS) with $375 million in net assets and 2337 shareholders. Leaving her previous job because she was tired of the unduly long hours, counseling difficult clients, and maintaining an adequate book of business, Gladstone accepted the Nuval offer of a $210,000 salary with stock options and other key benefits. As a single mother, Gladstone is delighted with the new position and the opportunity to spend more time with her children.

Six months after being hired, Gladstone arrives at her office and finds a memo on her desk from the Chief Executive Officer (CEO) and majority shareholder of the company (52% stake), Patrick A. Whitney. The memo discusses a parcel of land located in Annandale Virginia that Nuval purchased 12 years earlier for $1,765,000, and which the Company still uses as its principal warehouse. The warehouse is well situated for Nuval and aptly serves the Company's needs. Moreover, the price of the land has significantly appreciated (to around $3.8 million). In the memo, Whitney expresses his desire that Nuval sell the land (and the warehouse), realize the profit, and move the warehouse to a less expensive location. Coincidentally, Whitney personally owns a parcel of land near Dover, Delaware, which he purchased ten years earlier for a previous (and now terminated) business venture, and which he believes would be the perfect location for Nuval's warehouse. Without disclosing the amount for which he purchased that property ($575,000), he proposes selling the property to Nuval.

While Gladstone is reading the memo, Whitney stops by her office to discuss the proposed sale. After discussing the memo's contents, Whitney adds, "I want to remind you how important this transaction is to me. I, of course, am going to recuse myself. However, I would like you to take charge of the board meeting and see this deal through. I will be upset, to use a polite word, if I don't get at least $1.5 million for the property."

The Board of Directors of Nuval is composed of five persons: Whitney; Whitney's daughter Lauren, who is also Treasurer and Executive Vice President; Collin Wilhelm, an acquaintance of Whitney's and fellow member of the Crooked Tree Country Club; Roberta Razzano, a well-respected business professor at a nearby college, and Luis Rodriguez, who is a successful local entrepreneur. Neither Razzano nor Rodriguez has a business or personal relationship with Whitney.

Gladstone is concerned about the conflicts of interest dilemmas posed by the proposed sale. Moreover, she is worried about applicable disclosure requirements, such as those set forth in Item 404 of SEC Regulation S-K.[46] Considering the circumstances, how should Gladstone present the proposed transaction to the Board of Directors? What potential problems does the situation raise? Are there any alternative solutions?

---

[46] Item 404 of SEC Regulation S-K requires disclosure of transactions with the corporation by: (1) directors; (2) director-nominees; (3) executive officers; (4) five percent shareholders; and (5) members of the immediate family of the primary reporting persons involving more than $120,000 made within the past year in which such persons have a direct or indirect material interest. *See* Item 404, Regulation S-K, *as adopted*, SEC Securities Exchange Act Release No. 54294A (2006). This proposed transaction, if consummated, would be required to be disclosed to the SEC and to the investing public under Item 404.

SCENARIO XII

COUNSEL AS DIRECTOR?

■ ■ ■

The practice of the general counsel serving as a corporate director to a business enterprise, whether that person is an in-house lawyer or a partner in a law firm, has been widespread for decades. From the client's perspective, the specialized training, unique experience, and analytical skills of its corporate counsel are a valued resource to a board of directors when making business decisions.[1] Additionally, attorneys see this dual role as a means of strengthening the relationship with their clients as well as a way to help ensure continued legal business and financial stability for their law firms. Indeed, with the weakening of long-term relationships and the intense competition for retaining corporate representation in recent years, the solidification of this relationship is paramount.[2]

Although the practice of corporate counsel serving as director remains relatively common, the propriety of attorneys acting in this dual capacity has long been criticized. Because an attorney/director must play dual roles as counsel and director, this arrangement raises a variety of issues pertaining to professional responsibility, potential conflicts of interest, and enhanced liability exposure.

For example, the application of the attorney-client privilege will be assessed on an ad-hoc basis depending upon whether the attorney/director was acting as legal counsel or as a director. By assuming this dual function, therefore, the corporation's

---

[1] *See* Carrey, *Corporate Lawyer/Corporate Director: A Compromise of Professional Independence*, 67 N.Y. St. B.J. at 6 (Nov. 1995); Kim, *Dual Identities and Dueling Obligations: Preserving Independence in Corporate Representations*, 68 Tenn. L Rev. 179 (2001).

[2] *See* Cheek & Lamar, *Lawyers as Directors of Clients: Conflicts of Interest, Potential Liability and Other Pitfalls*, PLI No. B4–6940, 712 PLI Corp. 461, 463–464 (1990); Veasey & Di Guglielmo, *The Tensions, Stresses and Professional Responsibilities of the Lawyer for the Corporation*, 62 Bus. Law. 1, 15–17 (2006).

assertion of the attorney-client privilege may be subject to siege.[3] Also, by serving as director, counsel incurs the risk of having diminished ability to exercise independent judgment.

In these dual roles, counsel has a conflict between being a "team player" while at the same time rendering dispassionate legal advice that will be received with respect and without hostility by the inside directors.[4] [An inside director generally is one who has a significant employment relationship, such as being an executive officer of the corporation.] Moreover, the attorney/director may be denied legal malpractice insurance coverage by the carrier on the basis that the alleged impropriety did not involve the practice of law. Further, when counsel steps out of her attorney's shoes and acts as director, counsel's personal liability exposure is magnified. In such circumstances, courts frequently apply enhanced standards to analyze the propriety of the alleged wrongdoing.[5] Indeed, it has been asserted that lawyers who agree to sit as directors "have to be 'certifiably nuts' because of the likelihood of being sued."[6]

Despite the potential risks, however, many corporations exhort corporate counsel to serve as a director, due to perceived advantages that accrue to the client corporation. A primary benefit is the opportunity for the lawyer to be well informed concerning the corporation's affairs and to be in a position to provide legal advice when contemplated actions are first

---

[3] *Grimes v. LCC International, Inc.*, 1999 WL 252381 (Del. Ch. 1999). *See* M. Steinberg, *Corporate and Securities Malpractice* 251 (1992); Finklestein et al., *Attorney-Client Privilege: Potential Dangers of Having Corporate General Counsel Perform Multiple Roles*, 33 Rev. Sec. & Comm. Reg. 49 (2000).

[4] *See* Model Rules of Prof. Conduct, Rule 1.7 cmt. 35; Hershman, *Special Problems of Inside Counsel for Financial Institutions*, 33 Bus. Law 1435, 1439–1440 (1978); Lorne, *The Corporate and Securities Adviser, the Public Interest, and Professional Ethics*, 76 Mich. L. Rev. 425, 490–495 (1978); Riger, *The Lawyer-Director—A Vexing Problem*, 33 Bus. Law 2381 (1978).

[5] *See, e.g., Escott v. BarChris Constr. Corp.*, 283 F. Supp. 643 (S.D.N.Y. 1968); Hershman, *supra* note 4, 33 Bus. Law. at 1440 (1978) (asserting that "as a director, the General Counsel is likely to be held to a higher standard of care than other directors because of his [or her] unique access to information and expertise").

[6] *Lawyer-Directors Are Key Targets for Plaintiffs' Lawyers, ABA Group Told*, 21 Sec. Reg. & L. Rep. (BNA) 1272 (1989) (hereinafter "Lawyer-Directors"). *See* Stewart, *Lawyer Directors: Just a Bad Idea*, 189 PLI/NY 155 (2009).

presented or when problematic situations initially arise.[7] This enables counsel to be more effective in rendering advice to the board of directors, thereby preventing problems which could arise "due to the failure of the company to consult the attorney before taking an action or due to the . . . failure of management or the board of directors to recognize developing legal problems in their early stages."[8]

Because the attorney/director understands the legal implications of a potential decision, she can also act as a sounding board for corporate management.[9] This facilitates the flow of information between the board of directors and counsel because the attorney is more closely involved in the affairs of the client and is aware of the critical issues facing management.[10] Additionally, because the attorney/director, like the other board members, is subject to the same potential for liability as a director, the other directors may have greater comfort in the legal advice rendered by the attorney.[11]

From the law firm's perspective, economic necessities may dictate counsel serving as a director. An attorney's dual role enhances the relationship with clients and promotes continued legal business for the firm. Indeed, in some situations, senior executive officers may feel strongly that the company's general counsel should be an integral member of the "team," thereby insisting that such counsel serve on the board. To maintain the corporation as a client generating substantial legal fees, outside counsel may acquiesce in this arrangement.[12]

In general, applicable ethical rules contain no specific prohibition against an attorney serving as a corporate director.

---

[7] *See* Thurston, *Corporate Counsel on the Board of Directors: An Overview*, 10 Cumb. L. Rev. 791, 792 (1980) (citing Forrow, *Special Problems of Inside Counsel for Industrial Companies*, 33 Bus. Law. 1453, 1461 (1978)); Hawes, *Should Counsel to a Corporation be Barred From Serving as a Director?—A Personal View*, 1 Corp. L. Rev. 14, 17 (1978)).

[8] Thurston, *supra* note 7, 10 Cumb. L. Rev. at 792.

[9] *Id.* at 793.

[10] *Id. See* Cheek & Lamar, *supra* note 2, 712 PLI Corp. at 464; Zaffirini, *The Challenges of Serving as an Attorney/Director*, 33 Tex. J. Bus. Law No. 3, at 43, 44–45 (Fall 1996).

[11] Thurston, *supra* note 7, 10 Cumb. L. Rev. at 793; Veasey & Di Guglielmo, *supra* note 2, 62 Bus. Law. at 15–17; Zaffirini, *supra* note 10, 33 Tex. J. Bus. Law No. 3, at 45.

[12] *See* Lorne, *supra* note 4, 76 Mich. L. Rev. at 490–495.

In fact, the only guidance offered by the ABA Model Rules is included in the commentary to Model Rule 1.7, which touches upon the potential conflicts of interest that may exist when counsel serves as a director of the corporate client. Specifically, the Comment states:

> "A lawyer for a corporation or other organization who is also a member of its board of directors should determine whether the responsibilities of the two roles may conflict. . . . If there is material risk that the dual role will compromise the lawyer's independence of professional judgment, the lawyer should not serve as a director or should cease to act as the corporation's lawyer when conflicts of interest arise. . . ."[13]

Likewise, the American Law Institute's Restatement of the Law Governing Lawyers generally acquiesces in the counsel-director arrangement:

> "A lawyer's duties as counsel can conflict with the lawyer's duties arising from the lawyer's service as a director or officer of a corporate client. Simultaneous service as corporate lawyer and corporate director or officer is not forbidden under this Section. . . . However, when the obligations or personal interests as director are materially adverse to those of the lawyer as corporate counsel, the lawyer may not continue to serve as corporate counsel without the informed consent of the corporate client."[14]

A formal ethics opinion issued by the American Bar Association[15] provides additional suggestions to help an attorney/director avoid ethical violations and other problems. For example, the ABA opinion states that an attorney/director should:

---

[13] ABA Model Rules of Prof. Conduct, Rule 1.7 cmt 35. *See* Committee Report, *The Lawyer as Director of a Client*, 57 Bus. Law. 387 (2001) (stating that "[t]here is no ethical prohibition against a lawyer serving as a director of a client").

[14] *See* American Law Institute, *Restatement of the Law Governing Lawyers* § 135 cmt. d (2000).

[15] *Lawyer Serving as Director of Client Corporation*, ABA Comm. On Ethics and Professional Responsibility, Formal Op. 98–410 (1998).

"reasonably assure that management and the board of directors understand: (i) the different responsibilities of legal counsel and director; (ii) that when acting as legal counsel, the lawyer represents only the corporate entity and not its individual officers and directors; and (iii) that at times conflicts of interest may arise under the rules governing lawyers' conduct that may cause the lawyer to recuse himself as a director or to recommend engaging other independent counsel to represent the corporation in the matter, or to serve as co-counsel with the lawyer or his firm."[16]

Nevertheless, as the following discussion illustrates, serving as an attorney/director remains fraught with risk, including (1) the potential loss of the attorney-client privilege; (2) potential conflict of interest challenges and the perceived loss of independence; (3) a heightened duty of care; (4) increased liability risk under the securities laws;[17] (5) possible disqualification of the attorney's law firm; (6) vicarious liability for the attorney's law firm; (7) and possible loss of liability insurance coverage.

The first principal area of risk is the potential loss of the attorney-client privilege.[18] In general, the purpose of the

---

[16] *Id.* See Task Force on the Independent Lawyer, ABA Section of Litigation, *The Lawyer-Director: Implications for Independence* (1998); Committee Report, *supra* note 13, 57 Bus. Law. at 387–395; Kim, *supra* note 1, 68 Tenn. L. Rev. at 219–246.

[17] An attorney/director faces increased liability risk under both federal and state securities laws. For purposes of this illustration, this Scenario focuses on federal securities laws. For state securities laws, *see generally* Steinberg & Claasen, *Attorney Liability Under the State Securities Laws: Landscapes and Minefields,* 3 U. Cal. (Berk.) Bus. L. J. 1 (2005).

[18] The attorney-client privilege is discussed in Scenario IV herein. In *United States v. United Shoe Machine Co.,* 89 F. Supp. 357, 358–359 (D. Mass. 1950), the court set forth the following definition of the attorney-client privilege:

"The privilege applies only if (1) the asserted holder of the privilege is or sought to become a client; (2) the person to whom the communication was made (a) is a member of the bar of a court, or his subordinate and (b) in connection with this communication is acting as a lawyer; (3) the communication relates to a fact of which the attorney was informed (a) by his client (b) without the presence of strangers (c) for the purpose of securing primarily either (i) an opinion on law or (ii) legal services or (iii) assistance in some legal proceeding,

attorney-client privilege is to encourage full and frank communication between attorneys and their clients and thereby promote broader public interests in the observance of law.[19] In order to invoke the privilege while acting as both attorney and director, an attorney must render the advice in her role as a lawyer, rather than in her role as a director. If the information in question was communicated in the role as director, the privilege may be lost. However, although many attorney/directors regularly render business advice as well as legal advice, no clear test has been articulated to determine the issue of whether an attorney is acting as a director or as an attorney. Instead, courts traditionally have used a factual analysis.[20] For example, in *United States v. Vehicular Parking, Ltd.*,[21] the defendant in an antitrust case attempted to invoke the attorney-client privilege with respect to certain communications involving an attorney/director. The court, however, concluded that as a director, the attorney was involved in the promotion and management of the business so that "his communications involving business, rather than legal advice, were, therefore, not privileged."[22]

When an attorney/director performs dual roles, instances also may arise where an attorney's interests as counsel conflict with her duties as director. For example, one potential conflict of interest involves fee considerations—the attorney's self-interest in the corporation's continued retention of her law firm may conflict with her fiduciary duties as director.[23] Law firm revenues generated from these fees may place pressure on the firm and the attorney/director to maintain the relationship, and may make counsel reluctant to voice disapproval of certain actions.[24]

---

and not (d) for the purpose of committing a crime or tort; and (4) the privilege has been (a) claimed and (b) not waived by the client."

[19] *Upjohn Co. v. United States*, 449 U.S. 383, 389 (1981). *See* Scenario IV *supra*

[20] Thurston, *supra* note 7, 10 Cumb, L. Rev. at 811.

[21] 52 F. Supp. 751 (D. Del. 1943).

[22] *Id.* at 753–754. *See SEC v. Gulf & Western Ind., Inc.,* 518 F. Supp. 675 (D.D.C. 1981); *Federal Savings & Loan Ins. Corp. v. Fielding,* 343 F. Supp. 537 (D. Nev. 1972); Thurston, *supra* note 7, 10 Cumb. L. Rev. at 811

[23] Gould, *Should Lawyers Serve as Directors of Corporations For Which They Act as Counsel?*, 1978 Utah L. Rev. 711, 714 (1978).

[24] *See* Cheek & Lamar, *supra* note 2, 712 PLI Corp. at 470.

Related to these concerns is the issue of whether an attorney, who serves on the board of directors of a corporation which has a significant relationship with the attorney's firm, is considered "independent" for certain analyses involving the business judgment rule.[25] Generally, one of the rule's requirements is that subject directors making a board's determination must be disinterested, signifying that they are not engaged in self-dealing, do not have a disproportionate financial stake in the transaction, and are not under the control or domination of a director who has such a disabling conflict of interest.[26] An attorney/director, however, may promote the appearance of self-interest when voting on corporate action that would likely involve significant legal work for his law firm, or taking part in board discussions focusing on whether to reject the prospective sale of a particular corporate division which has generated substantial legal fees for his firm in the past. This appearance of impropriety is illustrated in *Steiner v. Meyerson*.[27] There, a director's law firm earned close to $1 million in revenues in representing the corporation. The court found that "[r]ealism. . . . requires one to acknowledge the possibility that a [law firm] partner bringing in close to $1 million in revenues from a single client in one year may be sufficiently beholden to,

---

[25] *See* Harris & Valihura, *Outside Counsel as Director: The Pros and Potential Pitfalls of Dual Service*, 53 Bus. Law. 479, 489 (1998). The business judgment rule provides an impressive shield from liability for directors, so long as they are disinterested, reasonably informed, have no disabling conflict of interest, and the decision made is rational. Gross negligence is the applicable standard for a plaintiff to hurdle in order to rebut the presumption of the business judgment rule. *See Aronson v. Lewis*, 473 A.2d 805 (Del. 1984). Note that, pursuant to the Sarbanes-Oxley Act (SOX), the attorney for a listed company that serves as a director may not be appointed to the audit committee. *See* SOX § 301(m)(3), *amending,* Securities Exchange Act § 10A(m)(3). Pursuant to Section 952 of the Dodd-Frank Act, enacted in 2010, similar independence requirements are mandated for compensation committee members. Moreover, pursuant to the rules of the New York Stock Exchange (NYSE), such an attorney-director may not be viewed, depending on the facts and circumstances, as an independent director. *See* NYSE, Inc. Listed Company Manuel § 303(A). *See also,* NASDAQ, Inc., NASD Manual § 4200(a).

[26] *See Aronson v. Lewis*, 473 A.2d 805 (Del. 1984); *Sinclair Oil Corp. v. Levien*, 280 A.2d 717 (Del. 1971); *Shlensky v. South Parkway Bldg. Corp.*, 166 N.E.2d 793 (Ill. 1960).

[27] [1995 Transfer Binder] CCH Fed. Sec. L. Rep. ¶ 98,857 (Del. Ch. 1995).

or at least significantly influenced by, that client as to affect the independence of his judgment."[28]

Due to an attorney/director's direct involvement in the activities of the corporation, there is also a greater risk for disqualification of the attorney and the attorney's firm in certain instances. Disqualification, for example, may occur if a plaintiff brings a lawsuit naming as defendants all of the directors, including the attorney/director. In this situation, the individual directors may utilize a "reliance on counsel" defense, which would conflict with the attorney/director's position that she relied on information provided to her by the other board members.[29]

Similarly, a court may disqualify an attorney/director from representing the client corporation when the attorney/director is called as a witness. The court in *Cottonwood Estates v. Paradise Builders,*[30] for instance, disqualified an attorney/officer from representing the defendant, stating:

> "This case demonstrates that [serving in a dual role as officer and attorney for a corporation] is fraught with danger. A lawyer owes his client a duty of loyalty and duty to exercise independent professional judgment. A lawyer representing a corporation has a duty to the corporate entity which may or may not be coexistent with any duty owed to the board of directors or officers. Here, the lawyer is being called into court to answer for his acts as an officer where his corporate ministerial duties conflicted with his professional duty to exercise independent judgment on behalf of his client."[31]

Additionally, Rule 3.7 of the ABA Model Rules of Professional Conduct, with certain exceptions, provides that a "lawyer shall not act as advocate at a trial in which the lawyer is likely to be a necessary witness."[32] Moreover, an

---

[28] *Id.* at 93,152. *See* Harris & Valihura, *supra* note 25, 53 Bus. Law. at 489.

[29] Thurston, *supra* note 7, 10 Cumb. L. Rev. at 808.

[30] 624 P.2d 296 (Ariz. 1981).

[31] *Id.* at 303. *See* Model Rules of Prof. Conduct, Rule 3.7; Cheek & Lamar, *supra* note 2, 712 PLI Corp. at 488–489.

[32] Model Rules of Prof. Conduct, Rule 3.7. *See* Block, Meierholfer, & Wallach, *Lawyers Serving on the Boards of Directors of Clients: A Survey of the Problems*, 7 Insights No. 4, at 3, 4–5 (April 1993).

attorney/director's law firm may be disqualified from representing the client corporation if it files for bankruptcy. Section 327(a) of the Bankruptcy Code "requires that an attorney retained by a corporation filing for protection under the Code be a 'disinterested person,'[33] which is defined to exclude anyone who has been a director or officer of the corporation within two years of the filing for reorganization."[34]

When an attorney serves as a director, he may be required to exercise a higher standard of care than that of certain other directors, thus resulting in greater personal liability exposure. In general, Section 8.30 of the Model Business Corporation Act requires that directors "discharg[e] their duties with the care that a person in a like position would reasonably believe appropriate under similar circumstances."[35] Developments in corporate and securities law signify, however, that attorney/directors must not only act with the due care ordinarily required of outside directors,[36] but also must adhere to higher standards premised on the attorney/director's unique skills and legal expertise—or in other words, the standard expected of an "ordinarily prudent attorney/director."[37]

A widely cited case dealing with the issue of an attorney/director's duty of care (also called "due diligence" in certain contexts) is *Escott v. BarChris Construction Corp.*[38] In *BarChris,* the plaintiffs brought an action for damages under Section 11 of the Securities Act of 1933 against the company, its officers, directors, accountants, and underwriters, alleging that the company's registration statement used to sell securities contained materially false and misleading statements. One defendant in the suit was the outside counsel for BarChris who was a director of the company, and whose law firm was the principal drafter of the registration statement at issue. Although

---

[33] 11 U.S.C. § 327(a).

[34] Block, Meierholfer & Wallach, *supra* note 32, 7 Insights No. 4, at 5; 11 U.S.C. § 101(13)(A), (D).

[35] Model Bus. Corp. Act § 8.30(b).

[36] Outside directors generally are defined as those directors who neither are employees nor have any other significant relationship with the corporation. *See* sources cited note 25 *supra*.

[37] Cheek & Lamar, *supra* note 2, 712 PLI Corp. at 490–491.

[38] 283 F. Supp. 643 (S.D.N.Y. 1968).

the claims against him concerned solely his role as a director, the court held:

> "[I]n considering [the defendant's] due diligence defenses, the unique position which he occupied cannot be disregarded. As the director most directly concerned with writing the registration statement and assuring its accuracy, more was required of him in the way of reasonable investigation than could fairly be expected of a director who had no connection with this work."[39]

In *Feit v. Leasco Data Processing Equipment Corp.*,[40] another case involving the attorney/director's due diligence defense under Section 11, the court opined that an attorney/director must undertake the strict investigatory obligations of an "inside" director. The court reasoned that the attorney/director was "so intimately involved in this registration process that to treat him as anything but an insider would involve a gross distortion of the realities of [the corporation's] management."[41] Supporting *BarChris*, the court stated that what constitutes satisfaction of a director's duty will vary with "the degree of involvement of the individual, his expertise and his access to the pertinent information and data [and] [w]hat is reasonable for one director may not be reasonable for another by virtue of their differing positions."[42] Thus, under the standards outlined in the Model Business Corporation Act and as enunciated in such cases as *BarChris* and *Feit*, attorney/directors are required to both perform a higher quality investigation and to act in a more prudent manner. Consequently, the attorney/director "is measured by a higher standard that takes into account his 'superior knowledge of, and access to, the relevant information.' "[43]

---

[39] *Id.* at 690. Under Section 11, except for the issuer which is strictly liable, all defendants have a due diligence defense. *See* M. Steinberg, *Understanding Securities Law* 225–240 (6th ed. 2014).

[40] 332 F. Supp. 544 (E.D.N.Y. 1971).

[41] *Id.* at 576. *See* Block, Meierholfer & Wallach, *supra* note 32, 7 Insights No. 4, at 6.

[42] 332 F. Supp. at 577–578. *See* Cheek & Lamar, *supra* note 2, 712 PLI Corp. at 495

[43] Thurston, *supra* note 7, 10 Cumb. L. Rev. at 821, *quoting*, Folk, *Civil Liabilities Under the Federal Securities Acts: The Barchris Case*, 55 Va. L. Rev. 1, 34–35 (1969). For another case recognizing that an attorney/director may be held to a higher standard of care, *see, e.g., In re Rospatch Securities*

Attorney/directors also may be held liable under the securities laws for "causing" a subject violation.[44] Attorney/directors should be especially wary of these provisions because their dual roles make them more vulnerable to being sued for "causing" a securities law violation.[45] Indeed, since the enactment of the Sarbanes-Oxley Act in 2002, the SEC has brought dozens of enforcement actions against attorneys.[46] The presence of the attorney as a director undoubtedly will enhance the SEC's scrutiny.[47]

An attorney/director also faces problems involving insurance coverage—in the event that an attorney/director becomes involved in litigation, there exists a distinct possibility that she will be denied coverage.[48] This is a significant concern because an attorney/director is more likely to be the target of a malpractice claim. Indeed, as perhaps overstated by one commentator, an attorney/director is "an irresistible target for plaintiffs . . . even when there is no evidence of legal malpractice in the usual sense because lawyers and law firms usually maintain large professional liability insurance policies."[49]

Litigation, [1992 Transfer Binder] CCH Fed. Sec. L. Rep. ¶ 96,939 (W.D. Mich. 1992) ("In these circumstances, [the attorney's] knowledge as a director cannot be separated from the knowledge of his law firm. In addition, the lawyer-director may also be held to a higher standard of care."). In addition to the risks arising under Section 11 of the Securities Act, attorney/ directors also may face greater liability risks under the state securities laws.

[44] *See, e.g.*, Section 15(c)(4) of the Securities Exchange Act (a person who was a "cause" of a failure to comply with the Exchange Act's reporting, proxy, or tender offer rules may be subject to an administrative enforcement action); Section 21(C)(a) of the Securities Exchange Act (cease or desist order may be imposed on a person who was a "cause" of the violation). *See also*, Albert, *The Lawyer-Director: An Oxymoron?*, 9 Geo. J. Leg. Eth. 413, 460 (1996); Cheek & Lamar, *supra* note 2, 712 PLI Corp. at 500.

[45] *See* Block, Meierholfer & Wallach, *supra* note 32, at 6.

[46] *See* M. Steinberg, *Attorney Liability After Sarbanes-Oxley* §§ 4.01–4.06 (2015); Callcott & Slonecker, *A Review of SEC Actions Against Lawyers*, 42 Rev. Sec. & Comm. Reg. 71 (2009).

[47] *See* Gill & Bautista, "An Overview of Recent Enforcement Actions By the Securities and Exchange Commission Against Attorneys," in *Gatekeepers Under Scrutiny: What General Counsel Need to Know About Lawyer & Director Liability* (Practising Law Institute 2004).

[48] *See* Block, Meierholfer & Wallach, *supra* note 32, 7 Insights No. 4, at 8.

[49] Albert, *supra* note 44, 9 Geo. J. Leg. Eth. at 463 (citations omitted).

Generally, an attorney/director has insurance coverage under two different types of policies: (1) professional liability insurance procured by the attorney/director's law firm (which insures the law firm and its attorneys against liabilities arising from the providing of legal services); and (2) directors' and officers' (D&O) liability insurance procured by the subject corporation (which insures the director from liability resulting from such person's conduct in her directorial capacity).[50]

Because the demarcation between professional advice as counsel and business conduct as director is not clear cut, the risk arises that an attorney/director will be denied coverage under the company's D&O insurance policy as well as the law firm's professional liability insurance policy.[51] Indeed, because professional liability insurance generally provides coverage for acts, errors, and omissions in the rendering of professional services while an individual is acting in the capacity of a lawyer, the insurer may deny coverage by asserting that the attorney/director's conduct was outside the scope of her role as counsel. On the other hand, the D&O insurer may contend that the actions of the attorney/director were not within the purview of her obligations as a director. Therefore, it is distinctly possible that an attorney/director will be denied coverage under both policies.[52] Likewise, the law firm with which the attorney/director is affiliated faces enhanced liability exposure. For instance, an attorney/director's law firm may be at greater risk for malpractice and negligent misrepresentation claims. Similarly, the law firm may be sued for controlling person liability under the securities laws.[53] Such claims are not

---

[50] Block, Meierholfer & Wallach, *supra* note 32, 7 Insights No. 4, at 8; Cheek & Lamar, *supra* note 2, 712 PLI Corp. at 499.

[51] *See* sources note 50 *supra*.

[52] *Id.*

[53] Section 20(a) of the Securities Exchange Act extends liability, subject to a good faith and noninducement defense, to anyone who "controls" another person that violates the Act or any rule thereunder. Although the term "control" is not defined in the Securities Acts, the SEC has defined the term to mean "the possession, direct or indirect, of the power to direct or cause the direction of the management and policies of a person. . . ." Rule 405, 17 C.F.R. § 230.405. If control is established, the burden shifts to the defendant to show that it acted in good faith and did not induce the primary violation. *See In re Rospatch, Inc. Securities Litigation*, [1992 Transfer Binder] CCH Fed. Sec. L. Rep. ¶ 96,939 (W.D. Mich. 1992), (upholding a control person claim against a defendant attorney and his law firm where the attorney was a director of the

surprising, because, as observed by one commentator, the attorney/director relationship ties the board of directors to the law firm and to the law firm's malpractice policy—a "very attractive" prospect for a plaintiff lawyer looking at a troubled company.[54]

Because of the enhanced risk of liability exposure, law firms should carefully assess whether to adopt a policy concerning their attorneys serving as directors on client boards. When implementing such a policy, a law firm should "carefully address all pertinent considerations, including those factors discussed above, to determine whether the attorney, the law firm, and the corporate client will be best served by such representation; and if so, what safeguards should be observed."[55]

Various commentators have suggested that law firms divide *minimizing liability* responsibilities between attorney/directors and other lawyers of the firm in such a manner that potential conflicts of interest and imputed liability claims are minimized.[56] One such way would be to erect a "wall"—precluding the attorney/director from performing any legal work for the corporate client, or removing him from participating in the billing process of such client.[57] Both approaches seek to minimize the connection between the lawyer's role as counsel and his role as director, thereby helping to avert vicarious liability claims and alleged conflicts of interest.[58] The use of such "walls", however, poses problems. First, the "walls" do not entirely eliminate the risk of conflicts of interest—although the attorney/director would not know precisely the extent to which his law firm is profiting from its relationship with the corporate-client, he would certainly be aware that the firm is benefiting in a significant way.[59] These

---

corporation, served on board committees, and he and his firm were heavily involved in the corporation's affairs).

[54] *See "Lawyer-Directors," supra* note 6, 21 Sec. Reg. & L. Rep. (BNA) 1272.

[55] Parker et al., *Law Firm Liability Under the Federal Securities Laws*, 6 Insights No. 3, at 19, 22 (March 1992).

[56] *See, e.g.,* Zaffirini, *supra* note 10, 33 Tex. J. Bus. Law at 53.

[57] *Id.* The concept of creating a "wall" also is discussed herein with regard to attorney disqualification. *See* Scenario VIII.

[58] Zaffirini, *supra* note 10, 33 Tex. J. Bus. Law at 53. *See* Parker, *supra* note 55, 6 Insights No. 3, at 23.

[59] *See* Zaffirini, *supra* note 10, 33 Tex. J. Bus. Law at 53.

"walls" also may impair the attorney-client privilege, given that their implementation may evidence that the attorney/director's role principally is business-related.[60]

A better alternative may be for counsel, rather than serving as a director, to attend all board of director and key committee meetings and meaningfully participate only in an attorney role. This route enables counsel to be informed and to provide advice as appropriate, but without losing her independence and facing the burdens accompanying a directorship. Indeed, this view was espoused by former SEC Chairman Harold Williams, who stated:

> "I am not convinced that it is possible to develop a conduct rule which adequately resolves the inherent conflicts in dual service. . . . I would suggest, however, that there is no impediment to having general counsel attend board meetings as an active participant. I believe it should be standard practice. Such a procedure would give the company and the board the benefits of counsel, without presenting the dilemma posed by dual service."[61]

The following Scenario highlights many of the ethical issues and potential liability concerns that arise from the counsel/director dilemma.

SCENARIO

Leon McIntyre, after traveling west to attend law school at UCLA, returned to his home town, Cleveland Ohio, to practice law. After learning the ropes in the corporate law section of a large Cleveland firm for five years, two of McIntyre's colleagues, both senior associates, and McIntyre leave the mega firm to start their own law firm called Haynes, McIntyre & Wallenstein, P.C. As anticipated, after six months, billables and collectibles are weak, yet fortunately, are improving. McIntyre thereupon is

---

[60] *Id.* at 54.

[61] Williams, *The Role of Inside Counsel in Corporate Accountability*, [1979–1980 Transfer Binder] CCH Fed. Sec. L. Rep. ¶ 82,318, at 82,375 (1979). *See* Veasey & Di Guglielmo, *supra* note 3, 62 Bus. Law. at 17 (stating that "it is our view that in most cases it is preferable for counsel not to be a member of the board").

approached by Sy Lucas, who he knew somewhat in high school and with whom he has become better acquainted in their church activities. Lucas is the chief executive officer of a publicly held company named Lukomas.com (the "Company"), the common stock of which is traded on the NASDAQ Small Cap Market.

Lucas informs McIntyre that the Company, which employs one in-house attorney, is looking for a law firm to be its outside general counsel and would like McIntyre's law firm to serve in that role. Lucas estimates that fees should approach $50,000 annually, if not more, and that a secondary public stock offering is tentatively planned one year from now which also should generate significant fees for McIntyre's firm (which would serve as the Company's counsel in that prospective offering). As a condition to this arrangement, Lucas explains that Lukomas.com needs a seventh director and that McIntyre must be that director. Without McIntyre's agreement to this proposition, Lucas tells McIntyre that the Company will retain another law firm to be its general counsel.

Should McIntyre and his law firm (Haynes, McIntyre & Wallenstein, P.C.) agree to represent Lukomas.com under the conditions set forth by Lucas? What, if any, diligence should be conducted by McIntyre and the law firm regarding Lukomas.com and its key executives, including Lucas? Does McIntyre's prospective dual roles as counsel for the Company and as corporate director raise ethical as well as potential liability concerns?

APPENDIX

ENGAGEMENT LETTER
(EXAMPLE 1)

Jagger Starr & McCarthy, LLP
Seven Citrus Grove
37th Floor
Miami, Florida 33058

October 1, 2015

Mr. Leonard J. Monroe
President, Monroe Enterprises, Inc.
Three Tropicana Lane
Fort Lauderdale, Florida 33317

Dear Mr. Monroe:

We appreciate your confidence in Jagger Starr & McCarthy, LLP and your decision to retain our firm to provide legal advice and representation. We believe the attorney-client relationship is best served by a clear understanding of the scope and financial terms of our engagement. The purpose of this letter is to set forth that understanding.

Identity of Client and Scope of Engagement:

We have been retained to provide the following legal services to Monroe Enterprises, L.L.C. ("the Company") in connection with litigation brought by Abso-Duet Corporation against the Company pending in Broward County, Florida.

If we undertake, at your request, additional legal work in the future for the Company, this letter will continue to define our relationship unless we enter into a subsequent letter agreement for that work. Once the work described herein (or any additional legal work we have undertaken at your request) has been completed, our engagement will end and, absent a specific request, we will have no further responsibility to advise you about changes in the law or later actions to be taken.

Billing, Administration and Work Assignments:

We try to take into account all relevant factors in setting our fees and related charges. The principal factor is the hourly rate, which is set in accordance with the seniority, expertise, and location of the lawyer or paralegal performing a given task.

Our policy with respect to our billing and fee arrangements, the assignment of additional lawyers and other pertinent matters are set forth in the attached Standard Terms of Engagement. Those provisions will apply unless this letter otherwise specifically addresses an issue.

We will bill you for expenses associated with your representation. These expenses—such as internal copying, computer research, telephone calls and air courier—will be billed on a cost basis absent a mark-up. Our internal costs for the aforementioned are reviewed periodically and adjusted to reflect changes in our cost structure.

We request advance payment for the work we anticipate performing. Our fees and charges for the work will be applied against this advance payment, and appropriate credit will be reflected on the statements you receive. Based on our analysis of the work to be performed, we believe a $25,000 advance payment is appropriate. The unearned portion of the advance, if any, will be refunded to you after this engagement has been completed. This prepayment of legal fees will be kept in an escrow account and drawn therefrom as invoices are rendered. If the need arises, we may request replenishment of this account.

We may contract with outside vendors to provide certain services associated with your representation, e.g., copying services. In such instances, we may bill you for such services prior to actually paying the vendor and/or pay the vendor upon receipt of your payment. Before proceeding, however, we would provide full disclosure as to the arrangement and obtain your consent. (See "Standard Terms of Engagement"—Disbursements and Charges)

Litigation Support Services:

As part of our engagement, we will provide the following litigation support services. First, we will provide optical scanning of all pleadings and correspondence at no cost to you. Second, we will provide optical scanning of all documents obtained through discovery for $0.35 per page. Third, we will provide coding for these documents which captures essential information about each document for $65.00 per hour. Fourth, we employ a litigation support technology specialist who will supervise litigation support services for this Matter, such as database development, input, retrieval and categorization of data and evidence for all legal and discovery proceedings, and preparation of electronic displays using Powerpoint or similar software for hearings and trial at an hourly rate of $95.00. We believe this represents a substantial savings for our clients since this work is frequently performed by paralegals charging considerably higher rates.

Conflicts of Interest:

We have procedures designed to avoid acceptance of engagements that would create a conflict of interest. Based on the information you provided, we have reviewed our records and have discovered no conflict that would preclude our representation of you in the engagement described in this letter. Please note that unless a subsidiary or other affiliate is described herein as a client, we do not consider such subsidiary or other affiliate to be our client in determining conflicts of interest or for any other purpose.

It is possible that a new or existing client might seek our advice or representation in a matter that involves you, directly or indirectly. Under the various codes of professional responsibility that govern the practice of law, a lawyer may not represent a client in a matter that is directly adverse to the interests of another existing client, absent informed consent. Competing economic interests are not, however, matters of direct adversity, and we would, therefore, be free to accept such other engagements without your consent.

We may be asked to accept an engagement that is considered to be in direct conflict with our engagement with you. If so, if we determine that (i) we would not be hindered in continuing to represent your interests in a fair and aggressive manner, (ii) our representation of you will not be adversely affected by undertaking the new engagement, or (iii) our independent professional judgment will not be materially limited by undertaking the new engagement, and (iv) the new engagement would not involve the use or disclosure of any confidential information about you, and if you concur in our judgment, after full disclosure, on those issues, we would hope that you would consent to the other engagement.

You hereby acknowledge that we do not represent any individual who is listed as a director, officer, or shareholder of the Company.

If the terms of this letter are satisfactory, please sign a copy in the space provided, and return it to me with the advance payment of $25,000. We appreciate the opportunity to be of service to you.

Very truly yours,

_____

Luis M. Salazar

for Jagger Starr & McCarthy, LLP

Agreed:

Monroe Enterprises, Inc.

By: _____

Leonard J. Monroe

President

Enclosure

Jagger Starr & McCarthy, LLP—Standard Terms of Engagement

FEES. Unless a specific alternate fee arrangement is set forth in the engagement letter, our fees are calculated based upon the fair value for the services we render after taking into consideration many factors, including but not limited to the complexity or novelty of the work performed; the seniority, experience, practice area and location of the lawyers, paralegals or law clerks performing the work; the time period within which the work is required to be completed; the likelihood that the engagement will preclude our acceptance of other employment; the number of hours required to perform the work; the nature and length of our professional relationship with the Client; the results obtained; and the fees charged for similar services. Hourly rates (determined using the forgoing factors) are established for lawyers, paralegals, law clerks, and other staff timekeepers, both for our internal cost accounting records and for matters where we have agreed to base our fees primarily or exclusively on the number of hours worked. Those base rates are adjusted periodically, in light of the factors enumerated above, as well as cost of living and market considerations.

WORK ASSIGNMENTS. The lawyer with whom the Client deals primarily may assign responsibility for completing some of the Client's work to other lawyers or personnel in the firm under his or her supervision, and may use other firm lawyers where specialized help is needed. The supervising lawyer will continue to be responsible for the Client's engagement, however. We assign tasks among lawyers, paralegals, and law clerks to produce the highest quality work in the most efficient and cost-effective manner. Our firm functions on the principle that a team represents a client more effectively and efficiently than an individual lawyer. Accordingly, although a number of lawyers may work on a particular engagement, we avoid, and will not charge, for redundancy.

RESPONSES TO AUDITORS' INQUIRIES. We are frequently asked to provide information to auditing firms regarding legal matters on which we are representing a client. We respond to those inquiries with the same level of care and professionalism that we use to handle the Client's other legal work. Moreover, if an auditing firm requests information on the Client's behalf, that request will be deemed to be the Client's consent for us to disclose that information to that firm.

DISBURSEMENTS AND CHARGES. Most matters involve disbursements and charges for various products and services incidental to our legal work, such as document duplicating services, travel, long distance telephone and telecopier services, computerized research (such as LEXIS and Westlaw), courier services, and postage. Some services will be provided by our firm and others by third party vendors. We may advance nominal charges from our Client's account to pay certain vendors. Invoices from other vendors (such as printer, expert witnesses, process servers and court reporters) will be forwarded to the Client directly for payment. We manage our own telephone network, printing and document duplication services. We generally use our in-house printing and document duplicating services rather than third party services, due to timing and confidentiality concerns. We will handle these services however the Client requests. We set our charges for these services based upon our fully burdened cost of providing them to the Client.

TRAVEL. We generally record the time spent traveling in furtherance of the Client's engagement at the hourly rates established for the Client matter and take that time into consideration in calculating a fee. Any time spent working on the Client's matters or those of another client while traveling will reduce the amount of any such traveling time considered in calculating the fee and will not be double billed. Air travel is booked at coach rates unless otherwise previously approved by the Client or unless the air travel is transoceanic or overnight, in which case we generally book business or comparable class.

OVERTIME. If the Client's work requires our non-exempt personnel to work overtime, we will ask the Client to reimburse us for those expenses. For safety reasons, or lack of readily available alternative means of transportation at night in some of our markets, it may be necessary to use taxi or car hire services rather than normal bus, train, or subway commuting. Such expenses are an appropriate cost of the Client's engagement, and we will pass them along at our direct cost, with no markup.

STATEMENTS. We render monthly statements for fees, disbursements, and charges. Separate invoices are normally produced for each legal matter being handled. The Client also will receive a monthly statement which shows any past due invoice, by number and date, for each Client's matters.

PAYMENT. Each statement is due upon presentation. Payment is expected within 30 days. Failure to pay statements promptly may result in temporary or permanent cessation of service. Payment of statements should be made in U.S. dollars, by wire transfer or in checks or drafts payable to Jagger Starr & McCarthy, LLP. Please note the date and identification number of the statement being paid, and return the remittance copy of our statement.

DISENGAGEMENT. The Client may terminate our engagement by written notice to the Firm. Such termination does not, however, relieve the Client of the obligation to pay for all services rendered and disbursements and other charges paid or incurred on behalf of the Client or in connection with our engagement. We also reserve the right to withdraw from our representation if, for example, the Client fails to honor the terms of the engagement letter, or the Client fails to cooperate or follow our advice on a material matter for any fact or circumstance which would or could, in our view, render our continued representation unlawful or unethical. If we elect to withdraw, the Client will take all steps necessary to free us of any obligation to perform further services, including the execution of any documents necessary to complete our withdrawal, and we will be entitled to be paid for all services rendered and all costs and expenses incurred on behalf of the Client up until the date of the withdrawal.

ENGAGEMENT LETTER
(EXAMPLE 2)

Jeter Greenberg & Suzuki, P.C.
One Unitas Square
1927 Yankee Boulevard
Syracuse, New York 13246

July 26, 2015

Mr. Hylton J. Horning
Chief Executive Officer
Cross-Jupiter Cargo, Inc.
3333 Savannah Road
Albany, New York 12209

Dear Mr. Horning:

We are pleased that Cross-Jupiter Cargo, Inc. ("the Company") has retained us to represent your Company in connection with the Company's contemplated acquisition of Tier Three Cargo Corporation. This letter sets forth the basic terms of our engagement.

We are committed to performing services for you with the utmost loyalty that an attorney owes to his or her client and in accordance with the Rules of Professional Conduct. It may be helpful for us to state the general principles that govern this area. We will, unless you consent otherwise, keep your confidences and avoid any conflict with your interests with respect to this and any other matter in which we are engaged by you. However, as you may know, we represent many other clients in a variety of geographical and subject-matter areas. We therefore undertake this representation and any future representation of you on other matter(s) on the understanding that we are free to represent other client(s) on matters in which you may be adverse or may have an adverse interest, so long as such matters are not substantially related to the work we are doing for you and do not allow for the use of confidential information you have provided to us. If this understanding is not acceptable to you, please notify me immediately. If you want us to consider your corporate parents, subsidiaries, or affiliates in our preclearance process of new matters, please inform me promptly, and please send us (i) a written list of your corporate affiliates; and (ii) a periodic updating of that list.

The lawyer with whom you deal primarily may assign responsibility for completing some of your work to other lawyers or other personnel in this law firm under his or her supervision, and may use other firm lawyers where specialized help is needed. The supervising lawyer will continue to be responsible for your entire assignment, however, and will be available to discuss the use of other personnel with you. It is our goal to assign tasks among lawyers, law clerks, and document clerks in a way that produces the highest quality of work at a reasonable price.

Our fees are ordinarily based on hourly rates for lawyers and various other time chargers such as paraprofessionals. Our rates, of course, reset from time to time, generally at the start of each year. Our current rates for matters such as this range from $220 to $625 for partners, $205 to $350 for "of counsel," $125 to $215 for associates, and $75 to $115 for most categories of paraprofessionals. My current rate is $375, and Ms. Jennifer McGrudy's rate, who will be working on this matter, is $195. We may adjust the charge downward or upward based on other facts such as the novelty or complexity of the issue and problems encountered, the extent of the responsibility involved, the result achieved, the efficiency of our work, the customary fees for similar legal services and other similar factors that will enable us to arrive at a fair fee under the circumstances. Pursuant to our normal practice, our bills also include direct charges for such items as travel expenses, postage, telephone calls, faxes, duplicating, computer network services, computerized research, and secretarial overtime.

In addition, if this engagement requires substantial disbursements by us to third parties, such as consultants, accountants, or other experts, we may request an advance from you of the amounts involved. Otherwise, your financial obligations to us will be reflected in our routine billings.

We will send you monthly statements for our services. (If you have any special policies with respect to information you want in our statements, please advise us promptly so that we can avoid confusion or delay.) Please review our bills when you receive them so that any questions you may have are raised in a timely fashion. We request that our statements be paid within thirty days of receipt, and we reserve the right to discontinue providing legal services, after notice, if our statements are not paid within a reasonable time.

You hereby acknowledge that we do not represent any individual who is listed as a director, officer, or shareholder of the Company.

We look forward to working with you on this matter. If you have any questions about any of the arrangements detailed in this letter, please do not hesitate to contact me.

Very truly yours,

_____

H. Albert Chiu

For Jeter Greenberg & Suzuki, P.C.

Agreed:

Cross-Jupiter Cargo, Inc.

_____

Hylton J. Horning

Chief Executive Officer

MULTIPLE REPRESENTATION LETTER

Luckman Payton & Sayers LLP
1035 Michigan Avenue
Suite 4700
Chicago, Illinois 60611

August 3, 2015

Mr. Colin Dupres
1301 Elmhurst Drive
Chicago, IL 60604

Ms. Jennifer Plassius
724 East Juniper Place
Chicago, IL 60611

Re: *Consent to Multiple Representation*

Dear Mr. Dupres and Ms. Plassius:

You have requested that our law firm, Luckman Payton & Sayers LLP, represent each of you in the preparation of organizational documents for Dexford Appraisal, LLC.

Our representation of clients is governed by the Illinois Disciplinary Rules of Professional Conduct, as adopted by the Supreme Court of Illinois and State Bar of Illinois.

A lawyer has the duty to exercise independent professional judgment on behalf of each client. When a lawyer is requested to represent multiple clients in the same matter, he can do so if he concludes that he can fulfill this duty with regard to each of the clients on an impartial basis and obtains the consent of each client after an explanation of the possible risks involved in the multiple representation situation. Further, if at any time during the representation it is determined that, because of differences between the joint clients, a lawyer can no longer represent each of the clients impartially, then the lawyer must at that time withdraw from representing all of the clients.

I am hereby advising each of you of your right to obtain separate legal counsel to represent you in all matters. I strongly recommend that course of action to you. I understand that each of you understands this but nevertheless wants our Law Firm to represent both of you in connection with the preparation of the documents referenced above. Based on the information you have provided, we have concluded that we can represent each of you on an impartial basis. In determining whether you should consent to this joint representation, however, you should carefully consider the following matters.

The first matter involves the attorney-client privilege. Although the law is not settled, we believe that any information disclosed by you to us in connection with this representation will not be protected by the privilege in a subsequent legal proceeding asserted by or against one of you involving the other. Moreover, we believe we cannot effectively represent each of you if information disclosed to us by one of you must be preserved by us in confidence from the other. If we are to represent you, it will only be with the express understanding that each of you has waived the attorney-client privilege to the extent, but only to the extent, that the privilege might otherwise require us to preserve in confidence information disclosed by one of you to us from the other.

An additional point is that, if either of you divulges information to anyone except the other one or members of my firm, the privilege would probably be waived, at least in part. The extent of that loss is not clear. It might relate only to the actual content of the specific communication. It could, however, involve related information.

Second, at this time there does not appear to be any difference of opinion between you with regard to the terms of the LLC member agreement or any of the other documents. However, it may turn out, upon further consultation, that one or more of you may have varying opinions with respect to the tax classification of the entity, valuation of contributed assets, allocations of profits and losses, sharing of expenses, distributions, buy-out provisions, management or other matters. It is our duty to explore each of these issues with you. Should we determine that there are material differences between you on one or more of these issues that you cannot resolve on an amicable basis or that we conclude cannot be resolved on terms compatible with the best interests of each party involved, then we must at that time withdraw from the representation. If this occurs, we will, if you wish, assist each of you in obtaining new counsel. If we must withdraw, there may be an added expense caused by the representation by a new law firm.

We understand that each of you will be responsible for payment of our legal fees, filing fees and any other out-of-pocket expenses.

As is true with all legal services, we cannot and do not guarantee the results of our representation. We cannot and do not make any warranties express or implied with regard to our representation.

If you are willing to consent to our joint representation based on the disclosures and conditions listed above, please so indicate in the spaces provided below and return one copy of this letter to us.

Very truly yours,

_____

Q.B. Cutler for Luckman Payton & Sayers LLP

We consent to your joint representation of us on the conditions set forth in this letter.

Date:

_____

Colin Dupres

Date:

_____

Jennifer Plassius

MULTIPLE REPRESENTATION PROVISION

Sandler Chase & Murphy, P.C.
23 Comic Way
Century City, California 90067

September 28, 2015

Ms. Jessica J. Bandera
22579 21st Street
Santa Monica, California 90405

Dear Ms. Bandera:

As we discussed, this Firm will be representing other clients in this Matter (the contemplated acquisition of "A to Z 24/7 Convenience Stores LLC") in addition to yourself. The co-clients are Lucky Beverage, Inc. and Mr. Luke Conners. Although your interests and those of the co-clients currently appear to coincide, there is a potential conflict of interest in every multiple representation. For example, you or the co-clients or one or more of them may subsequently decide to pursue different and inconsistent courses of action if circumstances change or for some other reason. You understand that if such a conflict arises the Firm may be forced to withdraw from representing one or more of its clients and that, as a result, you could incur additional expenses and inconvenience in securing substitute counsel.

The confidentiality of your communications to the Firm cannot be as secure in the case of multiple representation as they would be if you were separately represented. Secrets or confidences that you share with this Firm may be disclosed to the co-clients, and the privilege that ordinarily shields attorney-client communications from disclosure to third parties could be lost in the future if a co-client becomes adverse to you and discloses such communications to third parties. Of course, as in every representation, the Firm will in every other respect maintain the confidentiality of all privileged or proprietary materials provided to us by you in the course of our representation.

By your signature below you confirm your agreement to the terms of this multiple representation and your waiver of any actual or potential conflicts that may exist as a result of the Firm's joint representation of you and the Firm's co-clients in this matter.

Jessica J. Bandera
Dated: September 28, 2015

WAIVER OF CONFLICT LETTER

MANTEL RIPTEN & CABRERA LLP
300 Triple Way
Brooklyn, NY 11201

May 30, 2015

Board of Directors
Ruth Foods Corporation
230 Slugger Avenue
Brooklyn, NY 11201

Re: Waiver of Conflict–Ruth Foods Corporation

Dear Board Members:

As you know, Mantel Ripten & Cabrera LLP (the "Firm") has served as counsel to Ruth Foods Corporation (the "Company") and has represented the Company with respect to various matters, including the Company's efforts to obtain financing. The Company has reiterated its request that the Firm assist the Company with respect to those efforts.

The Firm has identified a potential source of financing for the Company (the "Investment Opportunity"). However, that financing would be derived from an existing and longstanding client of the Firm and/or associated entities of that client (hereafter, the "Maris Entities"). The purpose of this letter is to confirm that you are aware of this representation and that you waive any such conflict. In order for us to assist in this potential financing, it is necessary that both the Company and the Maris Entities: (i) acknowledge their awareness of this Firm's conflict of interest stemming from our prior representation of both potential parties to the Investment Opportunity; and (ii) waive the conflict of interest that exists, with the understanding that this Firm will then represent the Maris Entities in connection with the Investment Opportunity and not the Company.

We do not believe that our prior representation of the Company or of the Maris Entities will adversely affect our professional responsibility owed to the Company or to the Maris Entities with respect to the Investment Opportunity.

However, you must be aware that through its representation of the Company the Firm has become aware of certain non-public information adverse to the Company and individual members of the Board which would be disclosed to the Maris Entities. By signing this waiver letter you expressly recognize that such adverse information would be disclosed and consent to that disclosure.

The Company should and must retain separate counsel to represent it with respect to the Investment Opportunity. As required by the Rules of Professional Responsibility, the Firm will not represent the Maris Entities and will not assist in the Investment Opportunity absent a waiver by the Company and separate counsel being retained by the Company.

By execution of this letter in the space provided below, we are requesting that you waive any existing conflict of interest with respect to the Investment Opportunity as outlined above.

Please indicate your acknowledgment and consent by signing a copy of this letter in the space provided below and returning it to us.

Very truly yours,

MANTEL RIPTEN AND CABRERA LLP

By: _____

R. Steller Brock

AGREED TO AND ACCEPTED:

RUTH FOODS CORPORATION

By: _____

    C. Striker Kershaw

    Chairman, Board of Directors

    Chief Executive Officer

TERMINATION OF ENGAGEMENT PROVISION

This engagement will terminate at the end of the matter described in this letter. In any event, unless we agree otherwise in writing, this engagement will be deemed terminated if the matter has been inactive and the Firm has had no occasion to perform any legal services in connection with it for a period of one year. You will have the right to terminate this engagement at any time and for any reason. The Firm also reserves the right to do so if our statements are not timely paid, or for any other reason required or permitted by the applicable rules of professional conduct.

JOINT DEFENSE AGREEMENT

This Joint Defense Agreement is entered into by and among the Parties and by and among counsel for Kilarney Industries Corp. and counsel for Mack McLiew and Sylvia Abbott on or about this 17 day of August 2015. Kilarney Industries Corp., Mack McLiew and Sylvia Abbott are referred to herein as the "Parties."

WHEREAS, the undersigned are aware of the proceeding being conducted by the U.S. Department of Justice (DOJ), and the respective clients of the undersigned have been requested to provide information to the DOJ or expect that they may be requested or compelled to provide information to the DOJ; and

WHEREAS, the undersigned believe that it is in the mutual interest of their clients to pursue a joint defense in connection with this proceeding; and

NOW, THEREFORE, IT IS AGREED as follows:

1. The Parties agree to pursue a joint defense effort, for the sole purpose of facilitating their joint defense of such claims or charges as may be made against them, their officers, agents or affiliates in connection with or arising out of the above-referenced DOJ proceeding.

2. The Parties agree that members of the joint defense team will share information for the sole purpose of furthering such joint defense, and that all information so exchanged will be kept confidential and will not be revealed to persons outside the joint defense team. The confidential pooling of information among members of the joint defense team is not intended to

waive any attorney-client privilege or work product privilege that may be applicable to such material.

3.   The joint defense team includes:

(a) The Parties;

(b) Their attorneys, including Dustin J. Gray of the law firm of Hansen, Avila, Hu & Tresh, PC—counsel for Kilarney Industries Corp; Suzanne A. Torres of McKinney Swarz, RLLP—counsel for Mack McLiew; and Joseph J. Lazzano of Harrison Knoor & Sweeney, LLC—counsel for Sylvia Abbott; co-counsel who are associated with the same law firms as any of the aforementioned attorneys and who assist in the joint defense effort; and any in-house counsel of the respective Parties who assist in the joint defense effort.

4.   The Parties agree that all information shared pursuant to this agreement shall be used solely in connection with the above-referenced DOJ proceeding and any related proceedings resulting from it.

In order to memorialize this ongoing joint defense effort, the Parties, through their authorized attorneys, execute this Agreement on the dates set opposite their respective names.

Date: <u>August 17, 2015</u>   By:

                                      _____

                                      DUSTIN J. GRAY

Date: <u>August 17, 2015</u>   By:

                                      _____

                                      SUZANNE A. TORRES

Dated: <u>August 17, 2015</u>   By:

                                      _____

                                      JOSEPH J. LAZZANO

"TIPS" TO AVOID MALPRACTICE

(1) *Client "In-Take" Procedures*—It is surprising how little due diligence many law firms undertake when determining whether to accept a new client. Frequently, only a conflicts check is conducted with little or no scrutiny by firm lawyers regarding the prospective client's background. Some lawyers view their job as "fixing the client's dilemma" as soon as practicable. Unfortunately, the scenario too often arises that the client's dilemma becomes the lawyer's problem. Clients with previous regulatory problems, bankruptcy history, and fraud actions fall into this category. Steps that should be taken to minimize the in-take of unsavory clients include, for example, after receiving prospective client consent, making thorough inquiry of predecessor counsel, having discussions with the client's accountant and predecessor accountants (if feasible), conducting searches on LEXIS-NEXIS, Google, WestLaw, and other search engines, and making appropriate client references with third parties.

(2) *Written Letter of Engagement*—Before accepting a client, an attorney should insist on the execution of a letter of engagement setting forth the essentials of the representation. A letter of engagement should contain, for example, the identity of the client(s), the scope of the engagement, the amount of any retainer required, the fees to be charged by the attorneys, paralegals, and other personnel working on the matter(s), the costs (such as duplicating, courier fees, and court costs) to be incurred by the client(s), the terms upon which counsel may withdraw from the representation, and multiple representation disclosures (and client consents) that are applicable.

By executing a letter of engagement that clearly sets forth and limits the scope of the engagement, malpractice liability exposure may be minimized. For example, a number of courts hold that, in connection with drafting a client's offering documents, counsel owes the client a duty to conduct due diligence (including the making of independent inquiry) with respect to the accuracy and sufficiency of the disclosures made.[1] If the scope of the engagement has been limited so that counsel does not undertake this task (and such is clearly stated in the

---

[1] *See e.g., FDIC v. O'Melveny & Myers,* 929 F.2d 744 (9th Cir. 1992), *rev'd on other grounds,* 512 U.S. 79 (1994).

engagement letter), attorney liability normally should be averted. Of course, if significant "red flags" come to counsel's attention, limitations on the scope of engagement may not provide shelter for the subject attorney.[2]

(3) *Written Letters to the Client and/or Memos to the File*—Frequently, counsel renders oral legal advice to a client, declining to provide any written back-up to the advice proffered. When the client does not follow that advice and problems surface based on the issues covered by such advice, the danger exists that the client will assert that no such advice in fact was ever given. Without any written documentation to support that such advice indeed was provided, the affected client's suit for malpractice may withstand motions for summary judgment, thereby leaving the issue to the factfinder (namely, the jury) to determine who is telling the truth. In such event, settlement may be the most viable alternative.

To avoid this situation, counsel would be prudent to write the client confirming the oral advice rendered. Indeed, when the significance of the oral advice is clear, counsel customarily should follow-up in writing. Often, however, only with the benefit of hindsight does the importance of the oral advice emerge. Moreover, writing of continuous letters to clients may well be time-consuming, incur seemingly unnecessary legal fees, and impair client relations. To accommodate these concerns, when an attorney orally counsels a client on an apparently significant issue, writing a "Memo to the File" to document electronically and time date the oral advice given would be prudent. This "solution" is practical, takes at most five to ten minutes, and maintains good client relations. If consistently and adequately implemented, this practice lessens the risk of attorney malpractice exposure.

(4) *Termination and Change of Scope Letters*—When a law firm completes the matter(s) with respect to which it was retained, a letter of termination or disengagement should be

---

[2] *See generally* M. Steinberg, *Attorney Liability After Sarbanes-Oxley* (2015); Donohue, *Attorney Liability in the Preparation of Securities Disclosures Documents—Limiting Liability in the Face of Expanded Duties,* 18 Sec. Reg. L. J. 115 (1990); Warren, *The Primary Liability of Securities Lawyers,* 50 SMU L. Rev. 383 (1996); Razzano, *Is the SEC Targeting Lawyers?,* 36 Sec. Reg. L.J. 4 (2008); Zacharias, *Lawyers as Gatekeepers,* 41 San Diego L. Rev. 1387 (2004)

sent to the client setting forth such termination. Alternatively, a termination provision may be included in the engagement letter.

A disengagement letter is helpful in at least two important ways. First, it eliminates the argument that the subject party reasonably believed that the law firm was still engaged in the representation, being responsible to address pertinent legal dilemmas. Second, a termination or disengagement letter greatly aids in distinguishing present from former clients for attorney conflict of interest purposes. Undoubtedly, the conflict rules are far more stringent with respect to current clients. An effectively written termination letter significantly reduces a law firm's exposure to successful disqualification motions as well as malpractice actions.[3]

A practice that evidently is not customarily implemented today is to write an existing client a letter communicating that the scope of representation has changed. Such a letter should effectively diffuse a client's assertion that, although the firm had not billed the client with respect to the alleged deficient matter(s), the client, as a current client looking to the scope of representation as set forth in the engagement letter, reasonably believed that the law firm continued to be its counsel with respect to such matter(s).[4] An example illustrates this situation. At the inception of the representation, the engagement letter provides that the law firm Doolittle & Cartright, P.C. represents Jana Tarzana, Inc. with respect to general corporate work, securities offerings and SEC filings, transactional matters, and trademark infringement litigation. At that time, Doolittle & Cartright is the only law firm representing Jana Tarzana in corporate/securities matters, thereby clearly serving as the outside general counsel with respect to those matters. Ten months later, Jana Tarzana elects to hire three additional law firms to service its corporate/securities work. Indeed, within two years of its original retention as counsel to Jana Tarzana, Doolittle & Cartright's representation is limited to sporadic transactional work and trademark infringement litigation. Subsequently, due to misappropriation perpetrated by its insiders, Jana Tarzana becomes insolvent. Plaintiff's counsel on

---

[3] *See* Attorneys' Liability Assurance Society, Inc., *Loss Prevention Manual* Tab 1, p. 14 (1998).

[4] *See In re Reexplore Inc. Securities Litigation*, 685 F. Supp. 1132 (N.D. Cal. 1988).

behalf of aggrieved shareholders initiates suit in state court against Doolittle & Cartright alleging that as general outside counsel to Jana Tarzana the law firm was negligent and substantially assisted the fraud. These allegations may survive motions to dismiss and for summary judgment, thereby becoming issues for the jury.

An appropriately phrased letter to the Client (here Jana Tarzana, Inc.) setting forth changes in the scope of the engagement would have greatly diminished the risk that the subject law firm could have reasonably been viewed by the client as maintaining its position as general outside counsel. In addition to lessening liability exposure for the law firm, client misunderstanding on this subject would be avoided. The client will be informed that, if it so elects, it must select another law firm to act as outside general counsel or, alternatively, must reinvigorate the relationship with the subject law firm. Given the stakes implicated, prudent counsel today should endeavor to write such "change of scope" letters to affected clients.

(5) Multiple Representation—Client Waiver

Potential conflicts of interest arising from multiple representation arise with regularity. Such potential conflict dilemmas occur in both the transactional and litigation settings. A common perception held by attorneys is that conflicts may be waived by the affected clients with their informed consent after such clients are provided with adequate disclosure of the applicable circumstances and consequences of such joint representation. However, although such informed client consent is a necessary prerequisite, it alone is not sufficient. In addition, even if informed client consent is procured, in order to undertake (or continue with) the multiple representation, a disinterested lawyer should reasonably believe that such lawyer will be able to provide competent and diligent representation to each client.[5] This latter condition adds uncertainty to the propriety of proceeding with multiple representation in troublesome situations, irrespective of client consent. Particularly (but not solely) when the clients are relatively unsophisticated, the attorney should be wary of undertaking joint representation. Examples where prudent counsel normally should avoid multiple representation include representing: the

---

[5] *See* ABA Model Rule 1.7 & cmt. 15.

buyer and seller in the sale of a business; the corporation and its publicly-held subsidiary in a related party transaction; and the corporation and its directors in a derivative action involving serious allegations of insider wrongdoing.[6] In such situations, separate counsel normally should be retained.

(6) Supervision of Associates

Although obvious in theory, lapses at times occur relating to inadequate supervision of recent law school graduates. Perhaps due to (1) the entry of dozens of new associates each year in major law firms, (2) the time and client pressures placed on more senior attorneys, and (3) the mammoth size of many firms, thereby sometimes culminating in the inefficient allocation of oversight resources, the risk exists that inexperienced associates will be unduly left on their own to perpetrate malpractice. Fortunately, as a general proposition, law firms are astutely addressing these concerns in an effective manner to diminish their liability exposure, properly train their associates, and aptly serve their clients.

(7) Senior Partner Oversight Dilemmas

Unlike the associate supervision issue, numerous law firms ignore or neglect an equally important dilemma: that a senior partner who has leverage in the firm monopolizes "his" (or "her") client over a period of time, loses the requisite degree of objectivity, and becomes co-opted (with the firm) in the client's misconduct. Unfortunately, this scenario occurs with some frequency. The reasons why there is a dearth of co-partner oversight are relatively straightforward: the senior partner has a stable of premier clients generating handsome revenues and prestige for the law firm; other senior lawyers with clients of their "own" have affinity and respect for the subject partner; these lawyers trust that the subject partner will provide capable representation; and lower-tier attorneys in the firm fear reprisal if they become too active in questioning the advice rendered by the senior partner. To alleviate this situation, each law firm should assess its own culture to develop a suitable response. It is clear, however, that an increasing number of attorney liability cases invoke the senior partner lack of objectivity dilemma.

---

[6] See In re Oracle Securities Litigation, 829 F. Supp. 1176 (N.D. Cal. 1993); Messing v. FDI, Inc., 439 F. Supp. 776 (D.N.J. 1977); discussion in Scenario VII herein.

(8) Investing in Clients

Being an investor in a client or taking fees in stock increases the threat of liability. The anticipation of lucrative economic returns may justify this risk.[7] However, the presence of such an economic stake enables plaintiffs' lawyers to posture before the jury the motivations underlying counsel's alleged misconduct in concealing or aiding the client's fraud. Simply put, without the consummation of the offering involving materially misleading disclosure documents, the attorneys' remuneration would have been greatly diminished. Jurors earning $45,000 annually will listen intently when informed that a successful public offering resulted in the defendant law firm's receipt of stock then valued at $1 million. Law firms electing to invest in clients or take their fees in stock should be cognizant of their enhanced liability exposure.

(9) Counsel Serving as Director

For the lawyer in a small firm seeking to procure publicly-held corporations as clients, acting as an "outside" director may be a justifiable economic risk. Of course, a lawyer should do so only if adequate director and officer liability and attorney malpractice insurance is procured. For attorneys with more established practices, serving in the dual role of counsel and director makes little sense. Case law makes clear that the attorney/director is subject to enhanced standards. Concerns relating to privilege preservation and insurance coverage arise with some frequency. Accordingly, prudent counsel should attend board of director and appropriate committee meetings serving only as counsel.[8]

---

[7] See American Bar Association, *Acquiring Ownership In A Client In Connection with Performing Legal Services*, Formal Opinion No. 00–418 (2000); discussion in Scenario X herein.

[8] See *Escott v. BarChris Construction Corp.*, 283 F. Supp. 643 (S.D.N.Y. 1968); E. Veasey & C. Di Guglielmo, *Indispensable Counsel—The Chief Legal Officer in the New Reality* (2012); Block, Meierholfer & Wallach, *Lawyers Serving on the Boards of Directors of Clients: A Survey of the Problems*, 7 Insights No. 4, at 3 (April 1993); *Lawyer-Directors Are Key Targets for Plaintiffs' Lawyers, ABA Group Told,* 21 Sec. Reg. & L. Rep. (BNA) 1272 (1989) (asserting that attorneys who serve as directors of their clients "have to be 'certifiably nuts' "); Williams, *The Role of Inside Counsel in Corporate Accountability,* [1979–1980 Transfer Binder] CCH Fed. Sec. L. Rep. ¶ 82,318, at 82,375 (1979) (presented as then SEC Chairman); discussion in Scenario XII herein.

Conclusion

In conclusion, corporate/securities counsel today often labors in a "minefield" where scrupulous adherence to ethical standards and the conducting of "self" due diligence are key components of avoiding liability. The "tips" provided in this Appendix are not guarantees. But effective implementation of the suggestions proffered should go a long way to decrease the risk of liability.